BRAIN QUEST

GRADE 4
WORKBOOK

Written by Barbara Gregorich
Consulting Editor: Patty McKee

Workman Publishing • New York

This book belongs to:

ISBN 978-1-5235-1738-1

New and updated text by Jen Agresta and Jennifer Szymanski; educational review by Anne Haywood, Peg Keiner, and Jonathan Coor

Illustrations by Anthony Lewis, Kimble Mead, and Scott Dubar, with cover illustrations by Edison Yan

Workbook series design by Raquel Jaramillo

30th Anniversary Edition Revision produced for Workman by WonderLab Group, LLC, and Fan Works Design, LLC.

Workman books are available at special discounts when purchased in bulk for premiums and sales promotions as well as for fundraising or educational use. Special editions or book excerpts can also be created to specification. For details, please contact special.markets@hbgusa.com.

WORKMAN, BRAIN QUEST, and IT'S FUN TO BE SMART! are registered trademarks of Workman Publishing Co., Inc., a subsidiary of Hachette Book Group, Inc.

Distributed in Europe by Hachette Livre, 58 rue Jean Bleuzen, 92 178 Vanves Cedex, France.

Distributed in the United Kingdom by Hachette Book Group, UK, Carmelite House, 50 Victoria Embankment, London EC4Y 0DZ.

Workman Publishing Co., Inc., a subsidiary of Hachette Book Group, Inc.
1290 Avenue of the Americas
New York, NY 10104
workman.com • brainquest.com

Printed in the USA on responsibly sourced paper.

First printing April 2023
10 9 8 7 6 5 4 3 2 1

Dear Parents and Caregivers,

Learning is an adventure—a quest for knowledge. At Brain Quest, we strive to guide children on that quest, to keep them motivated and curious, and to give them the confidence they need to do well in school and beyond. We're excited to partner with you and your child on this step of their lifelong knowledge quest.

BRAIN QUEST WORKBOOKS are designed to enrich children's understandings in all content areas by reinforcing the basics and previewing future learning. These are not textbooks, but rather true workbooks, and are best used to reinforce curricular concepts learned at school. Each workbook aligns with national and state learning standards and is written in consultation with an award-winning grade-level teacher.

In fourth grade, children read and write across all subjects as they strive to understand their world and express their own ideas. They are challenged with more complex and exciting connections in math, science, and technology. They build on natural curiosity in science and social studies as they make observations, collect data, ask questions, and explore maps and models.

We're excited that BRAIN QUEST WORKBOOKS will play an integral role in your child's educational adventure. So, let the learning—and the fun—begin!

It's fun to be smart!®

—The editors of Brain Quest

HOW TO USE THIS BOOK

Welcome to the Brain Quest Grade 4 Workbook!

Approach your work in this book with a **growth mindset**, the idea that your abilities can change and grow with effort. With time and practice, you can achieve your goals. Think of mistakes as opportunities, not setbacks. Effort pays off—you can do this!

The **opening page** of each section has a note for parents and caregivers and another note just for kids.

Notes to children give learners a preview of each section.

Notes to parents highlight key skills and give suggestions for helping with each section.

Place a sticker here to show your excitement about starting a new section.

67

READING

What is your favorite genre of book to read? Whether it's fantasy, history, or poetry, comprehension skills are key to understanding and enjoying what you read. Let's break down language arts!

PARENTS By fourth grade, children have transitioned from *learning to read* to *reading to learn*. Reading widely strengthens their skills and introduces them to a range of content, like how-to manuals, schedules, recipes, fictional stories, nonfiction, poetry, news, and more. In this section your child will work with various genres and will analyze texts for main ideas and supporting details.

For additional resources, visit www.BrainQuest.com/grade4

Read the directions on each page before you begin.

Do you have experiences with these topics in your life? Making connections to the content helps you learn!

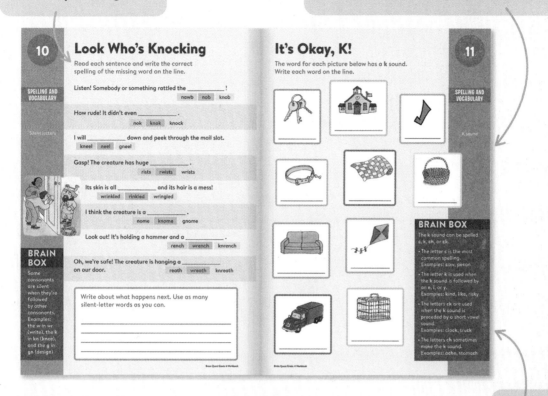

Brain Boxes offer friendly explanations of key concepts.

Cut out the Brain Quest Mini **Smart Cards** from the back to play and learn on the go!

After you complete each chapter, place a sticker on the **progress map** to mark your achievement.

You can use stickers to decorate the **certificate** and hang it up when it's complete!

CONTENTS

SPELLING AND VOCABULARY

Homophones, synonyms, antonyms, prefixes, suffixes—there's a lot to learn as you improve your spelling and expand your vocabulary. Luckily, the more you know how words work, the easier it will be. Let's go!

PARENTS A robust vocabulary is key to reading comprehension. Most vocabulary is learned indirectly through hearing words spoken and listening to or reading books. You can help expand your learner's vocabulary as they encounter new words by defining the words, giving examples in the framework of their daily life, and encouraging them to develop their own examples.

PLACE A
STICKER
HERE

For additional resources, visit www.BrainQuest.com/grade4

Strike Up the Band!

Circle each misspelled **irregular vowel word** in Malia's essay. Then write the correct spellings on the lines below.

BRAIN BOX

There are a number of **irregular vowel** spellings, including:

short a = **au** as in laugh

short e = **ea** as in head, **ie** as in friend, **ue** as in guess

short u = **ou** as in rough, **oe** as in does

long a = **ei** as in eight, **ai** as in train, **ay** as in frayed

long e = **ei** as in receive, **ie** as in believe, **ea** as in peas

long o = **ow** as in low

A Night to Remember
By Malia

It had been a (tuff) few weeks! Our band had been practicing a lot to get redy for our winter concert. Every day, we eether met before school or stayed after to practice. It was hard work, but we beleeved in ourselves. The nite of the concert, each roe of the auditorium was filled with our frends and families. (We were afrade the heavy rane would keep them away.) I gess we're ready, I thawt. We were nervis, but we plade our best. The music was joyus. I was so pleesed with our performance. And we went out for pizza afterward! Mostly, I was happy because I tried my best. I will tresure the memory of that evening forever!

tough

_____   _____
_____   _____
_____   _____
_____   _____
_____   _____
_____   _____

Alphabet Soup

Fill in the missing vowels to complete the words with **irregular vowel spellings.** Use the vowel combinations in the boxes below.

| ou | ea | oe | y | ei | eo | ie |

d<u>ou</u>ble   alth _ _ gh   n _ _ ghbor   w _ _ ther

tr _ _ sure   d _ _ s   s _ mbols   h _ _ ght

y _ _ ng   p _ _ ple   thr _ _ d   ch _ _ f

Irregular vowel spellings

Write each correctly spelled word below. Then write the vowel sound made by the irregular vowels in each word.

Word Vowel Sound

Word	Vowel Sound
double	short u

Look Who's Knocking

Read each sentence and write the correct spelling of the missing word on the line.

Listen! Somebody or something rattled the _____ !

nawb   nob   knob

How rude! It didn't even _____ .

nok   knok   knock

I will _____ down and peek through the mail slot.

kneel   neel   gneel

Gasp! The creature has huge _____ .

rists   rwists   wrists

Its skin is all _____ and its hair is a mess!

wrinkled   rinkled   wringled

I think the creature is a _____ .

nome   knome   gnome

Look out! It's holding a hammer and a _____ .

rench   wrench   knrench

Oh, we're safe! The creature is hanging a _____ on our door.

reath   wreath   knreath

BRAIN BOX

Some consonants are silent when they're followed by other consonants. Examples: the **w** in **wr** (write), the **k** in **kn** (knee), and the **g** in **gn** (design)

Write about what happens next. Use as many silent-letter words as you can.

_____

_____

_____

_____

It's Okay, K!

The word for each picture below has a **k** sound. Write each word on the line.

_____

_____

_____

K sound

_____

_____

_____

_____

_____

_____

_____

BRAIN BOX

The **k** sound can be spelled **c**, **k**, **ch**, or **ck**.

- The letter **c** is the most common spelling.
  Examples: **c**ow, pe**c**an

- The letter **k** is used when the **k** sound is followed by an **e**, **i**, or **y**.
  Examples: **k**ind, li**k**e, ris**k**y

- The letters **ck** are used when the **k** sound is preceded by a short vowel sound.
  Examples: clo**ck**, tru**ck**

- The letters **ch** sometimes make the **k** sound.
  Examples: a**ch**e, stoma**ch**

Scratches and Strums

Underline the letters that make up the three-consonant blend in each word in the boxes below. Then circle the hidden words in the puzzle.

The words go across or down.

SPELLING AND
VOCABULARY

throat	throne	through	thread	thrash
scrub	scream	scrapbook	scratch	scramble
strum	stranger	straight	stream	stray

Three-letter blends

Q	V	R	X	O	K	U	B	G	V	Z	Q	S	T	R	A	N	G	E	R
E	J	S	Q	X	F	T	E	I	E	F	K	F	N	H	C	K	W	V	S
C	S	C	R	A	M	B	L	E	O	R	K	H	B	V	L	B	Q	R	G
J	F	F	L	Z	V	P	S	O	Z	N	S	V	L	A	F	Y	F	V	Q
K	B	C	S	V	C	A	C	R	V	Q	M	D	F	C	B	L	G	L	B
D	Z	J	Q	L	L	N	R	S	Z	U	A	G	H	Y	S	T	R	U	M
M	F	Q	A	Z	L	U	A	C	B	G	D	W	S	C	R	U	B	D	N
Q	K	A	E	Q	A	Q	P	L	T	U	U	F	C	G	Q	J	D	Q	V
W	D	R	X	R	P	H	B	S	N	T	K	P	R	T	H	R	A	S	H
T	P	A	Z	G	Q	A	O	C	P	R	J	F	E	N	D	D	C	M	F
O	M	F	E	Z	V	O	O	R	M	Y	C	P	A	M	I	O	L	D	Z
T	S	P	U	L	T	G	K	A	T	S	D	K	M	M	Y	A	R	H	E
H	T	H	B	A	K	A	P	T	C	Q	M	X	R	J	M	K	A	R	R
R	R	R	L	U	E	A	L	C	W	E	L	V	E	V	V	S	N	W	K
E	E	Q	S	A	M	B	W	H	T	M	A	K	T	H	R	T	K	K	Z
A	A	H	T	K	W	R	N	J	C	L	F	A	O	E	Y	M	Z	Y	M
D	M	E	R	X	W	T	Z	N	J	S	T	R	A	I	G	H	T	B
P	O	A	A	V	X	G	T	H	R	O	N	E	T	H	R	O	A	T	A
M	N	E	Y	N	K	E	O	T	H	G	J	N	U	A	V	S	J	T	A
F	G	B	H	E	O	B	T	H	R	O	U	G	H	X	P	S	J	S	U

BRAIN BOX

Some words have **three consonants** grouped together in a **blend**. In a blend, the sound made by each consonant can be heard in the pronunciation. Example: strange

Break It Down

Divide each word into syllables. Then write the number of syllables in each word on the line.

col/or/ful __3__   afterward _____

prob/lem __2__   slippery _____

swallow _____   nearest _____

parachute _____   frequent _____

automobile _____   curly _____

spotless _____   disrespect _____

excellent _____   awkward _____

president _____   journey _____

million _____   instant _____

usually _____   messenger _____

bunk _____   encyclopedia _____

Write two sentences in which you use at least three of the words above.

BRAIN BOX

A **syllable** is part of a word that can be pronounced with a single sound.

Example: so • fa

The word *sofa* has two syllables.

You usually divide words by sound following these rules:

Divide between two consonants.

Example: din • ner

Divide between a consonant and a vowel.

Example: o • pen

The Herd That Heard

Complete the sentences below by circling the correct group of **homophones**.

The flying machine was not fancy. It was a plain plane / plane plain .

The giant swallowed one less than nine. He eight ate / ate eight .

Wes's rabbit has very thick fur. The hair has hare / hare has hair .

Halima will work hard to win the pottery prize.
She will earn an urn / urn an earn .

Leather straps to control horses fell from the sky.
The sky rained reins / reined rains .

A tree grew alongside the shore. The tree was a beech by the beach / beach by the beech .

The sheep listened to the shepherd play his pipes.
The heard herd / herd heard .

The burst of thunder drove everybody away.
The rain reigned / reign rained .

The pirate threatened my shellfish. The pirate muscled my mussels / musseled my muscles .

The carpenter stopped sawing and fell asleep.
She was board by the bored / bored by the board .

BRAIN BOX

Homophones are words that sound alike but have different spellings and meanings. Example: ant and aunt

Write two sentences that use a homophone pair.

_____

_____

_____

_____

Amazing Islands

Akira is giving a report to her class about a place she would like to visit. Circle each incorrect **homophone** in the paragraph. Then write the correct spellings.

I Want to Visit the Galápagos

If I could go anywhere, I wood go two the Galápagos Islands. These islands are in the eastern Pacific Ocean, along the equator. I have wanted to visit them for sew long. Their are so many animals that are knot found anywhere else. Did you no that Galápagos tortoises can live up to 150 years and sleep up to 16 ours a day? And marine iguanas found in the Galápagos are the only see-swimming lizards in the hole world! If I were able to visit, I would definitely knead to look four Galápagos sea lions, witch usually stay close to shore. But of awl the animal species, I think the waved albatross is the won I find most interesting. These birds don't waive at you, but they have the largest wingspan of any bird in the Galápagos. Pears of them mate for life, and when they are courting, they make a noise that sounds like a cow's moo!

_____   _____

_____   _____

_____   _____

_____   _____

_____   _____

_____   _____

Great Minds Think Alike

Use a **synonym** from the colored boxes to replace the highlighted words in the sentences.

help	within	tale

throw	stop	ordinary	view

snack	quickly	leap

Synonyms

Harold wanted to watch the game from the bleachers, while Jin wanted to _____ it from the field.

The green frog could jump farther than the brown toad could _____.

The animal species was common, but it was definitely not _____!

Julie swam very fast, but not as _____ as the day before.

Look inside the book to find the index _____ it.

Be sure to halt your reading at the end of chapter 15; we're going to _____ the lesson there today.

The other team could pitch the balls much better than we could _____ them.

Marty didn't eat all her lunch, so she put the rest away to _____ on after school.

The fourth-grade class wanted to assist the animal shelter, so they decided to _____ by holding a supply drive.

It was a long story, but they all agreed it was a _____ worth hearing.

BRAIN BOX

Synonyms are words that have the same or nearly the same meaning. Example: hat and cap

Make Me Laugh

Think about the correct **synonym** of each word.
Write the synonym in the crossword puzzle.

Synonyms

Across

1. handbag
4. bake
6. chuckle
8. glad
9. pals
13. begin
14. error

Down

2. grin
3. see
4. seat
5. weep
7. ground
10. frighten
11. hop
12. clutter

Speech, Speech!

Rewrite Jared's speech for class president by replacing every highlighted word with its **antonym**.

Antonyms

Classmates!
Vote for me for class president! I will never help you. I promise to add less food to each lunch tray. We will eat only foods we hate. That means fewer cupcakes and more fish sticks. I promise that we will always have homework! Rules will be difficult to follow. So vote for me! Better days are not near. We will all be sad!

VOTE FOR ME

BRAIN BOX

An **antonym** is a word that means the opposite of another word. Example: hot and cold

Friends with Opposites

Complete each sentence by writing the **antonym** of the highlighted word.

The soles of Diego's loafers were smooth, but the soles of his sneakers were _____.

When they are nervous, Sybil becomes speechless while Max becomes _____.

Jacob's younger sister asked lots of questions, but his older sister always knew the _____.

The sisters' paper boats were alike, but their brother's couldn't have been more _____.

The lion did not like acting cowardly, so he decided to be _____.

Instead of facing a penalty for being the last to arrive, Anthony actually received a _____!

Just when Kayla's gloves seem to vanish, they somehow _____.

Isaiah was a very private person, while Michael's life was very _____.

Brain Quest Grade 4 Workbook

What Comes First?

Form new words by adding a **prefix** from the cards.

un-	re-	mis-	over-
not opposite of	again	bad wrong	too much above

Prefixes

common <u>uncommon</u>   calculate _____

capture _____   expose _____

fortune _____   represent _____

eventful _____   disturbed _____

achieve _____   excited _____

visit _____   locate _____

Write another word using each **prefix.**

_____   _____

_____   _____

BRAIN BOX

A **prefix** is a word segment that changes the meaning of a word when added to the beginning.

Distinct Words

Add the **prefix dis-** to each **root word** to create a new word. Then write the definition of the new word.

appear	to become visible
disappear	to become invisible

loyal	faithful to someone or something else

honest	truthful

orderly	neatly arranged

infect	to contaminate

BRAIN BOX

A root word is a word that stands alone and has no prefix or suffix. For example, *friend* is the root word in *friendly*.

What Comes Last?

Finish each sentence by adding a **suffix** from the cards to the highlighted word.

-ment	-less	-ward	-ful
action result	without	in the direction of	full of apt to

A group that governs is called a <u>government</u>.

The detective had no clue. He was _____.

Logan has no fear. He is _____.

As pioneers traveled west, they chanted "_____ ho!"

My puppy likes to play —she is _____.

To equip his workshop, Jose bought _____.

A person who has hope is _____.

Her bike is not worth much money. In fact, it might be _____.

Caitlyn had great success — she was _____.

Rocket ships fly up, so they soar _____.

Write another word using each **suffix**.

_____ _____

_____ _____

More Endings

Fill in the correct **suffix** for each word. Then draw a line from the word to the matching definition.

-able	-ish	-less
able to be	approximately	without lacking

laugh __ __ __ __   very bad or cruel

break __ __ __ __   somewhat green

fiend __ __ __   anonymous

power __ __ __ __   pleasant or delightful

name __ __ __ __   easy to read, or legible

harm __ __ __ __   funny or amusing

green __ __ __   endearing

read __ __ __ __   not dangerous

enjoy __ __ __ __   something that can be easily broken

lov __ __ __ __   helpless

Write three sentences about this broken robot.
Use one **-able**, **-ish**, or **-less** word in each sentence.

Tough Words

Read the following sentences. Draw a line to match each highlighted vocabulary word with the correct definition in the box below. Use the **context clues** to help you.

She practices good hygiene by brushing her teeth and washing her hands.

My candy seems to multiply . There are more pieces every day!

The boy marked the boundaries of the playing field with cones.

My brother throws the discus and the javelin in track and field.

My sister gets anxious when she has to speak in front of the class.

Mandy loved the view from their penthouse apartment.

Each slice of banana bread had its own individual wrapper.

There was much less pollution in the town after the power plant closed.

When Dad bakes, he likes to modify the recipes.

We didn't have a ruler, so we had to approximate the length.

hygiene	upper or top floor of a building
multiply	single or separate
boundaries	change
javelin	something indicating a limit
anxious	harmful substance in the air, water, or soil
penthouse	estimate or make a guess
individual	uneasy or worried
pollution	personal cleanliness
modify	increase in number
approximate	long slender shaft thrown in field events

BRAIN BOX

You can sometimes figure out a word's meaning by looking at the surrounding words. These words are called **context clues.**

Find all ten tough vocabulary words hidden in the word search below. The words go across or down.

| multiply | penthouse | modify |

| hygiene | anxious | individual | approximate |

| javelin | boundaries | pollution |

Vocabulary

H	F	W	U	J	G	V	Q	B	Q	L	X	M	G	M	D	N	J	B	D	T	Q
U	C	A	L	Q	N	D	X	R	D	Q	F	S	O	O	J	M	C	G	X	P	S
T	N	U	K	C	M	F	Z	F	E	P	R	A	M	D	G	E	J	W	L	Q	W
V	H	Y	K	D	W	F	H	P	C	Z	Y	H	B	I	Y	R	R	N	V	H	K
H	N	K	D	M	Z	V	G	W	M	X	Q	O	G	F	M	C	H	D	H	E	A
P	K	X	B	I	L	O	K	R	U	R	Q	U	S	Y	B	H	W	T	L	N	M
E	S	C	W	A	R	U	Z	S	L	B	V	H	C	Y	O	A	W	M	A	C	B
N	Z	V	W	P	O	L	L	U	T	I	O	N	R	V	U	N	T	U	P	Y	H
T	C	B	O	A	H	M	D	I	I	B	J	H	H	Y	N	D	B	Y	P	C	L
H	P	I	H	J	N	Z	J	Y	P	K	O	T	N	A	D	I	Y	R	R	L	F
O	H	Y	G	I	E	N	E	N	L	C	L	J	S	N	A	S	C	W	O	O	E
U	N	C	F	K	R	A	V	V	Y	Q	X	C	C	X	R	E	P	K	X	P	E
S	U	Q	T	A	J	E	K	H	W	M	Q	M	I	I	I	A	B	A	I	E	T
E	I	I	N	D	I	V	I	D	U	A	L	D	T	O	E	T	A	O	M	D	O
U	C	X	O	U	V	X	M	S	F	B	G	J	N	U	S	J	Y	K	A	I	P
E	I	V	V	O	P	L	T	O	G	L	M	N	A	S	R	I	C	S	T	A	L
J	H	J	A	D	L	A	J	A	V	E	L	I	N	F	W	T	U	A	E	A	A
U	A	W	B	E	D	S	F	S	C	Y	W	M	I	I	F	U	B	M	E	X	T
K	Q	P	X	S	U	N	K	V	T	F	H	I	M	A	X	Y	S	Y	B	I	C

There are two extra-tough words hidden in the word search.
If you find them, write them here.

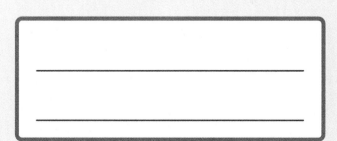

In Between

Each word in the colored boxes falls between two of the guide words listed below. Write each word on the correct line.

| renew | gristle | infuriate | insert | relevant |
| rhombus | engrave | guarantee | establish | elevation |

Using dictionary guide words

infrequent	_____	inheritance
remark	_____	reply
rhinoceros	_____	ribbon
innocent	_____	inspect
element	_____	elf
grumble	_____	guitar
escape	_____	estate
grimace	_____	grits
engineer	_____	enrage
relate	_____	reluctant

BRAIN BOX

Entries in a dictionary are listed in alphabetical order. At the top of each page of a print dictionary are two **guide words**. The word on the left is the first entry word on the page. The word on the right is the last entry word on the page. The words that fall alphabetically between the two guide words are included on the page.

Dictionary Time

Look up each of the vocabulary words in a dictionary. Write the first definition for each word.

generous	_giving and sharing often_
concentrate	_____
awkward	_____
accelerate	_____
gradual	_____
ignore	_____
refund	_____
locate	_____
harvest	_____
despise	_____

Vocabulary

Ask an adult before you go online.

In the dictionary, find four words you didn't already know. Write each word and its definition here.

_____ _____
_____ _____
_____ _____
_____ _____

Repurpose That Word!

Below are some of the longest words in the dictionary. How many other words can you make using the letters in each word? There are a couple of examples to get you started!

Vocabulary

incomprehensibility (noun): the state of being impossible or difficult to understand

time, hens,

_____

uncopyrightable (adjective): not able to be protected by copyright

cite, table,

_____

otolaryngologist (noun): an ear, nose, and throat doctor

tag, long,

_____

LANGUAGE ARTS

English has a lot of rules! They can feel intimidating, but learning them helps you understand language and be a better communicator.

PARENTS A strong understanding of grammar concepts—including punctuation, plurals, possessives, and parts of speech—helps children improve their reading and comprehension skills. As they learn to use more complex sentences, they improve their ability to make sense of ideas while reading. Practice combining small sentences into larger, more complex ones, and play with parts of speech by doing funny fill-in paragraphs together.

PLACE A STICKER HERE

For additional resources, visit www.BrainQuest.com/grade4

Together at Last

Write the compound word that goes with each picture.

Compound words

fingerprint

_____

_____

_____

_____

_____

_____

_____

_____

How many other compound words can you think of?
Write eight or more here.

_____ _____

_____ _____

_____ _____

_____ _____

Plurals Everywhere!

Write the plural of each word on the line. Then circle the hidden **plural nouns** in the puzzle. The words go across or down.

suffix <u>suffixes</u>   hobby _____   knife _____

chef _____   monkey _____   donkey _____

chief _____   baby _____   tray _____

enemy _____   family _____   tax _____

city _____   loaf _____   key _____

Plurals

```
M S E T B D K N I V E S A W P G Z
O X J F O T I R T J H O B B I E S
S H G O Y Y G C D Q K U F N Z T N
B Q V Q K S P J J J P J A X T K E
D O L O A V E S Y M F P M B A E M
O R F S K X R Q Z O C E I I X Y A
N G A B S X D A N N G M L P E S M
K M A K Y O O J A K E J I E S N U
E T R A Y S P V U E H X E F K Q T
Y V T Z X D V B S Y V B S X G K Q
S C I T I E S I A S F I Y D Y T I
P R Y L F O B J P W C H I E F S M
X H F F B B V K K I R F R Y V K L
N N Q E N E M I E S L T S U H R E
X R Z R B A B I E S Q P A C E W P
U L T Q W U Q N H C H E F S A L C
F W K H Z E B N S U F F I X E S M
```

BRAIN BOX

To spell the plural of most words, add **s**. Here are some exceptions:

• When a noun ends in a consonant followed by **y**, change the **y** to an **i** and add **es**.
Example: buggy → buggi**es**

• When a noun ends in **sh**, **ch**, **ss**, or **x**, add **es**.
Examples: brush**es**, witch**es**, dress**es**, fox**es**

• In some nouns that end in **f** or **fe**, change the **f** to a **v** and add **es**.
Example: shelf → shel**ves**

Plurals

Plural Fun

Write the **plural** of each word on the line.

boat _boats_   umbrella _____

church _____   visitor _____

brush _____   artist _____

newspaper _____   torch _____

bicycle _____   prince _____

thread _____   gearbox _____

wrench _____   princess _____

fox _____   bench _____

million _____   compass _____

quilt _____   hour _____

Write a four-line poem using the **es** plurals above.

_____

_____

_____

_____

_____

_____

Word Factory

Write the **contraction** for each set of words on the line.

cannot ___can't___   is not _____

I am _____   could not _____

should not _____   he is _____

you are _____   were not _____

I will _____   did not _____

are not _____   you will _____

Write two sentences that use at least two contractions.

BRAIN BOX

Contractions are formed by joining two words and replacing one or more of the letters with an apostrophe.

Examples:

She **is not** at school today.
She **isn't** at school today.

They will be the first to arrive.
They'll be the first to arrive.

Whose Leaves Are These?

Rewrite the phrases below using possessive nouns.

fender of the car *the car's fender*

breath of the dragon _____

scarf of the woman _____

books of Xander _____

ideas of the gremlin _____

calendar of Orma _____

plans of the man _____

smell of the tundra _____

hardships of the explorer _____

stickiness of the keyboard _____

leaves of the oak _____

BRAIN BOX

Nouns are made **possessive** by adding an apostrophe and s. Example: My mother's cooking is fantastic!

"The cooking of my mother" becomes "my mother's cooking."

Bear's Day Out

Change the possessive nouns in the sentences to plural possessives. You might have to change other words in the sentence too.

The computer's screen was flashing.

<u>The computers' screens were flashing.</u>

The whale's song was sad.

_____

The mechanic's wrench was greasy.

_____

A bear ate the camper's gear.

_____

The flower's petals were blown away.

_____

The catcher caught the pitcher's throws.

_____

Write in the missing apostrophes in the following sentences. The possessives should be plural.

The reporters stories won first prize.

I read the poets poems.

The clowns noses were bright blue.

The dragons breath was really stinky.

BRAIN BOX

You can change **singular possessive nouns** ending in s to the plural form by moving the apostrophe so that it follows the s. Be sure to make the verb plural too!

Example:

The **ostrich's** neck is long.
The **ostriches'** necks are long.

One Curious Creature!

Carlos wrote an essay, but he forgot to use **apostrophes**! Circle the words that are missing apostrophes. Then write the correct spelling of each on the lines below.

Apostrophes

My Favorite Animal

By Carlos

What animal looks like it borrowed a ducks bill, an otters furry body, and a beavers flat tail? Its the puzzling platypus! Found either at the waters edge or in lakes, rivers, and streams in eastern Australia and Tasmania, the platypus is one of natures most curious creatures. Besides its interesting appearance, the platypus is one of only two mammals that lays eggs. (The echidna is the other.) Male platypuses have a sharp, venomous spur on each back leg. Scientists think they use these spurs to compete with other male platypuses during breeding season. A platypuss webbed front feet allow it to paddle, and its beaver-like tail helps it steer as it moves through the water hunting for worms, crustaceans, and insects. Its bill has cells that help it sense movements and electrical fields given off by its prey.

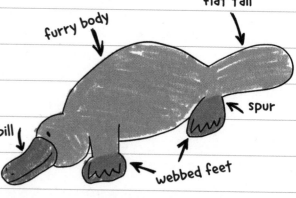

furry body

flat tail

bill

spur

webbed feet

_____   _____

_____   _____

_____   _____

_____   _____

Letter to a Friend

Read the following letter. If a word needs an **apostrophe**, write it in. If an apostrophe does not belong, cross it out.

LANGUAGE ARTS

Apostrophe review

Dear Gretchen,

Hi! How are you? I hope youre having fun at camp! Everythings the same as usual around here. My sisters room is even more of a mess now that were on vacation. Her shoe's are all over the floor, and so are her sweaters. Lilys' trench coat is on top of the beds canopy — how it got there, I dont know. Maybe she doesnt even know its there! On top of that, all the poster's on her wall are torn.

My twin brothers room is neat. Everything is in its place. Yesterday I wanted to borrow a sweatshirt from Lily, but hers was under the bed. So I borrowed either Jacks or Johns sweatshirt instead. Unfortunately, they noticed. "It's gone!" they shouted. "Who took it?" After I confessed, they ordered me to stay out of their bedroom. "Nothing thats ours is your's!" they said.

Well, I'll show them. Im knitting myself a sweater. Its beautiful! The sweater will be all mine. So there!

Anyway, I miss you and hope your bunkmate isnt as much of a slob as Lily.

Love, Emily

P.S. Here's a photo of Lilys messy bed!

Lily's room

Play by the Rules

Read each **capitalization** rule below. Circle do if the rule is correct; circle don't if the rule is incorrect.

1 You do don't capitalize past-tense verbs.

2 You do don't capitalize days of the week.

3 You do don't capitalize names of animals, such as monkey, giraffe, and elephant.

4 You do don't capitalize people's names, such as Hamid, LaVon, and Chase.

5 You do don't capitalize names of vegetables.

6 You do don't capitalize months of the year.

7 You do don't capitalize the exact names of schools and colleges.

8 You do don't capitalize the names of countries.

9 You do don't capitalize places like rivers, mountains, or hills unless they're named.

10 You do don't capitalize people's titles in front of their names, such as Professor Adams and Senator Jimenez.

11 You do don't capitalize the names of streets.

Landforms in Africa

These sentences each have at least one **punctuation** or **capitalization** mistake. Rewrite each sentence correctly.

The sahara desert covers the northern third of the continent.

_____

_____

victoria Falls is located along the Zambezi River, On the border between zambia and Zimbabwe

_____

_____

mount Kilimanjaro, in northeastern Tanzania, is the highest free-standing mountain in the world.

_____

_____

_____

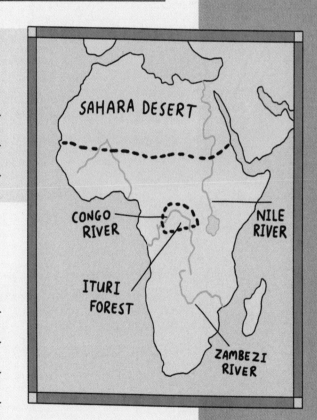

The Ituri Forest is a tropical Rain forest.
It is home to hyenas, antelopes, elephants, monkeys, chimpanzees, and many bird Species.

_____

_____

_____

_____

the two Longest rivers in africa are the Nile, in northern Africa, and the congo River, in central africa.

_____

_____

_____

QUICK FACT:
An estimated two thousand distinct languages are spoken in Africa— that's one-third of all the languages spoken in the world!

All Booked Up

Underline the titles in these sentences.

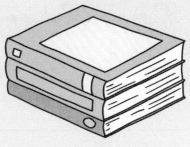

Underlining titles

Three books written by Kwame Alexander are The Crossover, Booked, and Rebound.

Kids interested in marine mammals might like the TV series called Secrets of the Whales.

A Sporting Chance is a book by Lori Alexander about how a scientist named Ludwig Guttmann created the Paralympic Games, a sporting event for athletes with physical disabilities.

Some movies about spelling bees include the fictional film Akeelah and the Bee and a documentary called Spellbound.

E. B. White wrote Charlotte's Web, a book about the friendship between a pig and a spider.

Lin-Manuel Miranda said he was inspired to write the musical Hamilton after reading a biography called Alexander Hamilton by Ron Chernow.

The Invention of Hugo Cabret is a book by Brian Selznick that was later turned into a movie called Hugo.

What are your favorite books, movies, and plays? Write them here, and don't forget to underline the titles.

BRAIN BOX

Underline the titles of movies, books, and plays when you're writing an essay by hand, and *italicize* them when writing on a computer.

Says Who?

Write in the missing **quotation marks** in the story.

Quotation marks

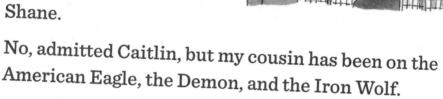

Shane and Caitlin had been on every ride in the amusement park—except one. As they stood in front of the Raging Bull, Shane could tell that Caitlin was nervous.

Have you ever been on a roller coaster? asked Shane.

No, admitted Caitlin, but my cousin has been on the American Eagle, the Demon, and the Iron Wolf.

Those are fun, said Shane, but not nearly as awesome as the Raging Bull!

Is it scary? asked Caitlin.

Not too scary, answered Shane. The first drop is 208 feet, but the speed is only 73 miles an hour. Shane shrugged. I've been on coasters that go over 100 miles an hour—zoom! Shane stopped talking. He looked at Caitlin. Hey, he said, you look kind of green. Don't worry about it. You'll be okay.

Are you sure? asked Caitlin.

Sure, said Shane. If you get too scared, just close your eyes!

Gulp, said Caitlin.

BRAIN BOX

Quotation marks show what is said by a person. Place quotation marks before the first word and after the ending punctuation of each quotation.

What Is It?

In this passage from *Five Children and It* by Edith Nesbit, five siblings are playing in a gravel pit near their new home. Read the passage and write in the missing commas.

Commas with quotation marks

Anthea suddenly screamed "Cyril! Come quick! It's alive! It'll get away! Quick!"

They all hurried back.

"It's a rat, I think," said Robert. "Father says they infest old places—and this must be pretty old if the sea was here thousands of years ago."

"Perhaps it is a snake" said Jane.

"Let's look" said Cyril, jumping into the hole. "I'm not afraid of snakes. If it is a snake I'll tame it, and it will follow me everywhere, and I'll let it sleep round my neck at night."

"No, you won't" said Robert firmly. He shared Cyril's bedroom. "But you may if it's a rat."

"Oh, don't be silly" said Anthea "it's not a rat, it's MUCH bigger. And it's not a snake. It's got feet; I saw them; and fur."

BRAIN BOX

Commas are used to separate quotations from the words that come before or after the quotation.

• When explanatory words come before the quotation, place the comma before the quotation marks. For example: He asked, "Where did you put it?"

• When explanatory words come after the quotation, place the comma inside the quotation marks. For example: "I put it in my desk," she answered.

• If a quotation ends in a question mark or exclamation point, do not insert a comma. "I can't believe you did that!" he exclaimed.

• If a quotation is broken up by explanatory words, insert one comma inside the first half of the quotation and another after the explanatory words. "I know," she answered, "but I didn't have a choice."

Now it's your turn. Write out a recent conversation you had with a friend. Use the rules for commas and quotation marks.

_____
_____
_____
_____
_____
_____
_____
_____
_____
_____
_____

The Majestic, Mysterious, Magnificent Ocean

Dive in and add in the missing **serial commas**.

Commas between items in a series

Earth's ocean is divided into five separate bodies of water: the Atlantic the Pacific the Indian the Arctic and the Southern oceans.

The ocean has zones where different plants and animals live. The three zones closest to the water's surface are the sunlight zone the twilight zone and the midnight zone.

The ocean is home to a diverse array of plants mammals invertebrates fish and more.

Some creatures, such as the sea star the sea squirt and the sea cucumber, can regrow body parts after losing them!

Many types of coral—including elkhorn staghorn and lettuce—can be found in the ocean.

There are about fifty thousand species of mollusks, including octopuses cuttlefish and squid.

Hawksbill green and Kemp's ridley are three endangered species of sea turtle.

Many people, such as scientists conservationists and citizens like you, are working to protect ocean ecosystems.

BRAIN BOX

Commas are used to separate words in a series of three or more. In a sentence, the last comma is placed before *and*. Example: Leo brought pencils, papers, string, and glue.

What's Wrong?

Rewrite the following sentences correctly.

did "you hear the concert" asked my brother rob.

"Did you hear the concert?" asked my brother Rob.

"What concert? i asked as I glanced at pages eleven twelve thirteen and fourteen of the book I was reading.

_____

_____

Punctuation review

My drum concert answered Rob.

_____

"No I answered, "Im reading Harry Potter and the goblet of fire.

_____

_____

cool!" said my brother. "Its even better than Harry Potter and the Prisoner of Azkaban

_____

_____

My plan is to read all seven books by the end of August, i said.

_____

"I have a plan too, said rob.

_____

And then he told me that his plan was to start a rock band become a rock star and make millions of dollars by the end of August.

_____

_____

good luck with that I replied. Now can I finish reading my book

_____

Friends and Fun!

Decide whether the words in the colored boxes are concrete or abstract nouns and write them on the lines below.

friendship	emotion	bread	appetite
table	napkin	chef	tomato
happiness	conversation	spices	chair
pizza	excitement	water	generosity

Concrete

_____
_____
_____
_____
_____
_____
_____
_____

Abstract

_____
_____
_____
_____
_____
_____
_____
_____

BRAIN BOX

A **concrete noun** names something tangible (something you can see, hear, feel, or touch). Examples: tiger, wind, friend

An **abstract noun** names something intangible (something you cannot touch), such as an idea, a feeling, a quality, a characteristic, or a state of being. Examples: kindness, fun, intelligence

And . . . Action!

Underline the **verbs** in the following sentences.

Verbs

"Bugs bug me!" James shouts as he swats at the insects.

I love when my friends laugh at the jokes I tell.

Jackson loads the boat while Jason raises the sails.

I buff the trophy until it gleams.

"I knead bread all day long, but I don't need to," Dad jokes.

Ginny matches all the socks, folds them, and stuffs them into her backpack.

Until Chris returns my football, I will hide his helmet.

Write three sentences of your own and underline all the **verbs**.

BRAIN BOX

A **verb** shows action by telling what a noun does. Examples: bounce, eat, walk, run

Dig It

Write the **past tense** of each verb below.

Irregular
past-tense verbs

get _____

drink _____

ring _____

sleep _____

hurt _____

hear _____

think _____

lay _____

dig _____

draw _____

go _____

ride _____

hold _____

grow _____

keep _____

give _____

Write two sentences using **irregular verbs** in the past tense.

_____

_____

_____

_____

_____

_____

_____

BRAIN BOX

Most **verbs** can be changed to the **past tense** by adding **d** or **ed**.

Irregular verbs have a special form in the past tense:

• Some change their vowel. Examples: **sing → sang, swim → swam**

• Some change their last letter. Examples: **build → built, flee → fled**

• Some change completely. Examples: **bring → brought, eat → ate**

• Some stay the same. Examples: **cost, hit**

This Is Strange

Circle Yes if the underlined word is a linking verb. Circle No if it is not.

Linking verbs

Yes No   The four-eyed alien <u>looked</u> strange.

Yes No   The cookies <u>tasted</u> delicious.

Yes No   The badger <u>dug</u> a tunnel.

Yes No   Fiora <u>is</u> my best friend.

Yes No   In autumn, the leaves <u>turn</u> yellow and red.

Yes No   Dad <u>walked</u> across the room.

Yes No   Samantha <u>felt</u> the water with her big toe.

Yes No   Sometimes my mother <u>becomes</u> angry.

Yes No   I love it when the temperature <u>turns</u> cold!

Yes No   The seeds <u>are</u> bigger today.

Yes No   Some farmers <u>grow</u> corn.

Yes No   Does that man <u>seem</u> sad?

Write two sentences that use linking verbs. Underline each linking verb.

BRAIN BOX

A **linking verb** connects a subject to a word or words that describe the subject and does not show action. Forms of the verb **be**, such as **is**, **are**, and **am**, are often used as linking verbs. Verbs like **appear**, **seem**, and **turn** can be linking verbs if **am**, **is**, or **are** can be substituted and the sentence still sounds logical.

Linking Verbs

Complete each sentence with a linking verb from the boxes below. Write each answer in the crossword puzzle.

| grows | are | tastes | looked | were | became |

| sounds | smell | is | am | feels | was |

Linking verbs

Across

3. There were no cars in the garage. It _____ empty to me.

4. If I win first prize, that means I _____ the best!

5. I love hummus. It _____ delicious!

7. Breakfast _____ my favorite meal.

8. Where _____ you yesterday?

9. My puppy _____ bigger every day.

10. The rubber ball _____ squishy when I squeeze it.

Down

1. My sister's music _____ beautiful.

2. The gorilla _____ angry when the zookeeper took the bananas away.

4. The man and the woman _____ married.

6. Why does sour milk _____ so bad?

8. Selene _____ upset because her ice cream fell on the ground.

50

Inside the Tunnels

Read the article. Circle the **nouns** and underline the **adjectives**.

LANGUAGE ARTS

Adjectives

An Underground World

Many large cities have underground spaces. The speedy subway trains in Washington, DC, travel deep underground, and you can tour Seattle's old underground streets. But you can't visit Chicago's famous underground—it is sealed off.

Chicago's underground is a fascinating series of tunnels. Digging began in 1899. Workers laid telephone cables and railroad tracks. The narrow tracks and wide tunnels allowed easy delivery of freight to many hotels and businesses.

Few people in Chicago knew or thought about the complex network of tunnels—until 1992, when the Chicago River burst through a small crack and flooded the huge tunnels. Hundreds of frightened employees evacuated tall office buildings as river water gurgled into ancient basements and sloshed up winding staircases.

If Chicago had repaired the leak when it was first reported, the cost would have been ten thousand dollars. But the city didn't repair it and the river broke through. The cost of repairing all damages came to one billion dollars.

BRAIN BOX

Adjectives are words that describe nouns.
Examples: wild, colorful, scary, three

Hot Dog!

Write the **er** and **est** forms of the **adjectives** below.

hot	_hotter_	_hottest_
kind	_____	_____
smelly	_____	_____
quick	_____	_____
nasty	_____	_____
breezy	_____	_____
funny	_____	_____
easy	_____	_____

Adjectives ending in er and est

List three more adjectives.
Then write the **er** and **est** form for each adjective.

Adjective	er	est
_____	_____	_____
_____	_____	_____
_____	_____	_____

BRAIN BOX

Add **er** to most short adjectives to compare two nouns. Example: taller

Add **est** to most short adjectives to compare more than two nouns. Example: tallest

When an adjective ends in a consonant followed by a **y**, turn the **y** to an **i** before adding **er** or **est**. Example: happier, happiest

Wait, There's More!

Complete each sentence with the correct form of the highlighted adjective. Add the word **more** or **most** or the suffix **-er** or **-est**.

Using more and most with adjectives

sad   That basset hound has the __saddest__ face I've ever seen.

troublesome   The mechanic said that my car's problem was _____ than yours.

starstruck   Layla is the _____ fan I know.

dark   Today's sky is _____ than yesterday's.

loyal   Who will prove _____ , you or me?

honest   There goes the _____ person on the block.

valuable   David's bike is _____ than mine.

outspoken   If you ask me, Tangia is too outspoken. She's the _____ person in the whole school.

Now it's your turn. Write two sentences using adjectives that require the use of the word **more** or **most**.

BRAIN BOX

Some **adjectives** with two or more syllables are preceded by the words **more** and **most** rather than adding the suffixes **-er** and **-est**. Example: more reliable, most reliable

How Did That Happen?

Complete each sentence with an **adverb** from the boxes below. Underline the verb the adverb describes.

never	here	then	slowly	yesterday
when	carefully	always	happily	hungrily

Adverbs

Turtles <u>move</u> ___slowly___ .

_____ did you arrive at school this morning?

No, an alien has _____ visited me.

Serena _____ looks both ways before she crosses a street.

I feel that I have been _____ before.

Ari felt sick _____ , but today he is feeling better.

He picked up the glass vase _____ so it wouldn't break.

Damien came home, but _____ he left.

She whistled _____ while she worked.

My dog looked _____ at the can of food.

BRAIN BOX

An **adverb** is a word that tells **how, when,** or **where** an action happens.

All About Adverbs

Circle the common **adverbs** hidden in the puzzle.
The words go across or down.

Adverbs

never	today	already	soon	yesterday
tomorrow	suddenly	seldom	usually	sometimes
early	often	always	now	finally

Q	N	D	V	T	U	U	S	U	A	L	L	Y	R	J	L	G
P	Z	Y	P	A	L	R	E	A	D	Y	I	G	Y	T	K	V
P	W	Y	L	F	P	Y	P	J	S	C	J	A	H	Z	H	R
R	T	E	J	I	S	E	T	P	N	O	W	Z	U	H	Y	S
E	K	S	C	L	Y	M	O	B	E	A	M	H	L	M	N	O
B	R	T	O	K	O	Q	M	D	D	L	H	H	T	V	O	N
N	K	E	A	R	L	Y	O	I	X	W	Y	I	O	D	F	E
P	C	R	P	U	X	D	R	A	X	A	Q	E	D	Y	T	V
W	R	D	E	C	B	G	R	E	K	Y	U	E	A	M	E	E
T	P	A	W	B	U	R	O	O	N	S	Z	L	Y	M	N	R
B	H	Y	B	E	J	E	W	R	Y	R	Y	S	K	U	G	V
C	G	E	V	P	C	G	W	S	U	D	D	E	N	L	Y	F
Q	R	M	C	Q	E	S	O	M	E	T	I	M	E	S	U	A
U	S	E	L	D	O	M	F	I	N	A	L	L	Y	L	L	O
H	W	E	W	G	M	F	S	C	F	W	K	A	N	W	M	I
R	Z	T	I	K	O	D	G	C	F	K	Q	C	X	T	N	K
E	O	U	B	S	O	O	N	V	O	C	K	D	U	N	A	B

Change It

Rewrite each sentence by changing the highlighted **adjective** into an **adverb**.

Adjectives into adverbs

The batter held the bat in a firm manner.
<u>The batter held the bat firmly.</u>

The astronaut looked at me in a strange way.

_____

_____

The collie dug a hole in a swift way.

_____

_____

Don't answer people in a mean way.

_____

Tegan divided the cookies in a fair way.

_____

The flimsy tree swayed in a weak way.

_____

My mother kissed me on the head in a tender manner.

_____

_____

Tell the truth in a bold manner.

_____

BRAIN BOX

Adjectives can often be changed into adverbs by adding the suffix -ly.

All About Pronouns

Decide which **pronoun** accurately completes each sentence below. There may be more than one possible answer.

A herpetologist is someone who studies reptiles and amphibians, sometimes going into the field to observe _____ .

Walter brought _____ own tent on the camping trip.

Burj Khalifa is the tallest building in the world. _____ is more than 160 stories!

After Ali made the final payment, the car was finally _____ .

Our science teacher, Mr. Cho, explained safe laboratory procedures to _____ .

The glass window had a large scratch across _____ .

After Stella and Sam left school, _____ went to volunteer at the food pantry.

Margot was training to be an equestrian. _____ had ridden horses _____ whole life.

Have you bought Norah a gift for _____ birthday?

Jodi and Kai love art. _____ is _____ favorite subject.

Brain Quest Grade 4 Workbook

BRAIN BOX

A **pronoun** is a word that replaces a noun or noun phrase.

Example: Abigail was not home.

The noun **Abigail** can be replaced by **she** or **they**:

She was not home.
They were not home.

The pronoun **they** can be used as a singular or plural pronoun, but it always uses a plural verb.

Don't Repeat Yourself

Draw a line from the underlined words to the **possessive pronouns** that can replace them. Some pronouns may be used more than once and some may not be used at all.

Possessive pronouns

Ronaldo uses <u>Ronaldo's</u> binoculars when he goes birdwatching.	my
The sprinters lined up to begin <u>the sprinters'</u> race.	your
Janie's and my favorite meal is the one <u>Janie's and my</u> mother makes on holidays.	his
The snake shed <u>the snake's</u> skin.	her
Marisol saw Angel Falls, the highest waterfall in the world, on <u>Marisol's</u> plane trip over southeastern Venezuela.	its
"<u>Sabrina's</u> goal is to be a volcanologist," Sabrina said. "I love studying geology!"	our
"How many days before <u>Pierre's</u> graduation, Pierre?" asked Aunt Céline.	their

BRAIN BOX

A **possessive pronoun** shows ownership. Possessive pronouns do not have apostrophes.

Examples:

The dog closed **its** eyes.

The girls closed **their** bedroom door.

This is **your** book.

Your vs. You're

Circle the highlighted word(s) that correctly complete each sentence.

Possessive pronouns and contractions

Sea otters hold hands while their they're sleeping on water so they don't drift away from each other.

A coyote commonly uses its it's howl to communicate with other coyotes.

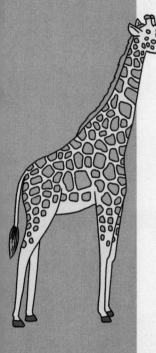

As they grow, hermit crabs exchange their they're shells for bigger ones.

No matter how swift your stroke, you're your no match for a dolphin: They can go more than 30 miles an hour!

A giraffe has seven bones in it's its neck.

Glasswing butterflies have transparent wings to avoid detection by they're their predators.

A ruby-throated hummingbird can beat its it's wings up to two hundred times per second!

All tigers have unique stripe patterns on their they're coats. No two are the same!

An axolotl can regrow it's its limbs.

If your you're wondering what kind of plant a coral is . . . it's its not a plant at all! A coral is actually an animal.

On the Move

Complete each sentence with a **preposition** from the boxes below. Use each word once.

with	between	for	over	on
under	below	from	behind	by

Prepositions

Mary laid the book ____on____ the table.

The socks were _____ Jaylen's bed.

He drove _____ the park on his way to work.

Vicki walks to class _____ Olivia.

The shy poodle hid _____ the sofa.

She likes to sit in _____ her mother and her father.

"Hey! Who took the costume _____ my locker?"

The pioneers set out _____ the western territories.

We walked _____ the bridge to get to the other side of the river.

Do you ever wonder what lies _____ the ocean surface?

Write a sentence using any of the prepositions above.

BRAIN BOX

A **preposition** shows how nouns and pronouns relate to other words in a sentence. A preposition usually shows where something is or when something happened. Example: The food fell **under** the table.

With or Without You

Circle the **preposition** in each sentence.
Then draw a line from the **preposition** to its **object**.
When you're finished, sort the words on the cards below.

Prepositions

"The flowerpot fell (on) my head," said the defendant.

Kris hid behind the bushes.

Sebastian stepped outside the line.

Hannah left without her lunch.

I parked my bike near the gym doors.

Emily was among the top five swimmers.

David raced down the ramp and up the stairs.

"You have until tomorrow," said the teacher.

We always eat breakfast at 7:30.

Grace received a letter from China.

My sister drew a line along the edge.

Angela climbed up the hill.

Put the ball in the basket.

Object

head _____ _____

_____ _____

_____ _____

_____ _____

_____ _____

_____ _____

Preposition

on _____ _____

_____ _____

_____ _____

_____ _____

_____

Life-Saving Technology

Fill in the missing **conjunctions**: **and**, **or**, **but**, or **so**.

Hurricanes are strong storms that can have winds of up to 150 miles an hour _____ more.

At one time hurricanes could not be predicted, _____ the development of technology such as radar _____ satellites has changed that.

At the National Hurricane Center, scientists use weather satellites to watch storms that are forming _____ track their movement.

Satellite data can tell scientists where the eye of a storm is going, _____ they won't be surprised if it changes direction.

Scientists can predict where hurricanes are going, _____ people have a chance to evacuate before the storm arrives.

Before these predictions, people had to depend on their own observations of wind direction _____ ocean currents.

BRAIN BOX

Conjunctions join or link words, phrases, and clauses. Examples: **and, or, but, so**

62

LANGUAGE ARTS

Conjunctions

Because!

Complete each sentence with a **conjunction** from below.

yet	so	while	because	since
or	if	either	unless	but

_____ I lost my notebook, I couldn't turn in the lesson.

Mr. Pilsen says he hates chocolate, _____ he ate a whole pound of it.

Nobody has talked to Dylan _____ he moved to Alaska.

_____ I counted the zucchini, the gardener read a magazine.

Max threw the ball to second base instead of third, _____ the runner scored.

" _____ you agree to wash the dishes, you won't eat," said the cook.

_____ he makes this free throw, Clive will win the prize.

_____ I lost my new gloves, _____ I left them at Dana's.

Daniel agreed to help me, _____ Caleb didn't.

It's So Simple

Make a **compound sentence** out of each pair of **simple sentences.** You may have to add some words or leave others out.

We wanted to have a picnic. The rain spoiled our plans.
We wanted to have a picnic, but the rain spoiled our plans.

I like to swim. My brother doesn't.
_____

The dog chased the truck. The cat followed.
_____

Simple and compound sentences

Learn to swim. If you don't, you will sink.
_____

Victor asked me for a dollar. I gave him one.
_____

Write two simple sentences about what you like at school. Then combine your sentences to make one compound sentence.

BRAIN BOX

A **simple sentence** has one **subject** and one **predicate.** The subject tells what the sentence is about. The predicate tells what the subject does or has done. A **compound sentence** is formed when you join two simple sentences together using a **conjunction.**

Single or Double?

Underline each **independent clause** in the following sentences. Then write whether the sentence is **simple** or **compound**.

Simple and compound sentences

<u>We rode our bikes with Elijah</u>, and then <u>we played baseball with Jeremiah.</u>

<u>compound</u>

Our team won, so we celebrated.

_____

My puppy bit the mail carrier.

_____

Maria and Hannah hid the cookies.

_____

The dragon's breath smelled like mint, but his feet smelled like wet cardboard.

_____

The bear destroyed the picnic tables and the garbage bins.

_____

Juan and Ryder spelled better than Clancy and Marco did.

_____

I changed my name to Javier, so that's what you should call me.

_____

BRAIN BOX

An **independent clause** is the main idea of a sentence. It expresses a complete thought or action. It can stand alone as a complete sentence.

Example:
I am a fourth-grader.
I like to ride bikes.

You can make a **compound sentence** by using a conjunction to join two or more independent clauses.

Example:
I am a fourth-grader, and I like to ride bikes.

That Depends

Underline the **dependent clause** in each **complex sentence**.

The tugboat pushed and pushed <u>until it could push no more</u>.

Omar called me after I had gone to bed.

When Rolf growls, everybody stands still.

I learned Arabic after I visited my grandfather.

Unless we run very fast, we will miss the bus!

Although I like football, I love soccer.

Before Vanessa said hello, Candace said goodbye.

You will win a hundred dollars if you answer correctly.

Now that I'm in fourth grade, I make my own lunch.

When you take a photo, first frame your shot in the viewer.

Jonathan sets the table while his father makes dinner.

Complex
sentences

Write a complex sentence about something you did yesterday. Underline the dependent clause.

BRAIN BOX

A **dependent clause** is part of a sentence that does not express a complete thought or action. A dependent clause sounds incomplete all by itself.

Example: <u>When I turned out the lights</u>, Baxter laid on his dog bed.

The underlined part of the sentence is the dependent clause.

A **complex sentence** contains one independent clause and at least one dependent clause.

Grammar Review

Read each clue. Write the answer in the crossword puzzle.

Grammar
review

Across

3. Use a _____ to separate the words that introduce a quote from the quotation itself.

5. An _____ is used to show ownership.

6. The titles of books should be _____ .

7. An _____ is a word that describes a noun.

8. A _____ is a word that replaces a noun or noun phrase.

11. A _____ is a word that names a person, place, or thing.

Down

1. Bathtub and football are both _____ words.

2. A _____ sentence contains only one subject and one predicate.

4. An _____ clause can stand alone as a complete sentence.

7. An _____ is a word that describes a verb.

9. A _____ is a word that shows action or being.

10. _____ is a very common conjunction.

READING

What is your favorite genre of book to read? Whether it's fantasy, history, or poetry, comprehension skills are key to understanding and enjoying what you read. Let's break down language arts!

PARENTS By fourth grade, children have transitioned from *learning to read* to *reading to learn*. Reading widely strengthens their skills and introduces them to a range of content, like how-to manuals, schedules, recipes, fictional stories, nonfiction, poetry, news, and more. In this section your child will work with various genres and will analyze texts for main ideas and supporting details.

PLACE A STICKER HERE

For additional resources, visit www.BrainQuest.com/grade4

Hockey Playoffs

Answer the questions using the hockey playoffs schedule.

Teams	Rink	Day	Times
Bergs vs. Martens	Taylor	Mon.	6:00
Hares vs. Giants	Stewart	Thurs.	6:00
Foxes vs. Bears	Sandusky	Mon.	6:30
Jays vs. Skates	Taylor	Thurs.	6:30
Glaciers vs. Hounds	Taylor	Wed.	6:30

Zach plays for the Skates. Which team will the Skates play against? _____

Which night of the week will Zach play? _____

His sister Johanna plays for the Hares. Which team will she play against? _____

Mr. Felsten drives the bus that takes kids to Taylor Rink. What nights must he work during the playoffs? _____

Of the three rinks, which start their games after 6:00?

_____

_____

If a player played on two teams, the Glaciers and the Bergs, could they play for both in the playoffs? Why or why not?

_____

Crush It!

Apple Butter and Potato Chip Sandwich

INGREDIENTS:
- 1 small bag of potato chips
- 1 tablespoon of apple butter
- 2 slices of bread

DIRECTIONS

1. Tear a small hole in the center of the potato chip bag to release the air inside. Lay the bag flat on the counter and slowly roll a rolling pin or unopened soda can over the bag to crush the chips.

2. After you finish crushing the chips, put the bag aside.

3. Spread the apple butter on one slice of bread.

4. Open the potato chip bag and cover the apple butter with the crushed chips.

5. Top the potato chips with the second slice of bread.

6. Enjoy your sandwich!

Answer the following questions.

What are the three foods you need to make this sandwich?
_____

What do you have to do before using the rolling pin?
_____

Is a can of soda a necessary part of this recipe? _____

How many slices of bread do you spread with apple butter?
_____

When do you place the crushed potato chips on the bread?
_____

Valdez the Vampire Robot

Read the **directions**.

How to Assemble Valdez

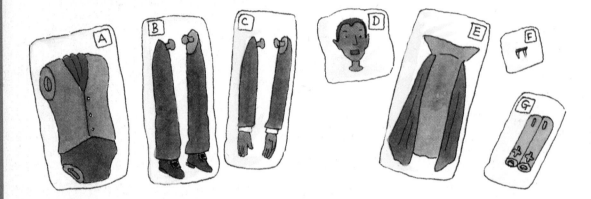

DIRECTIONS:

1. Remove the torso (A) from its wrapping.
2. Remove the legs (B) from their wrapping. Insert legs into bottom of torso.
3. Remove the arms (C) from their wrapping. Attach them to upper part of torso.
4. Remove the head (D) from its wrapping. Attach head to top of torso.

5. Remove the cape (E) from its wrapping. Fluff out the cape and tie one set of its strings to each shoulder.
6. Remove fangs (F) from their wrapping. Snap into place on Valdez's mouth.
7. Insert batteries (G) into back of torso.
8. To start the robot, press the button on Valdez's stomach.

Write the number 1 next to the first part you need. Then number the other parts in the correct order to put Valdez the Vampire Robot together.

_____ batteries   _____ legs   _____ torso

_____ fangs   _____ cape   _____ arms   _____ head

Come to the Table!

Answer the questions using the **table of contents**.

Healthy Cooking for Kids

Reading a table of contents

How many chapters are in this cookbook? _____

Which chapter will give you ideas about snacks to make before going to soccer practice? _____

Which chapter is most likely to have a recipe for pancakes? _____

On which page does the chapter containing smoothie ingredients start? _____

An index is an alphabetical list of subjects covered in the book. What is the first page of the index in *Healthy Cooking for Kids*? _____

Before you get started cooking, you want to make sure you understand kitchen safety rules. To which page should you turn? _____

BRAIN BOX

A **table of contents** is included at the front of a book. It gives you the title of each chapter and the page it begins on.

Concrete Canoes

Read the book page.

Concrete Canoes

Concrete is a building material. It's a **mixture** of cement, sand, gravel, and water. You can see concrete in your everyday life. There are concrete sidewalks, concrete blocks, and concrete buildings.

When you think of concrete, you probably don't think of something that floats. But it can! Getting concrete to float is a **challenge**. Each year, teams of college engineering students face this challenge. These students have the chance to create a concrete canoe and race it in a national contest.

First, a team designs a canoe. Then they build a **form** in the exact shape of the canoe. The form can be plywood, wire, or foam. Once the shape is exact, the team of young **engineers** mixes the concrete and pours it over the mold. After 30 days, when the concrete is **absolutely** dry, they **separate** the mold from the concrete canoe.

Finally, the students practice paddling their canoe. They have to practice if they want to win the concrete canoe contest. To win this **competition**, a team must score high or highest in several different categories. The last **category** is the toughest: Students need to keep their boat afloat and paddle across the finish line first to win the race against all the other canoes.

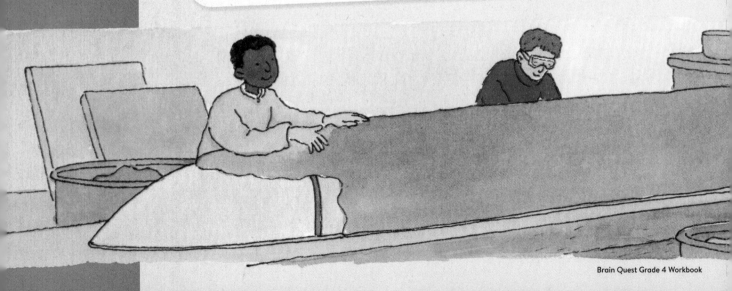

There are two definitions across from each highlighted word. Draw a line from the word to the matching definition. Use the **context clues** from the passage to help.

mixture

something made by stirring two or more things together

a plan to build something

absolutely

most certainly; without a doubt

not paying attention

Context clues

form

something that is foamy

a shape

category

a group of things within a larger group

a type of concrete boat

separate

organize

to pull apart; to divide into parts

challenge

something very difficult

to fight until the end

competition

entirely whole; not divided into parts

a contest; a struggle to win something

engineers

people who build boats

people who design things such as bridges

BRAIN BOX

Sometimes you can figure out what a word means by looking at the surrounding words, or **context clues.** Often, the words directly before and after an unknown word give enough information to explain the word's meaning. However, you may have to read the whole sentence to understand what the word means.

Who's That Vet?

Read the newspaper article and then answer the questions.

Animal Doc Honored at City Hall

Bassport—Wednesday, Feb 16—Bassport's own Kristen Bartos was honored at City Hall on Tuesday in recognition of her service to animals. "Ms. Bartos provides incredible care to our animals," said Mayor Braxley. "Without her devotion, many of our pets wouldn't live the long, healthy lives they do." The mayor then presented her with a statue designed by local sculptor Chauncey Smith. The statue features a dog being treated by a veterinarian. The

brass plate on the wooden base reads: "To Kristen Bartos, veterinarian, with thanks from all the citizens of Bassport."

Who is this article about? _____

What happened to this person? _____

When did it happen? _____

Where did it happen? _____

Why did it happen? _____

How was Kristen Bartos honored? _____

What is her job? _____

Who designed the statue? _____

What town does Kristen Bartos live in? _____

BRAIN BOX

A good newspaper article always answers the **"five Ws"**: Who? What? When? Where? Why? Often, the five Ws should be explained in the first sentence or paragraph of the article.

The Scenic Route

Read the book excerpt below, then read the **caption**.

The longest bridge in the world is the Danyang–Kunshan Grand Bridge, in eastern China. It is more than 100 miles long—about twice the width of the country of Jamaica! The bridge is located in the Yangtze River Delta, a region with a diverse landscape that includes rivers, lakes, streams, canals, and fields.

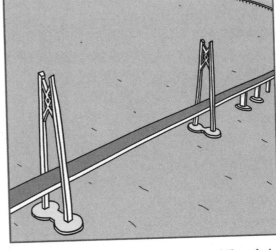

The bridge connects the Chinese cities of Shanghai and Nanjing.

This bridge is part of the Beijing-Shanghai high-speed railway and was built to transport high-speed trains. The construction of this massive marvel of civil engineering took four years and a workforce of about ten thousand people, at an estimated cost of between $8.5 and $10 billion. The bridge was designed to withstand the effects of earthquakes and extreme weather events such as typhoons.

Circle the sentences that explain information you learned only from the photo and caption, not from the article itself.

The bridge curves in places.

The bridge can withstand extreme weather events.

A workforce of ten thousand constructed the bridge.

The bridge crosses over water.

The bridge connects Shanghai and Nanjing.

The bridge is in eastern China.

BRAIN BOX

The text beneath a picture is called a caption. A **caption** usually gives you important information about the picture.

That's What I Mean

Underline the **main idea** in each sentence.

<u>This sentence</u>, which I wrote yesterday, <u>doesn't confuse me.</u>

My sister misses the bus nearly every morning.

Our team lost the game in the last inning.

Nadya took the key out of her purse and locked the door.

My camera fell and shattered.

I threw away the box because it was wet.

Half an hour later, Stephen felt much better.

When the cowboy put his foot in the stirrup, the horse bucked.

Every night at seven, Jesse calls his cat, Calico.

BRAIN BOX

Every sentence has a **main idea**. The main idea always includes the main subject of the sentence and a verb about the subject. Main ideas don't include adjectives, adverbs, or prepositional phrases.

In a complex sentence, the main idea can be challenging to find. One way to identify the main idea in a complex sentence is to cross out the dependent clause and look for the main idea in the independent clause.

What's the Big Idea?

Underline the **topic sentence** in each paragraph.

Elk are the second-largest type of deer. (The largest, of course, is the moose.) Female elk, called cows, weigh an average of 500 pounds. Male elk, called bulls, weigh an average of 650 pounds. And the antlers of an elk weigh a lot too. One pair of antlers can weigh 40 pounds!

Topic sentences

The kangaroo is a marsupial, but it is not the only one. The opossum is a marsupial, and so is the wombat. The koala is also a member of the marsupial family. All told, there are hundreds of kinds of marsupials.

Dogs are descended from wolves. Long ago, humans began to tame wolves. These early wolf pets are the ancestors of every dog in the world. As strange as it may sound, even the tiny Chihuahua and the heavy Saint Bernard can trace their roots back to wolves.

The onager is an interesting animal. Most American kids don't know it, but kids from India, Pakistan, Iran, and Syria probably do. An onager is a member of the horse family. It looks something like a donkey but is a bit larger. Unlike the donkey, the onager is very difficult to tame.

BRAIN BOX

A **topic sentence** states the **main idea of a paragraph.** The topic sentence is often the first sentence in a paragraph, but sometimes it can appear at the end of a paragraph.

Everywhere a Cow

Read the paragraphs about cows.

Cows Everywhere

The next time you're on a long, boring car trip, why not look at cows? All cows are not alike. In the United States, there are dozens of different breeds of cows.

A cow's color and patterns will help you tell one breed from another. The Holstein, for example, is a white cow with large black blobs of color all over its body. Then there's the Ayrshire, which is a white cow covered with red spots. The Black Baldy is almost all black, but it sometimes has a white face or white feet.

Another way to tell the different breeds apart is by unusual features. The Brahman, for example, has a large hump and ears that hang downward. If you happen to see a gigantic cow, it probably belongs to the Chianina breed. This all-white cow is the largest in the world. The Highland, on the other hand, is a very small cow. You'll recognize this breed right away because it has long horns and very shaggy hair.

If you look more closely you will notice other differences. The Guernsey has yellow ears. The Pinzgauer is orange around the eyes. And the Dutch Belted has a black tongue. But maybe you don't want to look closely enough to know!

BRAIN BOX

A **main idea** is explained and supported by details. Every good paragraph has one or more supporting detail.

Write the main idea and supporting details
for each paragraph you read.

First Paragraph

Main idea <u>All cows are not alike.</u>

Supporting detail <u>In the United States, there</u>
<u>are dozens of different breeds of cows.</u>

Second Paragraph

Main idea _____
_____

First supporting detail _____
_____

Second supporting detail _____
_____

Third Paragraph

Main idea _____
_____

First supporting detail _____
_____

Second supporting detail _____
_____

Fourth Paragraph

Main idea _____
_____

First supporting detail _____
_____

Second supporting detail _____
_____

The Logical Outcome

Read each story and then predict what will happen next.

Making predictions

"Oh boy, oh boy, oh BOY!" thought Angus. "I'm going to be rich!" They unpacked the shovel they had brought. Then they took a folded-up map out of their pocket. Carefully, they spread the old pirate map on the ground. Angus flexed their muscles and picked up the shovel. "Here goes!" they thought.

What will Angus do next?

_____

_____

_____

_____

John zoomed around the corner, leaning his bike low to one side. He barely avoided running down two dogs and one dog walker. John pedaled faster. Today would be the day he had no accidents. He wove between three people before they even knew he was there. He laughed as he heard their angry shouts. He turned back and waved at them. John turned forward and saw what he should have seen before—four men carrying a long, heavy board across the sidewalk. "Uh-oh," John said.

What will happen to John?

_____

_____

_____

_____

BRAIN BOX

You can make **predictions** about what will happen next by using information and clues you've already learned.

Reason It Out

Fill in each blank using a word from below.

inform	entertain	persuade

Writing that tries to _____ argues a point or tries to convince you to do or believe something.

Writing that tries to _____ provides information about a topic or explains how to do something.

Writing that aims to _____ wants to amuse you or bring you enjoyment.

Sort these books into the categories below.

Inform

_____

_____

_____

Entertain

_____

_____

Persuade

_____

_____

_____

What Are They After?

Read the advertisement.

READING

Persuasive writing

Glow-Glow T-Shirts!

Wanna rule?
You bet!
Easiest way?

Go-go for Glow-Glow,
the T-shirt everybody is wild about.
Glow-Glow rules the classroom!
Glow-Glow rules the sports arena!

Rule your school today—go for Glow-Glow!
Sizes: M, L, XL, XXL   Color: Glow-Glow Green

EARTH DAY

BRAIN FACT
The first Earth Day was celebrated on April 22, 1970. It was established to raise environmental awareness.

Use the advertisement to answer the questions about **persuasive writing**.

What is the Glow-Glow ad trying to persuade you to do?

_____

_____

BRAIN BOX

The goal of **persuasive writing** is to convince the reader to do something or to think a certain way. Persuasive writing uses techniques like highlighting key facts, appealing to the reader's emotions, making an argument, promising an outcome, or exaggeration.

The Glow-Glow ad states that everybody is wild about Glow-Glow T-shirts. What persuasive technique does this sentence use: fact, exaggeration, or promise?

_____

The Glow-Glow ad ends by stating, "Glow-Glow rules the sports arena!" What persuasive technique does this sentence use: fact, appealing to emotions, or promise?

_____

What Do You Think?

Circle **Fact** if the statement is a fact. Circle **Opinion** if it's an opinion.

The Kansas City Royals are awesome!	**Fact**	**Opinion**
A bicycle has two wheels.	**Fact**	**Opinion**
Crops need rain in order to grow.	**Fact**	**Opinion**
Nobody likes lima beans!	**Fact**	**Opinion**
Everybody should have a computer.	**Fact**	**Opinion**
A dictionary explains the meaning of words.	**Fact**	**Opinion**
Huge is another word for *gigantic*.	**Fact**	**Opinion**
Fourth-grade teachers are nice.	**Fact**	**Opinion**
A dog is man's best friend.	**Fact**	**Opinion**
South America is south of North America.	**Fact**	**Opinion**
Chickens lay eggs.	**Fact**	**Opinion**
Paris is a city in France.	**Fact**	**Opinion**

Fact and opinion

BRAIN BOX

A **fact** is something that can be **proven to be true**. Example: Earth is a planet that has air, water, and land.

An **opinion** states a personal view—it tells what someone **thinks, feels,** or **believes**. Example: Land is more important than water.

The Next Step

Read the article about Boston.

Many tourists visiting Boston walk the Freedom Trail, which includes sixteen stops. Each stop is dedicated to an important Boston event.

The first stop on the trail is the historic Boston Common. This is one of the oldest public parks in the country. In 1775, British soldiers camped on the Common and then went off to fight the colonists.

Across from the Common is the second stop, the Massachusetts State House. Its roof is covered with gold.

Like the first two stops, the third stop is full of history—not just Revolutionary War history, but also the events leading up to the Civil War. It is here, at the famous Park Street Church, that William Lloyd Garrison first spoke out against slavery.

Is this article organized by sequence? _____

What word in the second paragraph tells you which stop you are reading about? _____

In the third paragraph, what word tells you where you are in the order of stops? _____

This and That

Read about oceans.

Atlantic and Pacific

The Atlantic Ocean is the second-largest ocean on Earth. It covers about 20% of the Earth's surface. In addition, the Atlantic is the saltiest of the oceans. It got its name from Atlas, a Greek god.

The Pacific Ocean is the largest ocean on Earth, covering 32% of the Earth's surface. In fact, the Pacific covers more area than all the land on Earth. It is warmer than the Atlantic. It was named by the explorer Ferdinand Magellan. The name Pacific means *peaceful*.

Compare and contrast

In the paragraphs above, circle the words or phrases that compare or contrast the following information:

- The size of the Atlantic Ocean compared with other oceans

- The saltiest ocean

- The size of the Pacific Ocean compared with all the land on Earth

- The temperature of the Pacific Ocean compared with that of the Atlantic Ocean

- The famous figures behind the name of both oceans

Think about two sports, two movies, or two books that you like. Write one paragraph comparing and contrasting the two things.

_____

_____

_____

_____

BRAIN BOX

In a piece that compares and contrasts, the writer shows how two things are alike (**comparison**) and how they are different (**contrast**).

Cause and effect

Flat Tire

Read the story.

Declan strapped his bat and glove onto his bike, but in his hurry he left his repair kit behind. He pedaled furiously, trying to get to the baseball game on time. The Manatees were counting on him to drive in runs! Halfway to the game, on the emptiest stretch of road, Declan biked over a nail, and his front tire went flat.

"I can patch it and pump it up in no time," thought Declan. Then he realized that he had left his repair kit behind! He had no choice but to wheel his bike along the road. No friends or neighbors drove by. Nothing. Nobody. "I have to get to the game on time!" he thought. So he hid his bike behind some trees, grabbed his bat and glove, and began to run.

But by the time Declan reached the ballpark, the game was over. The Manatees had lost the game!

Write in the missing information to show cause and effect in the story about Declan.

Cause		Result/Effect
Declan left his repair kit behind.	→	He could not repair his flat tire.
_____ _____	→	He did not reach the game in time.
He did not reach the ballpark on time.	→	_____ _____
_____ _____	→	The Manatees lost the game.

BRAIN BOX

In a cause-and-effect piece, the writer shows how one thing causes another. The starting event is the cause. The result is the effect.

Step on a Crack

Finish each sentence with a word from below to show **cause** or **effect**.

because	so	since	caused

as a result of	due to	because of

Cause and effect

Irina raced down the sidewalk _____ she was late for art class.

_____ she was rushing, she tripped and fell on a crack in the sidewalk.

The hard fall _____ Irina to break her leg.

Luckily, a neighbor saw the accident and called 911. _____ the neighbor's quick thinking, an ambulance came right away.

By the time Irina's parents got to the hospital, a doctor had set the broken bone. He told Irina's parents her leg would be fine, _____ they felt relieved.

"_____ the fact that she is young," the doctor told them, "Irina's bones will heal quickly."

_____ her experience in the hospital, Irina now wants to be a doctor when she grows up.

BRAIN BOX

You can often tell when a sentence is showing cause and effect by recognizing certain words and phrases, such as **because, due to, since,** and **as a result of.**

Fact or Fiction?

Decide whether the book description is referring to a work of fiction or nonfiction. Then write either **fiction** or **nonfiction** on the line next to each.

Genre recognition

A manual that tells you how to build a bicycle _____

A book that features characters made up by the author _____

A magazine article that tells the life story of a person who lived a hundred years ago _____

A textbook about the history of your state _____

A travel guide that offers advice on the best places to visit in the American Southwest _____

A picture book that spins a fantastical tale about purple puppies _____

A school web page that lists who at your school has the fastest track times _____

A book with charts, graphs, and diagrams _____

The text of a virtual tour of the natural history museum _____

A comic book about a dog who is great at math _____

A short story about kids who meet an extraterrestrial _____

An encyclopedia entry about exoplanets (planets outside the solar system) _____

Write one more example of fiction and one more example of nonfiction that you find in your classroom or library.

_____

_____

_____

_____

BRAIN BOX

Fiction tells about made-up people and stories. Example: Any superhero book
Nonfiction tells about people and things that exist in the real world. Example: A book about seashells

Where and When

Read about each book. Underline all the words or phrases that tell you about the **setting**.

From the Mixed-Up Files of Mrs. Basil E. Frankweiler
by E. L. Konigsburg
On the first page of this book, Claudia decides to run away from home to the Metropolitan Museum of Art in New York City.

Setting

Stone Fox
by John Reynolds Gardiner
If 10-year-old Little Willy wins the National Dogsled Race, held every February in Jackson Hole, Wyoming, he can save his grandfather's farm.

Esperanza Rising
by Pam Muñoz Ryan
In 1930, Esperanza and her mother leave Mexico and cross the border to southern California. Although they were wealthy in Mexico, they are now poor. They join other Mexican migrants to work and live at a farm camp.

The Watsons Go to Birmingham—1963
by Christopher Paul Curtis
In the summer of 1963, Kenny's family travels from Flint, Michigan, to Birmingham, Alabama, to stay with his grandmother. The family has many experiences, including witnessing one of the darkest moments in civil rights history.

Describe one of your own favorite books below. Underline the words you use to tell about the setting.

_____

_____

_____

_____

BRAIN BOX

Setting tells **where** and **when** a work of fiction takes place.

The Best Guess

Read each paragraph. Then circle the correct **inference** or **inferences**.

Sophia looked in the mirror. "Impossible," she said. "Just impossible." She brushed and brushed, but nothing she did made her hair lie straight.

a. Sophia has curly hair.

b. Sophia doesn't care what her hair looks like.

c. Sophia cares what her hair looks like.

"Incredible!" breathed the professor as he looked inside the envelope. "Their mistake is my fortune!" He thought for a moment. "They'll come looking for these tickets," he muttered to himself. Removing the tickets from the envelope, he looked all around his office for the perfect spot.

a. The professor knows that somebody made a mistake.

b. The professor intends to hide the tickets.

c. The professor intends to pay for the tickets.

Catrina loved the sun more than anything. She especially loved the way the sunbeams came through the window and spread out on the carpet. Catrina leapt from the fireplace mantel to the easy chair, and from there to the floor. She curled up in the sunbeams and closed her eyes.

a. Catrina is a decorator.

b. Catrina is a cat.

c. Catrina is going to take a nap.

BRAIN BOX

An **inference** is a logical conclusion. You can make an inference by combining what you already know with what the author has told you.

Showing Character

Read the paragraphs on the cards. Then circle the highlighted words that complete each statement about the **characters** correctly.

Characters

"Look!" whispered Merrie. She tapped Clarissa on the shoulder as they got on the school bus. "WOW!" she exclaimed. "I just love how Max saves us seats each day. Isn't he the most amazing friend?"

Clarissa said nothing.

Merrie's character is shown through her speech thoughts .

She is a person who gets confused enthusiastic about things.

Clarissa's character is shown through her actions silence .

Clarissa probably thinks that Merrie Max is being silly.

Lucien lifted another domino from the box and then wiped his fingertips on his pants. Taking a deep breath, he slowly exhaled as he balanced the domino on end.

Lucien's character is shown through his thoughts actions .

He is a person who moves very carefully sadly .

BRAIN BOX

The people in a work of fiction are called **characters**. You can learn about the characters through their actions, thoughts, and speech.

"Drive to the basket," the coach encouraged me. "Drive and score, Josh!" He patted me on the back. "I have confidence in you." So I fought my way to the basket, surprised that I made it into the key. "There's no way I can score, though," I thought. "It'll never happen. I'm not a hero."

Josh's character is shown through his thoughts speech .

He is a person who thinks he is a hero has little confidence in himself .

A Real Character

Read this excerpt from the book *The Velveteen Rabbit* by Margery Williams.

The Skin Horse had lived longer in the nursery than any of the others. He was so old that his brown coat was bald in patches and showed the seams underneath, and most of the hairs in his tail had been pulled out to string bead necklaces....

"What is REAL?" asked the Rabbit one day, when they were lying side by side.... "Does it mean having things that buzz inside you and a stick-out handle?"

"Real isn't how you are made," said the Skin Horse. "It's a thing that happens to you. When a child loves you for a long, long time, not just to play with, but REALLY loves you, then you become Real."

"Does it hurt?" asked the Rabbit.

"Sometimes," said the Skin Horse, for he was always truthful. "When you are Real you don't mind being hurt."

"Does it happen all at once, like being wound up," he asked, "or bit by bit?"

"It doesn't happen all at once," said the Skin Horse. "You become. It takes a long time. That's why it doesn't happen often to people who break easily, or have sharp edges, or who have to be carefully kept. Generally, by the time you are Real, most of your hair has been loved off, and your eyes drop out and you get loose in the joints and very shabby. But these things don't matter at all, because once you are Real you can't be ugly, except to people who don't understand."

"I suppose you are Real?" said the Rabbit. And then he wished he had not said it, for he thought the Skin Horse might be sensitive. But the Skin Horse only smiled.

"The Boy's Uncle made me Real," he said. "That was a great many years ago; but once you are Real you can't become unreal again. It lasts for always."

The Rabbit . . . thought it would be a long time before this magic called Real happened to him. He longed to become Real, to know what it felt like; and yet the idea of growing shabby and losing his eyes and whiskers was rather sad. He wished that he could become it without these uncomfortable things happening to him.

Answer the questions about Skin Horse and Rabbit.
Support your answers with details from the story.

Is the Skin Horse a character who is trying to be kind or unkind to the
Rabbit? Provide support for your answer with examples from what he
says (his speech) or what he does (his actions or behavior).

_____
_____
_____

Characters

Is the Skin Horse a new toy or an old toy ? Do you know this through
his speech or his thoughts?

_____
_____
_____

Does the Skin Horse have happy or unhappy memories about
becoming Real? Do we know this through his speech or his actions?

_____
_____
_____

Was the Rabbit concerned or unconcerned when he realized he
might have hurt the Skin Horse's feelings? Do we know this through his
actions or his thoughts?

_____
_____
_____

BRAIN BOX

When you
draw a
conclusion,
you make
a guess
about the
most likely
outcome
based on the
evidence.

In the last paragraph, the Rabbit wants to become Real. Is he worried
or not worried about becoming Real? Do we know this through his
thoughts or his speech?

_____
_____
_____

What Happened?

Read the story.

Power!

Kyle looked at the new message on his computer. "Hello, Kyle," it said. "This is Hal, your computer." *Whoa, dude!* thought Kyle. *What's going on?* Kyle kicked aside a few pairs of sneakers, dumped the books off his chair, and sat down. Then he typed, "Your name isn't Hal. Your name, if you want to call it that, is Clover. You're a Clover computer, model number C7654C. Got that?"

Whirrrr! The sound was so loud that Kyle jumped back, falling off his chair. The whirring grew louder and louder. Kyle folded his arms over his head, just in case the computer exploded. At last the sound stopped.

Kyle peeked up at the desk. The computer screen was pulsing colors: red, purple, red, purple, red, purple. Kyle waited until the colors stopped, then he very carefully crawled back onto his chair. He placed his fingers on the keyboard and began to type.

Complete the sentences to tell about the key events in this story.

Kyle sees _____.

Kyle types _____.

The computer _____.

Kyle _____.

At last the sound _____.

Kyle _____ and begins _____.

It's All Connected

Open one of your favorite works of fiction. List the first five events in the plot on the lines below. Where you can, use the words **because** or **is caused by** to show how the events are connected to each other by cause and effect.

Understanding plot

Title of book or story

Plot

1.

2.

3.

4.

5.

BRAIN BOX

The **plot** is the events in a story that are connected by **cause** and **effect**.

Understanding
fables

Aesop's Fables

Read the fables. Then circle the correct answer to each question.

The Serpent and the File

A snake glided into a tool shop. As it slithered across the floor, the snake traveled over a metal file whose sharp teeth cut its skin. Furious, the snake turned and bit the file again and again. But the snake could not hurt the heavy iron tool. It had to give up its anger and continue on its way.

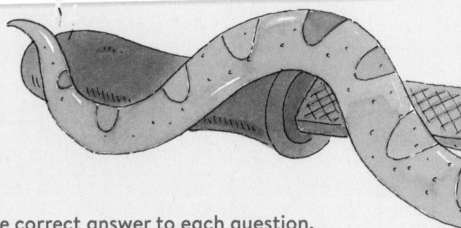

Circle the correct answer to each question.

The (iron   file   snake   tool shop) is the main character in this fable.

The main character has a problem with the (snake   iron   file).

Because the main character is hurt by the (tool shop   snake   file), it becomes (happy   angry   confused).

It (cuts   bites) the (snake   file) many times.

The lesson of a fable is called a moral. A moral gives some useful hints on how to live your life. The moral of "The Serpent and the File" is:

Don't go into tool shops.

It is useless to attack a nonliving thing.

BRAIN BOX

A **fable** is a story that teaches a lesson.

The Shepherd Boy and the Wolf

A shepherd boy watched over a flock of sheep near a village. The boy cried "Wolf! Wolf!" when there was no wolf—just to see the villagers run out of their houses to help him. When they arrived, the boy laughed. Again and again the shepherd boy cried "Wolf! Wolf!" just so he could laugh at the villagers. Then, at last, a wolf truly did come to kill the sheep. "Wolf!" cried the shepherd boy. "Help me! This is for real! A wolf is killing the sheep!" But not one villager paid attention to these cries, and not one villager came to help. The shepherd boy lost many sheep to the wolf.

The main character in this fable is the (village   boy   wolf).

The main character plays tricks on the (villagers   wolf   sheep).

The (sheep   villagers) will not come out because they think the boy is telling (the truth   lies).

The moral of this fable is:

A liar will not be believed, even when speaking the truth.
People who play tricks get chased by wolves.

The Real Meaning

Read about each **idiom.** Circle the sentence that uses the idiom correctly.

Understanding idioms

The idiom have one's head in the clouds has been around for four hundred years. It means to be dreamy and impractical.

Grungo the Giant was so tall that he had his head in the clouds.

Grungo the Giant couldn't be counted on to do anything because he always had his head in the clouds.

The idiom keep one's nose to the grindstone has been around for five hundred years. It stems from the idea that tools are sharpened by being pressed against a grindstone. It means to work hard and steadily.

Yoshi was rushed to the hospital because he kept his nose to the grindstone and cut it.

Yoshi won the prize because he kept his nose to the grindstone.

The idiom dog in the manger comes from Aesop's Fables, where a dog snarls to keep an ox from eating hay, even though the dog can't eat it himself.

Shane is a dog in the manger about kids using his swimming pool.

Shane is a dog in the manger, and Lightning is a horse in the stable.

BRAIN BOX

An **idiom** is an expression that means something different from what the words might seem to actually say. For example, **hold your tongue** is an idiom that means **be quiet.**

Hit the Books

Complete each sentence with the correct **idiom** from below.

| cool as a cucumber | hit the books | on his high horse |

| out of the woods | Greek to me | on pins and needles |

| wolf in sheep's clothing | the way the cookie crumbles |

Seraphina was very worried about the move, but her brother was _____.

I tried to understand my computer manual, but it was _____.

Takumi got a new book on Monday and lost it on Tuesday. "Oh well." He shrugged. "That's _____ _____."

Yancey has few friends, probably because he's always _____, acting like he's better than everyone.

Eula was _____ waiting to find out if she made the team.

After we finished playing Monopoly, Dad said, "Okay, kids, the fun is over. Time to _____."

Watch out for that tricky salesman. He's a _____.

We escaped the giants and the gnomes, but we weren't _____ yet.

Māui Brings Back Fire

Read this Māori legend.

Māui Brings Back Fire

Māui was mischievous when it came to fire. One day he put out every fire in the whole village. Now the people had no fire to cook with. They had no fire with which to keep themselves warm. Māui's mother told him, "You must go to the woman elder, Mahuika, and ask her for some fire."

So Māui traveled to the underworld and found Mahuika. She was very hungry because she couldn't feed herself. Everything she touched burst into flame, including her food. Māui speared some food. He held the food out to Mahuika and she ate and ate.

When she finished eating, Mahuika told Māui that he had been careless in the world of light. He had wasted the precious gift of fire. But because Māui had been kind to her, Mahuika would give him fire. She pulled off one of her fingernails and handed it to Māui. The fingernail burst into flames. Mahuika told Māui to take the fire into his world, light his fires, then bring back her fingernail.

Māui took the fingernail and left. As he carried it away, he decided to drop the fingernail into a stream and the fire hissed out. He went back to Mahuika. "I fell and lost your fingernail in a stream," he said. So Mahuika gave him another fingernail of fire to take back to his village.

But again Māui dropped the fingernail into a stream and the fire went out. He returned to Mahuika for another. Māui did the same thing with each fingernail until he had used all but one of Mahuika's fingernails. Mahuika became angry. "You have wasted my fire for the last time!" and she threw the last fingernail at Māui.

Māui jumped into the air and turned into a hawk as the flaming fingernail exploded beneath him. He flew out of the underworld, but the flames followed him all the way home. The gods came to Māui's rescue by creating wind, icy rain, overflowing streams, and an earthquake to swallow up Mahuika's fire.

When Māui arrived home safely, he turned back into a boy and held a glowing stick in his hand. He had fire, but people could no longer go to the underworld to find it. From that point on, they could only make fire by rubbing twigs from a kaikomako tree together.

BRAIN BOX

A **legend** is a story handed down from generation to generation that explains how things came to be. Every culture in the world has legends, and they are usually told out loud, not written down.

Legends

Answer the questions.

Why was Māui sent to find fire?

_____

_____

What adjectives would you use to describe Māui in this story?

_____

Where did Mahuika live?

_____

How would you describe Mahuika in this story?

_____

Why hadn't Mahuika eaten in so long?

_____

Why did Mahuika become angry with Māui?

_____

Why do you think Māui was so careless with Mahuika's fingernails?

_____

What happened when Mahuika threw her last fingernail at Māui?

_____

How do people have to make fire at the end of the legend?

_____

_____

Fill-In Fun

Read each sentence. Fill in a word that creates alliteration with the highlighted word or words.

Julius _____ for joy.

The plump porcupine ate my _____.

The _____ steered clear of the cute cub.

Howie has a horrible sense of _____.

Ned wore a nice _____.

Wes walloped _____ in Ping-Pong.

The turquoise turtle tried to _____.

The daring dragonfly darted between the _____ and the _____.

A pirate with a _____ patch would be unusual.

Lance liked _____ and _____ in his lunch box.

The wiggly worm worked its way across the _____.

Write two of your own examples of alliteration using any letters you like.

It's Just Like That

Underline the **simile** in each sentence. Then circle the two things that are being compared.

Our (classroom) was <u>as warm as</u> an (iceberg.)

Robert Burns wrote that his love was like a red, red rose.

Celia was as graceful as Godzilla.

Similes

Our teacher's understanding of history is as deep as the Pacific.

After Aiden tried to shave, his face looked like a jigsaw puzzle.

The two-year-old raced around the room like a hamster on its wheel.

"I wandered lonely as a cloud" was written by Wordsworth.

The football fluttered through the air like a sick duck.

The tired dog huffed and puffed like a steam engine.

My sister dances like a puppet.

The distant pueblos were as tiny as anthills.

Use these prompts to write three similes of your own.

My family is _____
_____

My friend is _____
_____

My bedroom is _____
_____

BRAIN BOX

A **simile** is a phrase that compares two things by using the words **as** or **like**. Example: Jason was **as tall as** a redwood.

Cold Fingers

Read the poem and then answer the questions.

The Muff

The muff
is a piece
of extravagant fluff
into which I stuff
both hands deeply,
up to the cuff.

It keeps them warm—
but not enough.

Due to the above
I now shove
freezing fingers
into a glove.

Which words in the first stanza rhyme with *muff*? _____

_____

Which of the rhyming words seems out of place
because of its spelling? _____

_____

Which words in the third stanza rhyme? _____

_____

Why do you think the author of this poem wrote a poem
instead of a story? _____

_____

BRAIN
BOX

A poem
sometimes
uses rhyming,
rhythm, and
alliteration
to tie things
together.

Snails: A Garden Poem

Read the **haiku** and then answer the questions.

Snails

Invaders from earth,
sliding on slime, eyes on stalks,
eat my green garden.

Haiku

How many syllables are in the first line?_____

How many syllables are in the second line?_____

How many syllables are in the third line?_____

Poems often surprise us by saying something different from what is expected. In the first line, the surprise is that the "invaders" are from _____, not from deep space.

Is this a good way to describe snails? Why or why not?
_____
_____

In the second line, what two things about the snails make it seem as if they are alien invaders? _____
_____

List the words with alliteration in the haiku. _____
_____

BRAIN BOX

Haiku is a form of poetry from Japan. A haiku verse has a certain number of syllables in each line.

Wolf Poem

Read the **cinquain** and then answer the questions.

Timber Wolf

Wolf nose

knows intruders;

wolf ears hear foreign sounds;

wolf eyes size up camera stand

and me.

Poets often repeat words for emphasis. What word is repeated three times in this poem? _____

Which two words in the poem are homophones? _____
_____

Which three of the wolf's senses are alert? _____
_____

In the fourth line, which two words repeat the **s** sound?
_____

Which two words rhyme in the fourth line? _____
_____

Who is "telling" this poem? _____

Read the poem aloud and write the number of syllables in each line. Did you end up with 2/4/6/8/2? If not, better count again!

BRAIN BOX

A cinquain is a five-line poem with 22 syllables. The syllables per line are 2/4/6/8/2.

Two Bears

Read the poem and then answer the questions.

Bears Consider Dinner

Sister bear,
let us shamble to the sea
and jump upon a seal;
or better yet, a walrus
makes a tasty meal.

Brother bear,
I've lost my taste for blubber.
I crave food that varies;
let us go vegetarian
and chow down grass and berries.

How many bears speak in this poem? _____

Do their words have quotation marks around them? _____

How can you tell when a different bear starts to speak? _____
_____

What does the first bear want to do? _____
_____

What does the second bear want to do? _____
_____

In the first stanza, the end of line _____
rhymes with the end of line _____.

BRAIN BOX

Dialogue is
conversation
between two or
more characters.
Usually dialogue
is shown
surrounded by
quotation marks,
but in this poem
the dialogue is
separated by
stanza.

Reading Review

Complete each clue. Then write each word in the crossword.

Across

2. A simile compares two things by using _____ or as.

4. Alliteration is the repetition of the same _____.

5. A _____ is a story that teaches a lesson. Aesop wrote hundreds of them.

7. The topic sentence states the _____ idea of the paragraph.

8. A work of fiction is about imaginary people and events. A work of _____ is about real people and events.

9. The people in a story are called _____.

Down

1. A _____ is an oral story that explains how things came to be.

3. A story that exaggerates a lot is a _____ tale.

4. The _____ is when and where a story takes place.

6. A caption is information under a _____.

WRITING

People write to share ideas, to teach, to entertain, and more. Why do you like to write? Let's learn how organizing our writing helps us share ideas more clearly with our audience.

PARENTS In this section, your child will practice a variety of skills for writing personal and persuasive essays, stories, emails, and more. Help your child brainstorm ideas by creating idea webs and story maps. Share the different kinds of communication and writing styles you use as an adult and point out how your writing changes based on the audience or subject.

For additional resources, visit www.BrainQuest.com/grade4

First Person

Read about **personal essays**.

A **personal essay** tells a story from the author's point of view. The following traits are characteristic of personal essays:

- They're usually written in the first person. The author's voice is "I."
- They're about a specific event or experience told from the author's unique perspective.
- They use descriptive language, vivid details, and dialogue.
- They often have a strong conclusion or point that the author wants to get across.

These writing prompts will help you think about a subject for a **personal essay**. Write one or two sentences to complete each prompt. Be sure to write in the first person.

The most surprising thing that happened to me this year was . . .

The worst experience of my summer vacation was when . . .

There's no place I'd rather live than _____, because . . .

One of my favorite days ever was definitely the day when . . .

BRAIN BOX

Narrative writing tells a story. Examples of narrative writing include **personal essays, fairy tales, short stories,** and **poems.** All fiction is narrative writing, but not all narrative writing is fictional.

Using a Story Map

Choose one of the writing prompts from page 110 to write a personal narrative. Fill in the following **story map** to think about how your personal narrative will be organized.

Character or characters
(including yourself)

_____

_____

Setting

_____

_____

_____

The Main Situation/Problem

_____

_____

_____

Major Event Number 1
(supports the situation or problem)

_____

_____

Major Event Number 2

_____

_____

_____

Summary/Conclusion

_____

_____

_____

BRAIN BOX

When writing a narrative, one way to organize it is to use a **story map**. Story maps help the writer think about the narrative in terms of **character, setting, story events,** and **conclusion.**

Drafting a Personal Essay

Using your story map on page 111, write a three-paragraph draft of your personal essay.

Remember to:

- Use the first person ("I").
- Include a topic sentence in each paragraph.
- Use descriptive language, vivid details, and dialogue wherever you can.
- Have a strong conclusion or point that you want to get across.

Title:

Author (your name):

Writing a Fairy Tale

Think of a good idea for a **fairy tale**. Plan when and where your story will take place by filling out the box below.

Setting

Where: _____

When: _____

Next, think about your main character and at least one other character.

Characters

Name of main character: _____

What does the main character want? _____

_____

_____

Name of another character: _____

What does this character want? _____

_____

_____

Name of another character: _____

What does this character want? _____

_____

_____

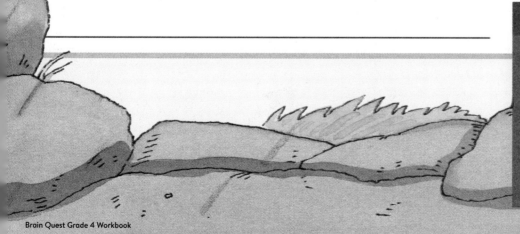

BRAIN BOX

A **fairy tale** is a story with make-believe characters, such as fairies, goblins, witches, and talking animals. Fairy tales are usually written for children.

What's Next?

Think of three things that will happen in your fairy tale. Write each event in the space below.

Events
1.
2.
3.

Write the first event of your fairy tale in the space below. Then, write the second event and explain how it is caused by the first event. Finally, write the third event and explain how it is caused by the second event.

Remember, a plot consists of a series of events that are either **causes** or **effects**.

Plot
First event of the fairy tale:
Second event of the fairy tale:
Third event of the fairy tale:

Remember, when writing about events, use words such as **because**, **because of**, and **as a result of**.

Friendly Letter

Write a letter to a friend. First, **inform** your friend of the things you're doing. Then try to **persuade** them to join you to do something (perhaps to go on a trip or attend camp together). Use the words in the boxes to strengthen your writing.

Writing to inform and persuade

Words to Persuade

please	again
to sum up	surely
definitely	why not
try	only
the best	amazing
secondly	finally
even	as you know

Words to Inform

and then	such as
when	usually
so	here
for example	next
including	another

BRAIN BOX

All writing has a purpose. The purpose could be to **inform**, **persuade**, or **entertain**. A piece of writing can have more than one purpose.

Sharing Good News

Write a draft email to your favorite relative telling them about something great that happened or something you're looking forward to. Use descriptive language and write in complete sentences.

BRAIN BOX

T.H.I.N.K. First!

When you write or post anything online, it's important to use **netiquette**, or internet etiquette. Keep courtesy and communication guidelines in mind every time you write an email or comment on a post or video. A good way to remember to use netiquette is to **T.H.I.N.K.** before you hit send: Are your words **True**, **Helpful**, **Inspiring**, **Necessary**, and **Kind**? Remember to **T.H.I.N.K.** before you post!

Haiku

Below is a **haiku** about autumn. Read it, then write a haiku about spring, summer, and winter below.

Writing a haiku

Autumn

Leaves turning colors _____ 5 syllables

Dropping with each gust of wind _____ 7 syllables

Fall days come quickly _____ 5 syllables

Spring

_____ 5 syllables

_____ 7 syllables

_____ 5 syllables

Summer

_____ 5 syllables

_____ 7 syllables

_____ 5 syllables

Winter

_____ 5 syllables

_____ 7 syllables

_____ 5 syllables

BRAIN BOX

A **haiku** verse has a total of 17 syllables: 5 in the first line, 7 in the second, and 5 in the third.

That's the Idea

Read about **idea webs**.

Idea web

Tamara is using an **idea web** to help her write about her new closet. She writes her **topic sentence** in the big circle. Each time she thinks of something to describe, she writes it in a small circle.

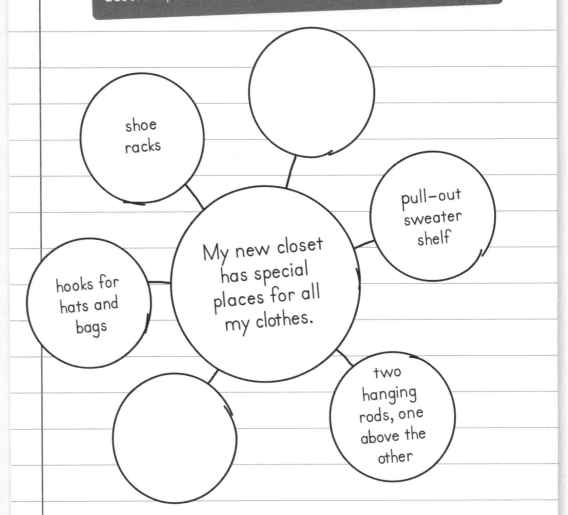

My new closet has special places for all my clothes. All my sweaters go on a pull-out shelf. My shoes go on a shoe rack, and my hats and bags go on special hooks. My new closet also has two hanging rods. One is above the other, so I can hang my pants on the bottom rod and my shirts on the top one. I love my new closet!

The topic sentence becomes the first sentence of her paragraph. She uses each item in the smaller circles as a **supporting detail**.

BRAIN BOX

An **idea web** can help you organize your thoughts before you start writing about a subject.

Pick a subject to write about. Make an **idea web** to help you brainstorm. Write your topic sentence in the big circle.

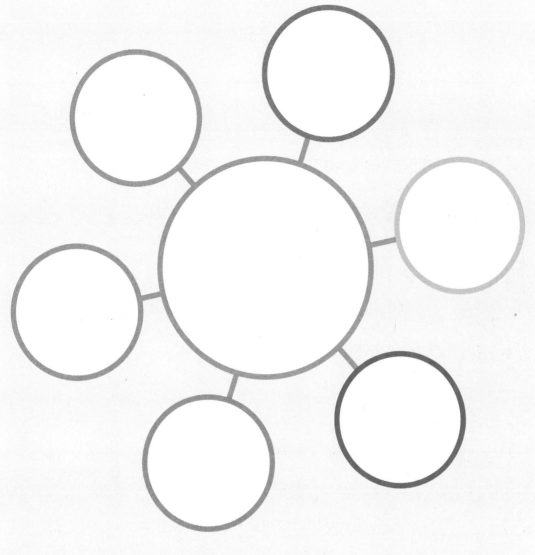

After you finish your idea web, write your paragraph below.

Taking Notes

Read the notes about the lynx, a type of wildcat.

Idea web

—short tails

—long legs and big paws

—mostly live in forested areas

—very thick fur coat

—tufts of fur on tips of ears

—most are spotted for camouflage

—many live in North America, like Canada and Alaska

—mostly live in habitats that are cold and snow-covered

—about 30 pounds

—long, pointy teeth

—high-altitude environments

—some live in Russia, Scandinavia, parts of Europe

—most are light brown and gray

BRAIN BOX

Nonnarrative writing explains, reports, or informs. Examples of nonnarrative writing include journalism, research reports, recipes, and instruction manuals.

Nonnarrative writing usually requires taking **notes.** These are brief facts written down to help you remember them later.

In the idea web, write details about what the lynx looks like and where it lives. Write a topic sentence in the center circle.

Idea web

short tails

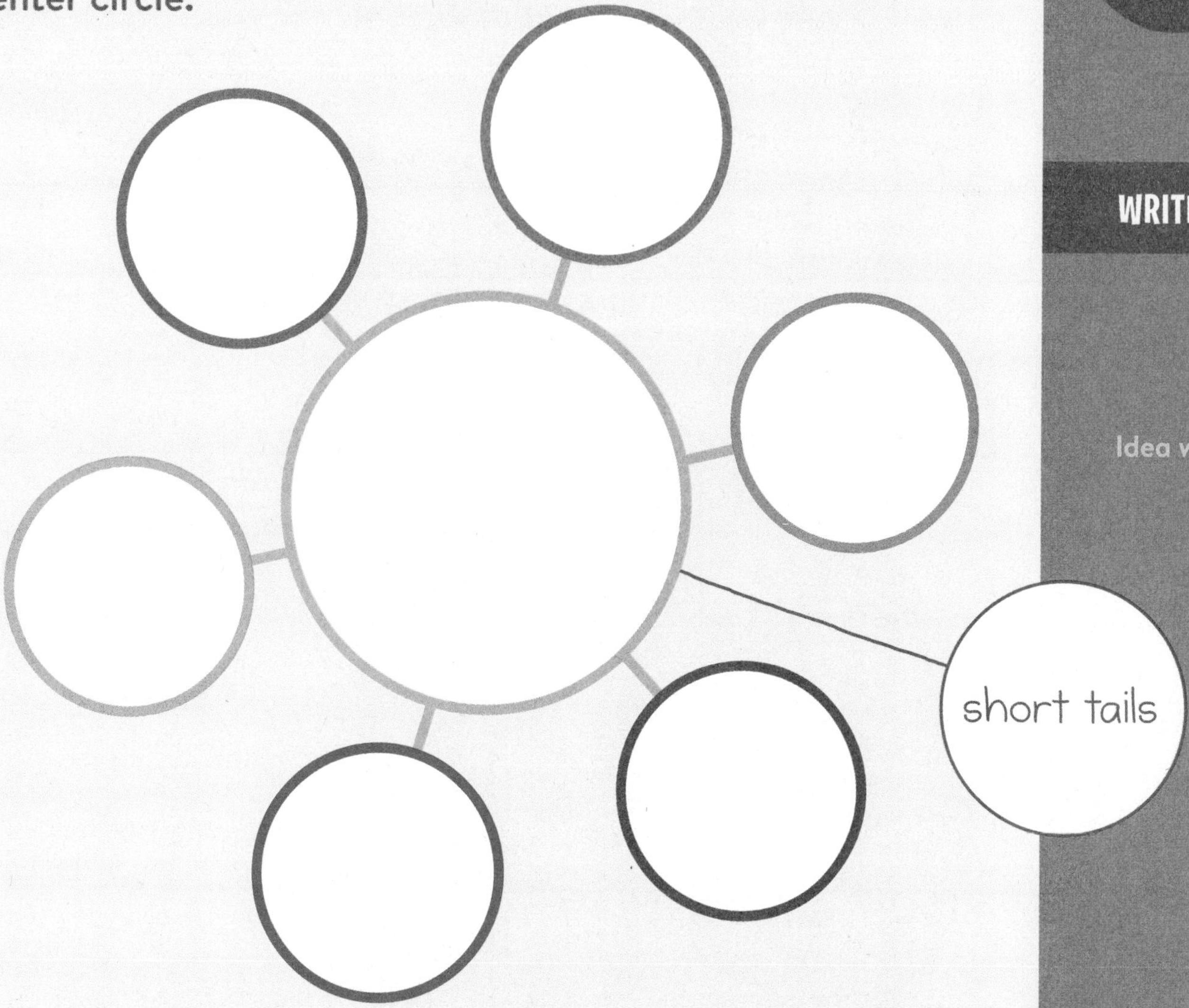

Use your idea web to write a paragraph about the lynx. Begin with the topic sentence in the center circle. Use the notes in the smaller circles in your idea web as supporting details.

Badminton and Tennis

Read the notes in the **Venn diagram**.

Comparing
things

This Venn diagram is about tennis and badminton, two sports that are alike but also have many differences.

BADMINTON

- underhand serve
- serve inside baseline
- play with shuttlecock
- shuttlecock must not bounce

BOTH

- play with rackets
- play on court
- court has net
- Olympic sports
- two-person or four-person game

TENNIS

- overhand serve
- serve outside baseline
- play with ball
- ball may bounce

The blue circle lists all the things that are unique to badminton.

The yellow circle lists all the things that are unique to tennis.

The part where the circles overlap lists all the things the two sports have in common.

BRAIN BOX

A **Venn diagram**, which is two circles that intersect, is a useful tool when comparing and contrasting subjects.

Use the notes in the Venn diagram to write two paragraphs comparing badminton and tennis. In the first paragraph, write about how the two sports are alike. In the second paragraph, write about how they differ from each other.

Comparing things

They're Connected

Read about what happened on December 16, 1773. Research the subject in an encyclopedia or on the internet. List as many effects as you can on the page below.

Using cause and effect

Cause
On December 16, 1773, a group of American colonists dumped 342 tea chests from British ships into the waters of Boston Harbor.

Ask an adult before you go online.

Effects
• The British government closed the port of Boston.

BRAIN BOX

A **cause** is why an action happens. An **effect** is what happens as a result of the action.

Be a Journalist

Write a **newspaper article** about Valdez the Vampire. Use the reporter's notes below. Make sure you include the five Ws.

The five Ws

Who: Valdez the Vampire

What: Called press conference

Why: Going vegetarian, will drink only tomato juice, not blood

When: Midnight, Friday, October 31

Where: At Crumbling Castle, long believed to be haunted

BRAIN BOX

A newspaper article answers the five Ws: who, what, when, where, and why.

126

Narrowing
a topic for
a report

Make Your Choice

Use this page to help you prepare to write your report.
First choose a topic.

Here are the first three steps to writing a good report:

1. **Choose a topic.** If you are given a topic, this step is already done. Otherwise, look for subject matter you are interested in.

2. **Do some quick research.** For quick research on a subject, a dictionary, an encyclopedia, and reliable internet sites are all excellent sources.

3. **Narrow your topic.** For example, if your topic is *dogs*, you could narrow your topic to be about a specific breed of dog.

Topic

_____

_____

_____

_____

Quick research

_____

_____

_____

_____

Final topic of my report

_____

_____

_____

_____

Once you have a final topic, it's time to do more research and take some notes. Use at least three different sources in your research.

Use authoritative sources. These sources are reliable, or trustworthy, and give only true information. Authoritative sources include encyclopedia entries, magazine articles, and books about your topic. An interview with someone very knowledgeable on your subject is also considered an authoritative source.

Look for reliable internet sources, too, like online encyclopedias, magazines, and books and the websites of universities, nonprofit research organizations, and government agencies—their URLs end with .edu, .org, and .gov. Museum websites are also great sources.

To decide whether a source is authoritative, ask yourself, "Do I know who wrote or published this?" Look for authors or publications whose authority is widely recognized among experts in that subject.

Double- and triple-check your facts by making sure they are up-to-date and by finding the same facts in multiple sources.

Imagine that you are researching a report on the peacock mantis shrimp. After each of the sample sources below, write whether it is **authoritative** or **not authoritative**.

A page called "Fast Facts: Peacock Mantis Shrimp," published on the website of the American Museum of Natural History

_____

A fan website created by someone who likes animals

_____

A library book about underwater animals

_____

An advertisement selling "amazing underwater cameras"

_____

A print magazine article written by a well-known marine biologist

_____

An article in *Encyclopedia Britannica* called "Mantis shrimp"

_____

TRY THE LIBRARY! You can log in to a research portal through some local public libraries and access authoritative sources just for kids. You can also ask a librarian, at either your school or your local library, to get recommendations for sources.

Take Your Notes

Use these mini index cards to take notes as you research your report topic. Consult at least three sources, and write the name of a source on each card. Write down interesting facts and details.

How to take notes

Use quotation marks if you want to use an exact quotation. Note who the quotation is from.

Source:

Source:

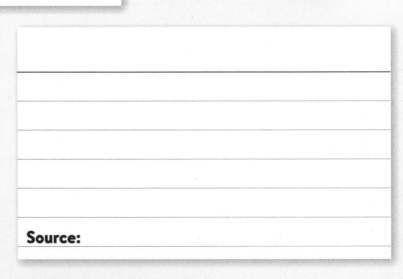

Source:

Use as many cards as you need.
If you need more, use real index cards.

Make Your Plan

Once you finish your research, think about the best way to organize your report. Should it be written chronologically (in time order)? Organized by subtopic or cause and effect? Choose a way to structure your report based on the topic and your notes. Then fill in the idea webs.

Organizing your notes

Prewrite Your Report

Once you've finished organizing your notes, it's time to **prewrite**. Fill in the **outline** below using the information from your notes.

Topic:

1st Paragraph Topic Sentence:

1st Supporting Detail:

2nd Supporting Detail:

3rd Supporting Detail:

2nd Paragraph Topic Sentence:

1st Supporting Detail:

2nd Supporting Detail:

3rd Supporting Detail:

3rd Paragraph Topic Sentence:

1st Supporting Detail:

2nd Supporting Detail:

3rd Supporting Detail:

BRAIN BOX

An **outline** is a way of organizing information by main idea and supporting details.

Your Final Report

Now write your final report. Remember to begin each paragraph with a topic sentence. Fill out your paragraphs with supporting details. Use interesting language and details in your writing.

Using exact nouns

To Be Exact

Write an **exact noun** for each general noun.

plant	tulip
dog	
celebrity	
vegetable	

Write six sentences, one for each **exact noun** in the boxes below. If you don't know what a word means, look it up in a dictionary.

surgeon	brook
gasoline	governor
telescope	lavender

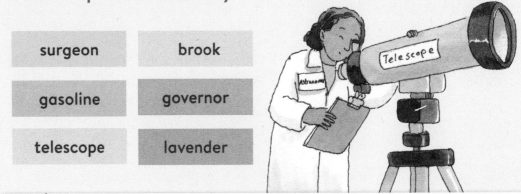

Be Precise

Write a **vivid verb** for each general verb.

walk	
drive	
eat	
stir	

Write six sentences, one for each **vivid verb** below. If you don't know what a word means, look it up in a dictionary.

frowned   sniffed   yelped   signaled

fled   pondered

BRAIN BOX

Use **vivid verbs** to make your writing come alive.

Example: He was **acting confused**. He was **floundering**.

It's All in the Details

Make each sentence more interesting by rewriting it using your own **adjectives** and **adverbs**.

Using descriptive words

Luis painted a line on the sidewalk.

Luis quickly painted a yellow line on the crooked sidewalk.

We took a walk.

My favorite shirt has a stripe.

Mom made an announcement.

Darla's dog looked at her.

The bike ride was bouncy.

I got drenched in the rain.

The weather is cold.

The spy studied the code.

BRAIN BOX

Adding **descriptive words** such as **adjectives** and **adverbs** makes your writing more interesting and more exact.

Put 'Em Together

Combine each set of sentences into one sentence. Use the words **because**, **but**, **and**, or **which**. Change the order of the sentences if needed.

WRITING

My dog is scratching himself. He has fleas.
<u>My dog is scratching himself because he has fleas</u>.

Rewriting sentences

Kayla and Cyrah are friends. Kayla and Iniko are not friends.
_____

I earn money by doing chores. My father pays me when I wash the car.
_____

Omar went to the farmers market. He needed fresh vegetables to make a salad.
_____

My state has a state flower. It has a state bird and a state insect.
_____

The name Mississippi means "Great River." Indigenous people named the Mississippi River. The Mississippi River is a powerful river.
_____
_____
_____
_____

BRAIN BOX

You can combine sentences to make your writing more interesting by:

- Joining two independent clauses with a conjunction such as **and**, **but**, or **because**

- Changing an independent clause into a dependent clause by adding the word **which**

- Writing words in a series separated by commas

US Interstates

Rewrite this paragraph so it reads more smoothly. Combine the ten sentences into no more than five new sentences.

Combining sentences in paragraphs

The directions of US interstate highways are not hard to understand. They are easy to understand. All the even-numbered highways travel east. They also travel west. I-80 starts in New York City. I-80 ends up in San Francisco, California. All the odd-numbered highways run north. They run south as well. I-35 begins in Texas. It ends in Minnesota.

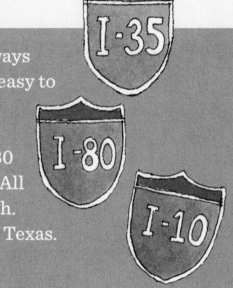

On the Run

Correct each **run-on sentence** by rewriting it below.

Correcting run-on sentences

The knight charged the castle, the drawbridge was going up.

The knight charged the castle because the drawbridge was going up.

Jeans are very popular, they are stylish and comfortable.

I don't like heights, we live on the 25th floor.

Gophers are cute, they are awesome diggers.

The planets travel around the sun, they travel in an ellipse, which is an oval shape.

Lance drops candy wrappers everywhere, he is a litterbug.

The remote control stopped working, its battery was dead.

BRAIN BOX

A **run-on sentence** is two or more sentences connected without punctuation between them. They can usually be corrected by:

• Breaking the run-on sentence into two separate sentences

• Adding a conjunction, such as **and**, **but**, or **because**

Brain Quest Grade 4 Workbook

Make It Smooth

Use the **transitional words** in the boxes below to rewrite this paragraph.

Using
transitional
words

first	next	then	another

second	third	finally

To make a chocolate milkshake, you need milk, chocolate ice cream, and a blender. Put two scoops of ice cream in the blender. Add one-half cup of milk. Close the lid of the blender. (If you don't, you'll get milk everywhere!) Press the MIX button for six or seven seconds. Press the LIQUEFY button for six or seven seconds. Take the lid off the blender. Pour the milkshake into a glass. Yum!

BRAIN BOX

Transitional words
help make a smooth
connection between one
part of a sentence or
paragraph and another.

Make the Mark

Here are some common **proofreading marks** you can learn and use.

Symbol	What it means	Example
a̲ (triple underline)	capitalize	The pacific Ocean is the largest ocean in the world.
A (slash)	make lowercase	There are 25,000 Islands scattered throughout the ocean.
∧	insert letter to spell correctly	The Pacific Ocean is so wide that it touches the coasts of Indonesia and Colobia. (m inserted)
∧ (comma)	add a comma	It is home to incredible whales, sharks, and coral reefs.
⊙	add a period	The Pacific Ocean gets its name from the word for peaceful. It isn't always peaceful, though.
℘	delete or take out	The area the Pacific Ocean covers is bigger larger than the area covered by all the dry land on Earth.
¶	start a new paragraph	The Pacific Ocean has the deepest trenches in the world. ¶The Indian Ocean is another beautiful ocean.

Proofreading marks

BRAIN BOX

Proofreading marks show what to correct when you edit.

Ice *Brrreakers*

Below is a single paragraph, but it should be three. Break it up by underlining the three topic sentences. Then write the correct proofreading mark where each new paragraph should begin.

Using paragraph structure

Deserts cover one-fifth of Earth's land surface. Most people think of them as being hot and dry, but an area doesn't have to be hot or dry to be called a desert. A desert is the name for a place that gets very little rainfall—less than 10 inches per year. The two largest deserts in the world are in Earth's polar regions: the Arctic and the Antarctic. At the southern end of the globe lies the Antarctic Desert—the world's largest desert. It is about 5.5 million square miles and covers the continent of Antarctica. Scientists there have recorded temperatures as low as –144 °F! The second-largest desert in the world is the Arctic Desert. It has a surface area of about 5.4 million square miles. Extending across the northern end of the globe, it covers parts of Norway, Finland, Sweden, Canada, Alaska, Iceland, Greenland, and Russia. The lowest recorded temperature during Arctic winter is –93.3 °F!

Meet Rita Dove

Proofread the paragraphs below using the correct proofreading marks from page 139.

Rita Dove was the first Black American to be Named poet laureate (LAW-ree-at) of the united states. A poet laureate is selected by the librarian of the US Congress to encourage people to appreciate reading and writing Poetry They usually do this by giving talks and readings. Dove was poet laureate from 1993 to 1995,

Rita Dove loved reading when she was a Child. She was a high school Presidential Scholar, an honor given to the country's most distinguished students. Rita Dove attended college at Miami University in ohio, graduating summa cum laude—meaning With highest honors. She also studied in germany and at the University of iowa

Rita Dove has won many Awards and written many Books, including *On the Bus with Rosa Parks* and *Thomas and Beulah*, which won the Pulitzer Prize for poetry. Rita Dove is also a teacher. She is a professor at the University of virginia.

Final Word

Whenever you finish writing something, remember to review and edit your work. Use this checklist to help—you can even tear it out and hang it near your desk.

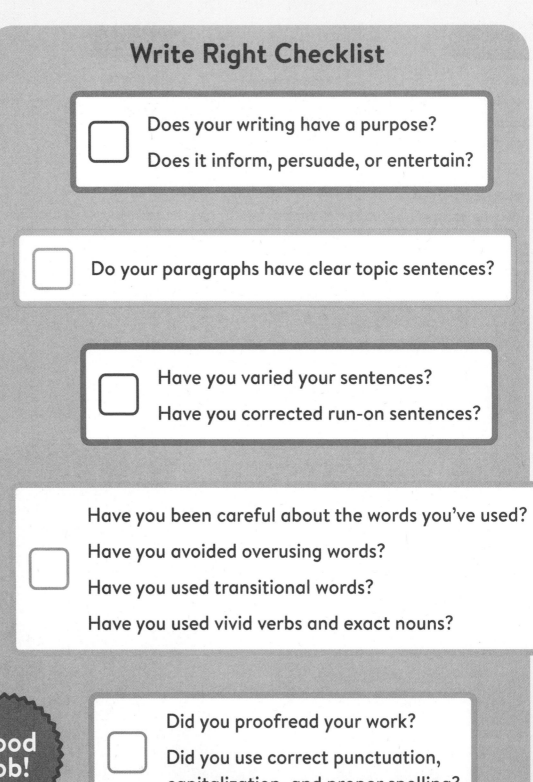

Write Right Checklist

☐ Does your writing have a purpose?

Does it inform, persuade, or entertain?

☐ Do your paragraphs have clear topic sentences?

☐ Have you varied your sentences?

Have you corrected run-on sentences?

☐ Have you been careful about the words you've used?

Have you avoided overusing words?

Have you used transitional words?

Have you used vivid verbs and exact nouns?

Good Job!

☐ Did you proofread your work?

Did you use correct punctuation, capitalization, and proper spelling?

MATH SKILLS

How can two numbers with the same digits have different values? When do you round a number up instead of down? Understanding how to think about numbers helps us work through more difficult math.

PARENTS In this section, your child will review place value, expanded notation, rounding, number patterns, and estimation. Help your child develop a growth mindset, where they learn that their abilities can be strengthened through hard work. If they say, "I can't do this math activity," encourage them to say, "I can't do this math activity yet." This helps build confidence and determination.

PLACE A
STICKER
HERE

For additional resources, visit www.BrainQuest.com/grade4

Building Skills

Circle the **6** in each number and write its **place value**.

4(6) ones _____

614 _____

168 _____

4,602 _____

6,190 _____

6 _____

Circle the **1** in each number and write its place value.

1,542 _____

145 _____

4,321 _____

9,810 _____

Circle the **3** in each number and write its place value.

5,302 _____

9,143 _____

735 _____

3,447 _____

BRAIN BOX

The **place value** of a digit in a number is determined by where it appears in the number.

Example: 2,547

thousands	hundreds	tens	ones
2	5	4	7

Write It Out

Write out the **expanded notation** for each number.

5,147 = [5,000] + [100] + [40] + [7]

7,975 = [   ] + [   ] + [   ] + [ ]

8,331 = [   ] + [   ] + [   ] + [ ]

2,704 = [   ] + [   ] + [   ] + [ ]

1,228 = [   ] + [   ] + [   ] + [ ]

6,977 = [   ] + [   ] + [   ] + [ ]

3,812 = [   ] + [   ] + [   ] + [ ]

5,548 = [   ] + [   ] + [   ] + [ ]

Expanded and standard notation

Write the **standard notation** for each expanded notation below.

Ten Thousands	Thousands	Hundreds	Tens	Ones	
40,000	+ 5,000	+ 200	+ 30	+ 9	= _____
20,000	+ 3,000	+ 400	+ 70	+ 6	= _____
50,000	+ 7,000	+ 500	+ 50	+ 7	= _____
80,000	+ 1,000	+ 600	+ 20	+ 3	= _____
40,000	+ 6,000	+ 900	+ 0	+ 8	= _____
10,000	+ 5,000	+ 100	+ 90	+ 2	= _____
30,000	+ 2,000	+ 800	+ 30	+ 9	= _____
70,000	+ 9,000	+ 700	+ 10	+ 2	= _____
90,000	+ 4,000	+ 300	+ 40	+ 4	= _____

BRAIN BOX

The **standard notation** for a number is the way it is typically written.

Example: 2,547

The **expanded notation** shows the place value of each digit in the number.

**Example:
2,000 + 500 + 40 + 7**

Computer Challenge

Read the clues and fill in the place-value charts to find out the computer's answers. Then write the number on the line.

Filling in place notation

This number has 5 tens.
It also has 9 thousands.
It has 8 ten thousands!
It has 2 hundreds.
This number has only 1 one.

Ten Thousands	Thousands	Hundreds	Tens	Ones

_____

This is a new number. It has 3 hundreds.
It has 7 thousands and 7 ones.
The number has 4 tens.
It has as many ten thousands as it can, which is 9.

Ten Thousands	Thousands	Hundreds	Tens	Ones

_____

The last number has 1 hundred.
It has 2 ten thousands, 7 tens, and 6 ones.
The number has 5 thousands.

Ten Thousands	Thousands	Hundreds	Tens	Ones

_____

Beach Ball Roundup

Round each number up or down. If you **round up** a number, write the answer in an inflated beach ball. If you **round down** a number, write the answer in a deflated beach ball.

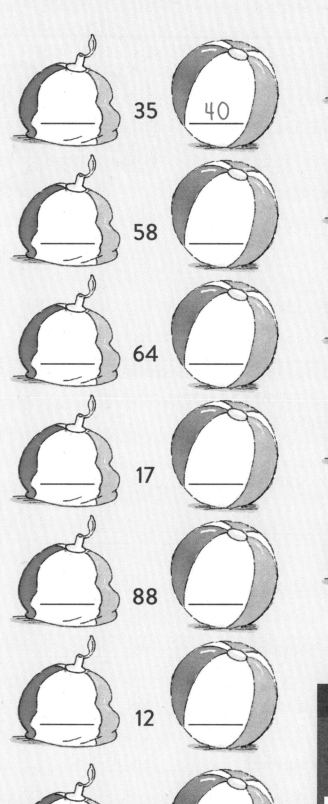

35   40

58   ___

64   ___

17   ___

88   ___

12   ___

55   ___

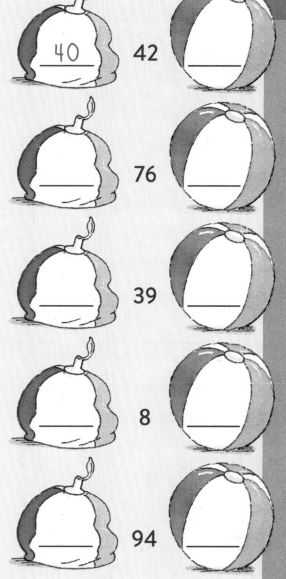

40   42

76   ___

39   ___

8   ___

94   ___

BRAIN BOX

Rounding is making a number simpler while keeping its value close to what it was. A rounded number is less accurate but easier to use.

Example: 82 rounded to the nearest ten is 80, because 82 is closer to 80 than 90.
But 87 rounds up to 90.

148

Up or Down

Round each number to its **nearest hundred**.
Write on the line whether you're rounding up or down.

MATH SKILLS

689 can be rounded __Up__ to __700__.

231 can be rounded _____ to _____.

449 can be rounded _____ to _____.

Rounding hundreds and thousands

758 can be rounded _____ to _____.

391 can be rounded _____ to _____.

862 can be rounded _____ to _____.

Round each number to its **nearest thousand.** Write on the line whether you're rounding up or down.

2,854 can be rounded _____ to _____.

7,125 can be rounded _____ to _____.

5,550 can be rounded _____ to _____.

1,820 can be rounded _____ to _____.

3,437 can be rounded _____ to _____.

6,501 can be rounded _____ to _____.

BRAIN BOX

When rounding to the **nearest hundred**, round up or down based on the number in the **tens place**. If the number is under 50, round down. If the number is 50 or higher, round up.

Example: 759 can be rounded up to 800.

When rounding to the **nearest thousand**, round up or down based on the number in the **hundreds place**. If the number is under 500, round down. If the number is 500 or higher, round up.

Example: 5,499 can be rounded down to 5,000.

Round the Mountain

Round each number.

Round 784,392 to the nearest ten thousand: _____

Round 815,295 to the nearest thousand: _____

Round 98,670 to the nearest ten thousand: _____

Round 564,195 to the nearest hundred: _____

Round 1,643,253 to the nearest hundred thousand:

_____

Round 3,845,211 to the nearest ten thousand: _____

Round 7,568,250 to the nearest hundred thousand:

_____

Round 237,874 to the nearest thousand: _____

Round 598,587 to the nearest ten thousand: _____

Round 1,471,932 to the nearest hundred thousand:

_____

BRAIN BOX

When rounding to the nearest **ten thousand**, round up or down based on the number in the **thousands place**. If the number is under 5,000, round down. If the number is 5,000 or higher, round up.

Example: 67,373 rounds up to 70,000.

When rounding to the nearest **hundred thousand**, round up or down based on the number in the **ten thousands place**. If the number is under 50,000, round down. If the number is 50,000 or higher, round up.

Example: 832,780 rounds down to 800,000.

Noted Numbers

Find the **patterns**. Fill in the missing numbers.

6	12	18	24	30	36

4	8	7	11		

8	20	32			

20	19	17	14		

12	13	15	18			

27	37	32	42			

7	8	11	16		

50	45	48	43		

BRAIN BOX

To figure out the **pattern** in a series of numbers, look at the relationship between each number and the number that follows.

Example: 8, 11, 9, 12, 10

8	11	9	12	10
+ 3	– 2	+ 3	– 2	+ 3
11	9	12	10	13

The pattern for this number series is +3, –2. The next number would be 13.

8 9 10 11 12 13

Make up your own number patterns and write them here. Then give them to a friend to solve!

Test-Run Time

Estimate how many minutes it will take each driver to finish the race based on the actual times of their test runs. Round up or down to the nearest ten. Then answer the questions below.

Name	Actual Time of Test Runs	Estimated Time
Helena	33	30
Graham	22	
Victoria	27	
Enzo	18	
Kathleen	15	
Pham	14	
Morgan	36	

Estimating numbers

Whose estimated time is the lowest? _____

Whose estimated time is the highest? _____

Whose estimated time would change if his
test-run time had been one minute more? _____

Whose actual time was two minutes
less than his estimated time? _____

Whose actual time was four minutes
less than his estimated time? _____

BRAIN BOX

An **estimate** is an approximate number. One way to estimate a number is to round it up or down.

Just About Right

Estimate the sums by rounding each number to the nearest ten.

43 + 28	rounds to 40	+ 30	= 70
7 + 12	rounds to ▢	+ ▢	= ▢
4 + 61	rounds to ▢	+ ▢	= ▢
9 + 24	rounds to ▢	+ ▢	= ▢
36 + 53	rounds to ▢	+ ▢	= ▢
8 + 74	rounds to ▢	+ ▢	= ▢
13 + 91	rounds to ▢	+ ▢	= ▢

Estimate the differences below by rounding each number to the nearest ten.

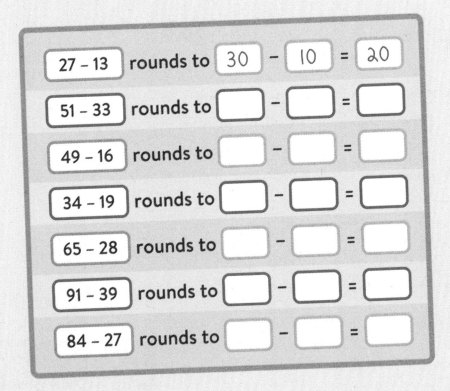

27 – 13	rounds to 30	– 10	= 20
51 – 33	rounds to ▢	– ▢	= ▢
49 – 16	rounds to ▢	– ▢	= ▢
34 – 19	rounds to ▢	– ▢	= ▢
65 – 28	rounds to ▢	– ▢	= ▢
91 – 39	rounds to ▢	– ▢	= ▢
84 – 27	rounds to ▢	– ▢	= ▢

Estimating sums and differences

What's That Sign?

Write <, >, or = in each box to show the relationship between the sets of numbers.

10 + 11 ☐ 5 + 16

28 – 4 ☐ 18 + 10

Greater than, less than

4 – 1 ☐ 7 – 4

45 – 9 ☐ 6 × 6

7 + 8 ☐ 8 + 5

4 + 4 ☐ 4 × 4

2 + 13 ☐ 7 + 9

17 + 9 ☐ 28 – 5

10 + 2 ☐ 6 + 6

12 – 2 ☐ 9 + 9

BRAIN BOX

In math:

• the symbol < means *less than.*

• the symbol > means *greater than.*

• the symbol = means *is the same as.*

Roman Numerals

Look at the chart comparing **Arabic numerals** to **Roman numerals**. Use the chart to write the Roman numeral equivalent to each number.

1	2	3	4	5	6	7	8	9	10
I	II	III	IV	V	VI	VII	VIII	IX	X

Roman numerals

20	50	100	500	1,000
XX	L	C	D	M

3 = _____

20 = _____

5 = _____

53 = _____

BRAIN FACT
Mathematicians in India invented Arabic numerals 1,500 years ago!

10 = _____

24 = _____

8 = _____

157 = _____

521 = _____

BRAIN BOX

The numerals we use to represent numbers are called **Arabic numerals**.

Roman numerals use letters to represent numbers.

1,555 = _____

It's Prime Time

Take a look at these numbers from 1 to 25. Circle only the **prime numbers**. (Hint: There are nine prime numbers between 1 and 25 . . . and 1 is not a prime number!)

Prime numbers

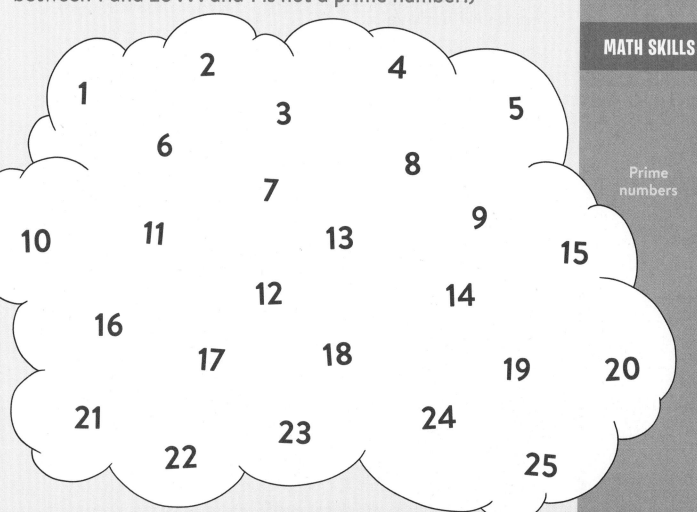

1   2   3   4   5   6   7   8   9   10   11   12   13   14   15   16   17   18   19   20   21   22   23   24   25

BRAIN BOX

A **prime number** is a number greater than 1 that can be divided evenly by only two numbers: 1 and itself.

Is 2 a prime number? Yes! 2 is a prime number because it is divisible only by 1 and 2.

Example:
2 ÷ 1 = 2
2 ÷ 2 = 1

Is 4 a prime number? No! 4 is not a prime number because it can be divided by more than two numbers: 1, 2, and 4.

Example:
4 ÷ 1 = 4
4 ÷ 2 = 2
4 ÷ 4 = 1

Is 13 a prime number? Yes, 13 is a prime number because it is divisible only by 1 and 13.

Example:
13 ÷ 1 = 13
13 ÷ 13 = 1

What about 15? No, 15 is not a prime number because it can be divided by more than two numbers: 1, 3, 5, and 15.

Example:
15 ÷ 1 = 15
15 ÷ 3 = 5
15 ÷ 5 = 3
15 ÷ 15 = 1

Going Down

Write each amount as a **negative number**.

A diving chamber is two hundred feet below sea level. | -200 |

The temperature is seventeen degrees below zero. | |

A submarine is three thousand, one hundred and eighty-nine feet below the surface. | |

The scientists drilled one thousand five hundred feet below sea level. | |

My brother isn't happy that the temperature is twenty below. | |

Sam owed their sister eighteen dollars and fifty cents but didn't have any money in their piggy bank. | |

The nation's budget was in bad shape. The government spent eight million dollars more than it had. | |

BRAIN BOX

The numbers that we use most often are **positive numbers**. This means they are **greater than 0**.

Numbers **less than 0** are called **negative numbers**.

A negative number always has a **minus sign** in front of it.

Example: **−20**

Left of Zero

Use the **number line** to answer the questions.

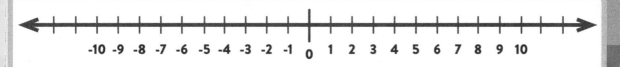

-10 -9 -8 -7 -6 -5 -4 -3 -2 -1 0 1 2 3 4 5 6 7 8 9 10

Negative numbers

What number is four units to the right of 0? _____

What number is four units to the left of 0? _____

On the number line above, does every positive number have a matching negative number? _____

How many units from 0 is +5? _____

How many units from 0 is –5? _____

If you stood on +3 and moved back 7 spaces to the left, where would you be? _____

If you stood on –5 and moved in a positive direction for 15 spaces, where would you be? _____

What is the opposite of +6? _____

How many units are there between +6 and its opposite?

_____

On the number line above, write the numbers 11 and 12 and also –11 and –12.

BRAIN BOX

A **number line** is a straight line that shows the relationship between numbers. **Opposite numbers** are in opposite positions on the number line, like 2 and -2.

I Must Be Going

Write the correct time on each digital clock.

Time

Seventeen minutes past ten o'clock

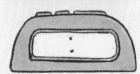

Fifteen minutes past twelve o'clock

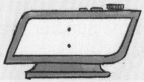

Half an hour past seven o'clock

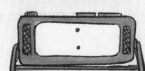

Twenty minutes before two o'clock

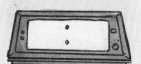

Nineteen minutes past eight o'clock

Thirty-three minutes past ten o'clock

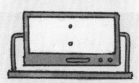

Ten minutes before six o'clock

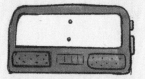

Fifteen minutes before one o'clock

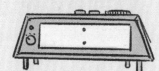

Noon

BRAIN FACT
The first digital clock was invented in 1956!

Half an hour before four o'clock

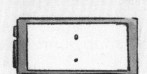

ADDITION AND SUBTRACTION

You're probably a pro at adding and subtracting by now. But are you *efficient*? Sometimes going step-by-step isn't the quickest or least complicated way to solve a problem. Think about which solution method works best for the problem and for *you*.

PARENTS Compensation, adding or subtracting by place value, decomposing, and the standard algorithm are all valid addition and subtraction strategies. Encourage your child to use the strategy that is most suitable for the equations and for how they think about math. Choosing appropriate strategies is an important higher-level problem-solving skill that will extend to nonmath situations as well.

PLACE A STICKER HERE

Heavy Lifting

Find the **sum**. Find the two heaviest weights and color them your favorite color.

ADDITION AND
SUBTRACTION

Adding tens
and hundreds

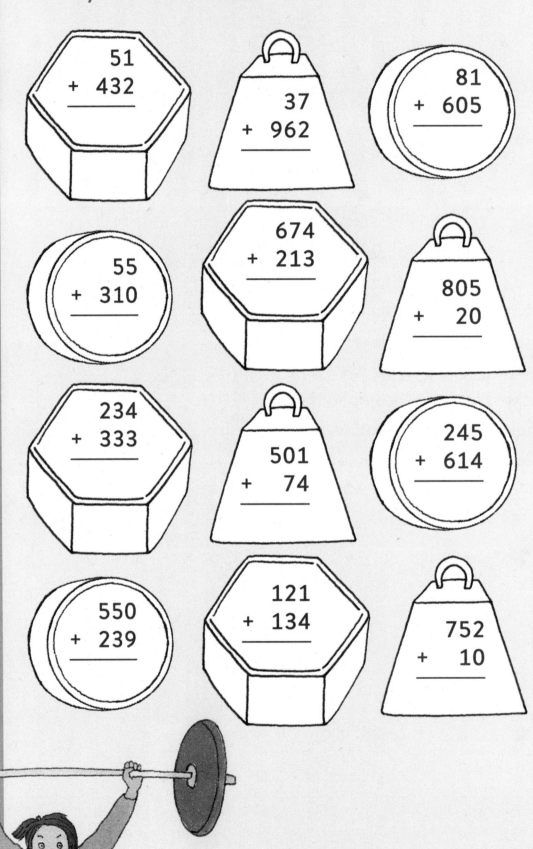

$$51 + 432$$

$$37 + 962$$

$$81 + 605$$

$$55 + 310$$

$$674 + 213$$

$$805 + 20$$

$$234 + 333$$

$$501 + 74$$

$$245 + 614$$

$$550 + 239$$

$$121 + 134$$

$$752 + 10$$

Favorite Number

Find the **sum**. Regroup if necessary. Now color all the tomato juice cans that add up to the same number red.

Adding hundreds and thousands

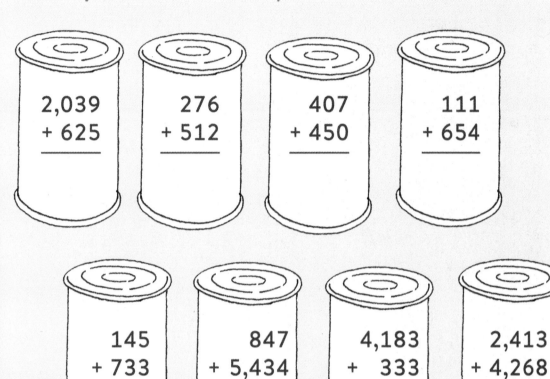

2,039
+ 625
___

276
+ 512
___

407
+ 450
___

111
+ 654
___

145
+ 733
___

847
+ 5,434
___

4,183
+ 333
___

2,413
+ 4,268
___

6,977
+ 2,045
___

1,287
+ 4,994
___

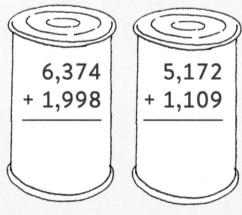

6,374
+ 1,998
___

5,172
+ 1,109
___

Ants and More Ants!

Add the number of ants in each anthill. Circle the anthill with the most ants. Put a triangle around the anthill with the fewest ants. Can you solve any of these problems using mental math?

Adding thousands

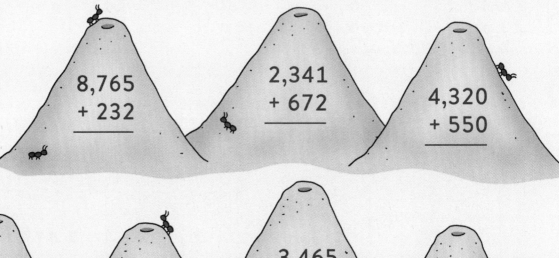

8,765
+ 232
_____

2,341
+ 672
_____

4,320
+ 550
_____

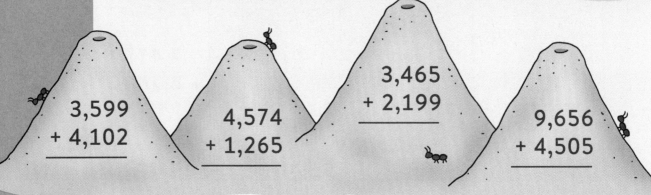

3,599
+ 4,102
_____

4,574
+ 1,265
_____

3,465
+ 2,199
_____

9,656
+ 4,505
_____

1,050 + 225 = _____   6,753 + 3,195 = _____

3,425 + 110 = _____   8,200 + 1,190 = _____

8,459 + 4,340 = _____

Heaviest Crate

Add the numbers to show how many pounds each crate weighs. Circle the lightest crate. Draw an **X** through the heaviest crate.

Adding ten thousands

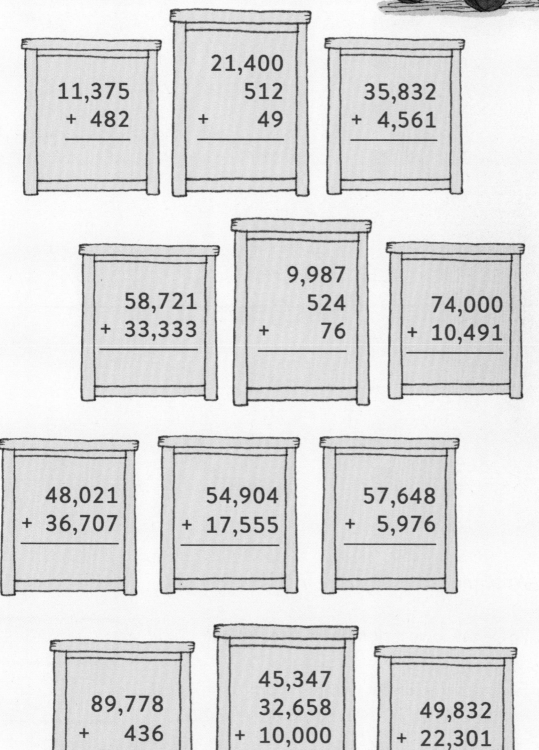

```
  11,375
+    482
```

```
  21,400
     512
+     49
```

```
  35,832
+  4,561
```

```
  58,721
+ 33,333
```

```
   9,987
     524
+     76
```

```
  74,000
+ 10,491
```

```
  48,021
+ 36,707
```

```
  54,904
+ 17,555
```

```
  57,648
+  5,976
```

```
  89,778
+    436
```

```
  45,347
  32,658
+ 10,000
```

```
  49,832
+ 22,301
```

Brain Quest Grade 4 Workbook

Hut, Hut, Hike!

Find the **difference**.

Subtracting hundreds

```
  463
- 322
_____
```

```
  845
- 723
_____
```

```
  491
- 380
_____
```

```
  976
-  41
_____
```

```
  890
- 740
_____
```

```
  743
- 231
_____
```

```
  989
- 787
_____
```

```
  627
- 515
_____
```

```
  178
- 145
_____
```

```
  978
- 863
_____
```

```
  237
- 203
_____
```

```
  869
- 759
_____
```

Write the highest number in the yellow box.

Write the lowest number in the red box.

Subtract the lowest number from the highest number. Write the number in the blue box.

Is this the quarterback's number? _____

Mitten Mania

Find the **difference**. Regroup if necessary.

$$\begin{array}{r} 310 \\ -\ 174 \\ \hline \end{array}$$

$$\begin{array}{r} 515 \\ -\ 88 \\ \hline \end{array}$$

$$\begin{array}{r} 674 \\ -\ 390 \\ \hline \end{array}$$

$$\begin{array}{r} 1,554 \\ -\ 1,076 \\ \hline \end{array}$$

$$\begin{array}{r} 4,474 \\ -\ 653 \\ \hline \end{array}$$

$$\begin{array}{r} 6,495 \\ -\ 1,045 \\ \hline \end{array}$$

$$\begin{array}{r} 8,313 \\ -\ 790 \\ \hline \end{array}$$

$$\begin{array}{r} 7,831 \\ -\ 1,264 \\ \hline \end{array}$$

Color the two mittens with the lowest answers green. Color the two mittens with the highest answers yellow.

Too Many Hot Dogs

Find the **difference**.

Subtracting thousands

$$6,375 - 3,174$$

$$2,347 - 205$$

$$9,042 - 16$$

$$8,755 - 7,418$$

$$5,555 - 4,446$$

$$5,120 - 386$$

$$9,722 - 8,876$$

$$5,413 - 1,019$$

$$4,144 - 876$$

$$2,781 - 2,764$$

Think about the whole problem and choose a subtraction strategy that works best with those numbers. Some problems are most efficiently solved using the standard algorithm, but others can be solved more quickly using compensation or decomposition.

Brain Quest Grade 4 Workbook

Too Much Hay

Find the **difference**.

```
 12,013
- 4,101
-------
```

```
 32,162
- 20,508
-------
```

```
 87,878
-    989
-------
```

```
 44,306
-  7,541
-------
```

```
 11,100
-  7,942
-------
```

```
 25,725
- 12,500
-------
```

```
 30,122
- 10,456
-------
```

```
 39,573
-  6,878
-------
```

```
 89,452
- 77,709
-------
```

```
 76,497
-  1,050
-------
```

```
 44,009
- 13,010
-------
```

```
 51,171
-    863
-------
```

Plus or Minus

Find the **sum** or the **difference**.

Addition and
subtraction
review

10,500
+ 10,642
_____

22,450
-     397
_____

61,611
+ 5,720
_____

9,873
+ 5,181
_____

43,872
+ 33,422
_____

55,982
+ 7,348
_____

18,498
+ 2,450
_____

99,999
- 68,789
_____

24,600
- 4,654
_____

52,000
- 45,370
_____

10,500
- 3,075
_____

48,756
+ 3,903
_____

MULTIPLICATION AND DIVISION

> Knowing multiplication facts and understanding place value are the keys to mastering more complex math. Let's apply what we know to multidigit multiplication and division problems!

PARENTS Learners build on their understanding of place value and regrouping as they multiply and divide one-, two-, and three-digit numbers. This practice will help your child build fluency toward more complex problem-solving and mental math. Offer an extra sheet of paper and encourage your child to show the steps of each problem as they solve it.

Sets

Fill in the missing number to **multiply** each set.

Multiplying as repeated addition

$$2 \times 2 = 4$$

$$\boxed{} \times \boxed{} = \boxed{}$$

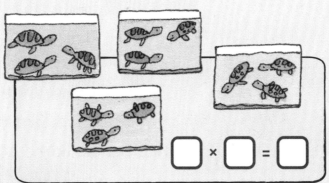

$$\boxed{} \times \boxed{} = \boxed{}$$

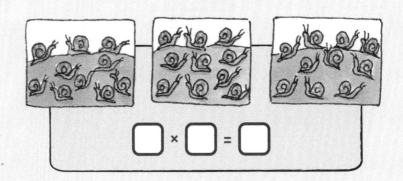

$$\boxed{} \times \boxed{} = \boxed{}$$

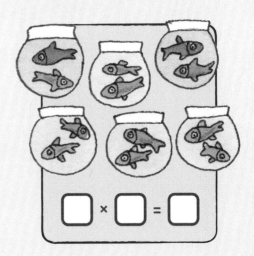

$$\boxed{} \times \boxed{} = \boxed{}$$

BRAIN BOX

Multiplication is a quick way to find the sum of the same number added to itself.

Example:

4 + 4 + 4 = 12

3 × 4 = 12

Another way to think of multiplication is adding groups. 3 × 4 is the same as adding 3 groups of 4.

Times Tables

Multiply.

$$\begin{array}{r} 2 \\ \times\ 2 \\ \hline 4 \end{array} \qquad \begin{array}{r} 5 \\ \times\ 3 \\ \hline \end{array} \qquad \begin{array}{r} 6 \\ \times\ 5 \\ \hline \end{array} \qquad \begin{array}{r} 3 \\ \times\ 4 \\ \hline \end{array} \qquad \begin{array}{r} 9 \\ \times\ 6 \\ \hline \end{array}$$

Multiplying
one-digit
numbers

$$\begin{array}{r} 9 \\ \times\ 1 \\ \hline \end{array} \qquad \begin{array}{r} 8 \\ \times\ 4 \\ \hline \end{array} \qquad \begin{array}{r} 4 \\ \times\ 2 \\ \hline \end{array} \qquad \begin{array}{r} 9 \\ \times\ 3 \\ \hline \end{array} \qquad \begin{array}{r} 9 \\ \times\ 7 \\ \hline \end{array}$$

$7 \times 8 =$ ___ $5 \times 5 =$ ___ $6 \times 2 =$ ___ $5 \times 4 =$ ___

$9 \times 4 =$ ___ $6 \times 7 =$ ___ $1 \times 3 =$ ___

BRAIN FACT
Any number multiplied by
1 always stays the same!

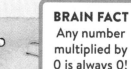

BRAIN FACT
Any number
multiplied by
0 is always 0!

$3 \times 0 =$ ___ $7 \times 7 =$ ___

The Facts About Factors

Fill in the missing **factors**.

__4__ × 8 = 32   6 × _____ = 36   3 × _____ = 15

_____ × 7 = 49   4 × _____ = 20   _____ × _____ = 25

Write all the possible factors for each number.

Factors and products

12

1 × 12 = 12
2 × 6 = 12
3 × 4 = 12

| 1 | 12 | 2 |
| 6 | 3 | 4 |

9

16

___ ___ ___

___ ___ ___

15

18

8

___ ___ ___

___ ___ ___

___ ___ ___

___ ___ ___

Finish the math sentences.

The product of 5 × 8 is __40__.

The product of 7 × 4 is _____.

The product of 9 × 2 is _____.

The product of 10 × 5 is _____.

The product of 2 × 11 is _____.

BRAIN BOX

The two numbers in a multiplication problem are called **factors**. The answer is the **product**.

Zeros

Multiply.

Multiplying
by zeros

```
   20         30         40         80         70
 ×  3       ×  2       ×  4       ×  5       ×  7
 ─────      ─────      ─────      ─────      ─────
   60
```

```
  500        900        300        100        600
 ×  3       ×  2       ×  3       ×  8       ×  6
 ─────      ─────      ─────      ─────      ─────
```

```
  200        400        700        800        200
 ×  9       ×  9       ×  5       ×  4       ×  5
 ─────      ─────      ─────      ─────      ─────
```

```
 1,000      5,000      3,000      8,000      2,000
 ×    3     ×    4     ×    4     ×    8     ×    6
 ──────     ──────     ──────     ──────     ──────
```

```
 4,000      7,000      9,000      6,000      7,000
 ×    2     ×    5     ×    9     ×    5     ×    6
 ──────     ──────     ──────     ──────     ──────
```

BRAIN BOX

When multiplying numbers ending in zero:

Multiply the ones, tens, and hundreds column in the usual order, from right to left.

```
Example:   400
         ×   5
         ──────
           2,000
```

or

Multiply the non-zero digits first.

```
Example:   400
         ×   5
         ──────
           2,000
```

Then count the numbers of zeros in the factors and write them on the end of the product.

Tens

Multiply. Regroup as needed. Show your work.

Multiplying two digits by one digit

$$\begin{array}{r} 35 \\ \times\ 7 \\ \hline \end{array}$$

$$\begin{array}{r} 72 \\ \times\ 2 \\ \hline \end{array}$$

$$\begin{array}{r} 11 \\ \times\ 9 \\ \hline \end{array}$$

$$\begin{array}{r} 48 \\ \times\ 6 \\ \hline \end{array}$$

$$\begin{array}{r} 93 \\ \times\ 4 \\ \hline \end{array}$$

$$\begin{array}{r} 19 \\ \times\ 7 \\ \hline \end{array}$$

$$\begin{array}{r} 37 \\ \times\ 6 \\ \hline \end{array}$$

$$\begin{array}{r} 90 \\ \times\ 8 \\ \hline \end{array}$$

$$\begin{array}{r} 53 \\ \times\ 7 \\ \hline \end{array}$$

$$\begin{array}{r} 22 \\ \times\ 5 \\ \hline \end{array}$$

$$\begin{array}{r} 84 \\ \times\ 3 \\ \hline \end{array}$$

$$\begin{array}{r} 89 \\ \times\ 4 \\ \hline \end{array}$$

$$\begin{array}{r} 58 \\ \times\ 8 \\ \hline \end{array}$$

$$\begin{array}{r} 34 \\ \times\ 6 \\ \hline \end{array}$$

$$\begin{array}{r} 71 \\ \times\ 9 \\ \hline \end{array}$$

$$\begin{array}{r} 33 \\ \times\ 4 \\ \hline \end{array}$$

$$\begin{array}{r} 77 \\ \times\ 4 \\ \hline \end{array}$$

$$\begin{array}{r} 25 \\ \times\ 1 \\ \hline \end{array}$$

$$\begin{array}{r} 12 \\ \times\ 9 \\ \hline \end{array}$$

$$\begin{array}{r} 67 \\ \times\ 3 \\ \hline \end{array}$$

BRAIN BOX

When you multiply, you might need to **regroup**. Here's how to regroup **tens**.

Step 1: Multiply the number in the ones place and regroup.

$3 \times 8 = 24$, so you write the 4 in the ones column and move the 2 above the tens column.

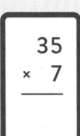

Example:
$$\begin{array}{r} \overset{2}{23} \\ \times\ 8 \\ \hline \end{array}$$
$3 \times 8 = 4$ **4**

Step 2: Multiply the number in the tens column. Add the number moved from the ones column.

$2 \times 8 = 16$
$16 + 2 = 18$

Example:
$$\begin{array}{r} \overset{2}{23} \\ \times\ 8 \\ \hline \end{array}$$
$2 \times 8 + 2 = 18$ **184**

Hundreds

Multiply. **Regroup** as needed. Show your work.

$$\begin{array}{r} \overset{1\ 1}{233} \\ \times\ \ 6 \\ \hline 1,398 \end{array}$$

$$\begin{array}{r} 190 \\ \times\ \ 4 \\ \hline \end{array}$$

$$\begin{array}{r} 312 \\ \times\ \ 9 \\ \hline \end{array}$$

$$\begin{array}{r} 253 \\ \times\ \ 7 \\ \hline \end{array}$$

$$\begin{array}{r} 384 \\ \times\ \ 3 \\ \hline \end{array}$$

Multiplying three digits by one digit

$$\begin{array}{r} 343 \\ \times\ \ 6 \\ \hline \end{array}$$

$$\begin{array}{r} 190 \\ \times\ \ 8 \\ \hline \end{array}$$

$$\begin{array}{r} 512 \\ \times\ \ 9 \\ \hline \end{array}$$

$$\begin{array}{r} 653 \\ \times\ \ 5 \\ \hline \end{array}$$

$$\begin{array}{r} 433 \\ \times\ \ 8 \\ \hline \end{array}$$

$$\begin{array}{r} 946 \\ \times\ \ 8 \\ \hline \end{array}$$

$$\begin{array}{r} 264 \\ \times\ \ 7 \\ \hline \end{array}$$

$$\begin{array}{r} 326 \\ \times\ \ 7 \\ \hline \end{array}$$

$$\begin{array}{r} 342 \\ \times\ \ 9 \\ \hline \end{array}$$

$$\begin{array}{r} 584 \\ \times\ \ 8 \\ \hline \end{array}$$

BRAIN BOX

Here's how to regroup **hundreds**.

Example:

$$\begin{array}{r} \overset{4\ 5}{268} \\ \times\ \ \ 7 \\ \hline 1,876 \end{array}$$

Step 1: Multiply the number in the ones place and regroup.

8 × 7 = **56**, so you write the 6 in the ones column and move the 5 above the tens column.

Step 2: Multiply the number in the tens column. Add the number moved from the ones column.

6 × 7 = **42**

42 + 5 = **47**

Step 3: Multiply the number in the hundreds column. Add the number moved from the tens column.

2 × 7 = **14**

14 + 4 = **18**

Aquarium Math

Multiply. Regroup as needed. Show your work.

Multiplying two-digit numbers

22 × 33	15 × 11	61 × 37	40 × 10	41 × 12

$$\begin{array}{r} {}_1\,66 \\ +660 \\ \hline 726 \end{array}$$

23 × 32	14 × 21	58 × 10	11 × 13	91 × 15

The aquarium has 27 tanks of tropical fish. Each tank contains 17 fish. How many tropical fish does the aquarium have in all?

_____

Pass the Fish Food!

Multiply. Regroup as needed. Show your work.

```
    1
   13
   56          83          39          36
 × 35        × 30        × 91        × 15
 ─────       ─────       ─────       ─────
    1
  280
+1,680
 ─────
 1,960
```

Multiplying two-digit numbers with regrouping

```
   58          45          72          37
 × 67        × 26        × 34        × 59
 ─────       ─────       ─────       ─────
```

```
   63          44          75          69
 × 42        × 53        × 68        × 59
 ─────       ─────       ─────       ─────
```

Miya bought a fish and fish food. She bought 19 boxes of fish food. Each box contains 12 pellets. How many fish food pellets does she have?

_____

BRAIN BOX

Here's how you multiply two-digit numbers:

Example:
```
    46
  × 12
  ────
```

Step 1:
Multiply the top number by the ones factor of the bottom number. Regroup.
```
    1
    46
  × 12
  ────
    92
```

Step 2:
Put a **0** in the ones column.
```
    46
  × 12
  ────
    92
     0
```

Step 3:
Multiply the top number by the tens factor of the bottom number.
```
    46
  × 12
  ────
    92
   460
```

Step 4:
Add the two products.
```
    46
  × 12
  ────
    1
    92
 + 460
  ────
   552
```

Three Levels

Multiply. **Regroup** as needed. Show your work.

Multiplying
three-digit
numbers with
regrouping

$$\begin{array}{r} {}^{1}234 \\ \times\ 21 \\ \hline 234 \\ +\ 4{,}680 \\ \hline 4{,}914 \end{array}$$

$$\begin{array}{r} 158 \\ \times\ 72 \\ \hline \end{array}$$

$$\begin{array}{r} 541 \\ \times\ 77 \\ \hline \end{array}$$

$$\begin{array}{r} 639 \\ \times\ 35 \\ \hline \end{array}$$

$$\begin{array}{r} 310 \\ \times\ 44 \\ \hline \end{array}$$

$$\begin{array}{r} 605 \\ \times\ 47 \\ \hline \end{array}$$

$$\begin{array}{r} 578 \\ \times\ 19 \\ \hline \end{array}$$

$$\begin{array}{r} 753 \\ \times\ 58 \\ \hline \end{array}$$

Chef Chanticleer has 103 very hungry people to cook for. He cooks a dozen eggs for each person. How many eggs does the chef cook in all?

_____

BRAIN BOX

Here's how to multiply a three-digit number by a two-digit number:

Example:

$$\begin{array}{r} {}^{32} \\ {}^{11} \\ 454 \\ \times\ \ \ 63 \\ \hline {}^{1} \\ 1{,}362 \\ +\ 27{,}240 \\ \hline 28{,}602 \end{array}$$

Step 1: Multiply the three-digit number by the number in the ones column. Regroup as needed.

Step 2: Add a zero below the ones column. Then multiply the three-digit number by the number in the tens column.

Step 3: Add the two products.

First Division

Fill in the boxes to write the **division** problems both ways. Write the answer too.

$12 \div 4 = 3$ → $4 \overline{)12}$ with □ on top

$9 \div 3 = \square$ → $3 \overline{)9}$ with □ on top

$21 \div 3 = \square$ → $\square \overline{)\square}$ with □ on top

$6 \overline{)24}$ with □ on top → $\square \div \square = \square$

$6 \overline{)18}$ with □ on top → $\square \div \square = \square$

BRAIN BOX

Division is the opposite of multiplication. It's the process of finding out how many times one number will fit into another number.

A division problem can be written two ways:

$15 \div 3 = 5$ or $3 \overline{)15}$ with 5 on top

Cricket Division

Divide to find the **quotient**.

$$5 \overline{)55}$$
$$\begin{array}{r} 11 \\ 5\overline{)55} \\ -5\downarrow \\ \hline 05 \\ -5 \\ \hline 0 \end{array}$$

$$3\overline{)18}$$

$$6\overline{)60}$$

$$4\overline{)20}$$

$$8\overline{)88}$$

Dividing two-digit numbers by one-digit numbers

$$2\overline{)46}$$

$$7\overline{)70}$$

$$7\overline{)56}$$

$$2\overline{)68}$$

$$3\overline{)21}$$

Divide to find the quotient.

49 ÷ 7 = _____   25 ÷ 5 = _____

63 ÷ 9 = _____   36 ÷ 4 = _____

56 ÷ 8 = _____   27 ÷ 3 = _____

BRAIN BOX

The number being divided is called the **dividend**. The number doing the dividing into is called the **divisor**. The answer to a division problem is called the **quotient**.

$$13 \leftarrow \text{quotient}$$
$$\text{divisor} \rightarrow 4\overline{)52} \leftarrow \text{dividend}$$

$$\text{dividend} \rightarrow 52 \div 4 = 13 \leftarrow \text{quotient}$$
$$\nwarrow \text{divisor}$$

To find the quotient in a division problem: **Example: $4\overline{)52}$**

Step 1: Divide into the tens.
$$\begin{array}{r} 1 \\ 4\overline{)52} \end{array}$$

Step 2: Multiply and subtract.
$$\begin{array}{r} 1 \\ 4\overline{)52} \\ -4 \\ \hline 1 \end{array}$$

Step 3: Bring down the ones.
$$\begin{array}{r} 1 \\ 4\overline{)52} \\ -4\downarrow \\ \hline 12 \end{array}$$

Step 4: Divide into the new number.
$$\begin{array}{r} 13 \\ 4\overline{)52} \\ -4 \\ \hline 12 \end{array}$$

If the divisor is larger than the first digit of the dividend, divide it into two digits, not one. For example:
$$\begin{array}{r} 8 \\ 4\overline{)32} \end{array}$$

What Remains

Divide. Show your work. Write the **remainder** next to the **r**.

$$3\overline{)37} \quad \frac{12\,r1}{}$$
$$-36\downarrow$$
$$\boxed{1}$$

$$2\overline{)13} \quad r$$

$$7\overline{)60} \quad r$$

$$5\overline{)11} \quad r$$

$$8\overline{)21} \quad r$$

Dividing two-digit numbers by one-digit numbers

$$3\overline{)74} \quad r$$

$$4\overline{)55} \quad r$$

$$8\overline{)75} \quad r$$

$$6\overline{)34} \quad r$$

$$7\overline{)41} \quad r$$

$$6\overline{)64} \quad r$$

$$8\overline{)99} \quad r$$

$$9\overline{)33} \quad r$$

$$4\overline{)75} \quad r$$

$$7\overline{)79} \quad r$$

BRAIN BOX

Sometimes the divisor doesn't go into the dividend evenly. Then you have a number left over. This number is called the **remainder**.

Example:

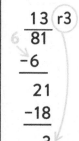

$$6\overline{)81} \quad 13\,r3$$
$$-6$$
$$21$$
$$-18$$
$$3$$

The answer is 13 r 3 (r for remainder).

Check It Out!

Divide. Then check your answer by **multiplying.**

Checking your answer

$$
\begin{array}{r}
18\text{r}1 \\
3\overline{)55} \\
-3\downarrow \\
\hline
25 \\
-24 \\
\hline
1
\end{array}
\qquad
\begin{array}{r}
18 \\
\times 3 \\
\hline
54 \\
+1 \\
\hline
55
\end{array}
$$

$2\overline{)71}$

$5\overline{)79}$

$8\overline{)63}$

$6\overline{)51}$

$9\overline{)95}$

$8\overline{)76}$

$4\overline{)49}$

$7\overline{)87}$

BRAIN BOX

You can check the answer to a division problem by multiplying. First, **multiply** the **quotient** by the divisor. Then **add** any remainder. The number you get should be the same as the dividend.

Sock Drawer

Divide. Show your work.

```
    166
2 )332
  -2↓
   13
  -12↓
    12
```

```
5 )840
```

```
7 )432
```

Dividing three-digit numbers by one-digit numbers

```
6 )111
```

```
4 )272
```

```
3 )515
```

```
8 )195
```

```
9 )476
```

```
5 )183
```

Glow-Glow has 789 T-shirts to put on sale in three different stores. How many shirts will it give to each store?

_____

BRAIN BOX

When dividing a three-digit number by a one-digit number:

Step 1: Divide into the hundreds.

Step 2: Multiply and subtract.

Step 3: Bring down the tens and then divide into the tens.

Step 4: Multiply and subtract again.

Step 5: Bring down the ones and divide into the ones.

Step 6: If there is a remainder, write it next to the answer.

Example:
```
     172r1
3 )517
  -3
   21
  -21
    07
    -6
     1
```

Missing Signs

Look at each problem and fill in the missing
+, − , ×, or ÷ sign that makes the equation correct.

Add, subtract,
multiply, or
divide

$$20 \boxed{} 6 = 120$$

$$264 \boxed{} 3 = 88$$

$$549 \boxed{} 510 = 39$$

$$28 \boxed{} 12 = 336$$

$$18 \boxed{} 45 = 63$$

$$645 \boxed{} 130 = 775$$

$$99 \boxed{} 55 = 44$$

$$89 \boxed{} 21 = 110$$

$$123 \boxed{} 5 = 118$$

$$167 \boxed{} 92 = 75$$

$$567 \boxed{} 7 = 81$$

$$375 \boxed{} 5 = 75$$

My Dear Aunt Sally

Solve the following problems by using the correct **order of operations.**

$4 + 4 × 5 = 4 + 20 = 24$

20

Multistep problems

$8 + 7 × 2 =$

$12 + 18 ÷ 3 =$

$5 × 3 - 11 =$

$24 ÷ 8 + 4 - 7 =$

$47 - 9 × 4 =$

BRAIN BOX

Order of operations tells you the order in which you should solve a math problem with multiple steps: Multiply, Divide, Add, and Subtract. Use the phrase **"My Dear Aunt Sally"** to help remember the correct order.

In the Middle

Find the average of each group of numbers.

Averaging

	Sum	Average
11, 7, 18	36	12
37, 55	___	___
8, 15, 9, 12	___	___
374, 156	___	___
20, 60, 80, 120	___	___
19, 27, 32	___	___
114, 264	___	___
32, 56, 87, 97	___	___
99, 77, 154	___	___
6, 10, 18, 18	___	___

Work Space

$36 \div 3 = 12$

BRAIN BOX

You can find an **average** by adding all of the numbers and then dividing the sum by how many numbers are in the group.

Example:
Find the average: 7, 12, 5, 12

Step 1: 7 + 12 + 5 + 12 = 36

Step 2: 36 ÷ 4 = 9

9 is the average.

I have a good average.

FRACTIONS AND DECIMALS

Fractions are pretty useful. Knowing how to divide one whole into smaller equal pieces comes in handy every day, especially when sharing with friends— you want to make sure everyone gets an equal share.

PARENTS This section starts with pictorial representations and gradually moves to numbers-only fraction equations. It is preferable to complete this section sequentially, as the skills build in complexity.

Parts of a Whole

Write a **fraction** to show which part of each whole is shaded.

Identifying numerators and denominators

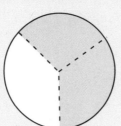

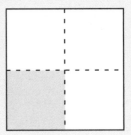

$$\frac{2}{3}$$

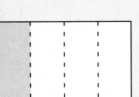

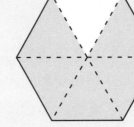

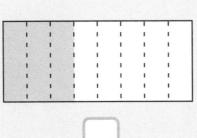

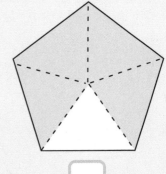

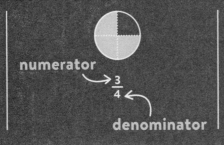

BRAIN BOX

A **fraction** shows parts of a whole. Fractions are written as one number on top of another, with a line between them.

numerator

$$\xrightarrow{}\frac{3}{4}$$

denominator

The bottom number of a fraction is called the **denominator**. It tells the total number of pieces in the whole. The top number is the **numerator**. It tells how many pieces of the whole you are talking about.

Name the Part

Fill in the missing **numerator** or **denominator** for each fraction.

Identifying numerators and denominators

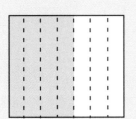

$$\frac{4}{\boxed{7}}$$

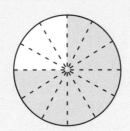

$$\frac{\boxed{}}{12}$$

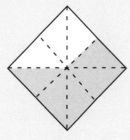

$$\frac{5}{\boxed{}}$$

$$\frac{7}{\boxed{}}$$

$$\frac{4}{\boxed{}}$$

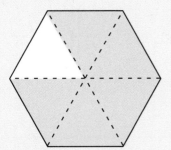

$$\frac{\boxed{}}{6}$$

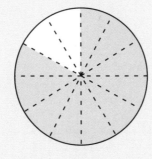

$$\frac{10}{\boxed{}}$$

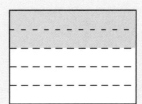

$$\frac{\boxed{}}{5}$$

Thomas cut a round birthday cake into 8 pieces. He ate 3 of the pieces. Write a fraction to show what part of the cake Thomas ate.

$$\frac{\boxed{}}{\boxed{}}$$

Up the Ladder

Add the fractions.

Adding fractions

$\dfrac{1}{3} + \dfrac{1}{3} = \dfrac{2}{3}$

$\dfrac{1}{4} + \dfrac{2}{4} = \dfrac{}{}$

$\dfrac{1}{5} + \dfrac{1}{5} = \dfrac{}{}$

$\dfrac{1}{6} + \dfrac{2}{6} = \dfrac{}{}$

$\dfrac{1}{7} + \dfrac{5}{7} = \dfrac{}{}$

$\dfrac{1}{8} + \dfrac{6}{8} = \dfrac{}{}$

$\dfrac{1}{10} + \dfrac{6}{10} = \dfrac{}{}$

$\dfrac{1}{12} + \dfrac{8}{12} = \dfrac{}{}$

HINT: Sometimes it helps to draw your own shaded diagrams to help you add fractions.

$\dfrac{\boxed{}}{10} + \dfrac{6}{10} = \dfrac{7}{10}$

$\dfrac{3}{8} + \dfrac{\boxed{}}{\boxed{}} = \dfrac{5}{8}$

$\dfrac{1}{\boxed{}} + \dfrac{1}{\boxed{}} = \dfrac{2}{4}$

$\dfrac{\boxed{}}{\boxed{}} + \dfrac{1}{3} = \dfrac{2}{3}$

$\dfrac{3}{7} + \dfrac{1}{\boxed{}} = \dfrac{4}{7}$

$\dfrac{1}{6} + \dfrac{\boxed{}}{\boxed{}} = \dfrac{3}{\boxed{}}$

$\dfrac{2}{5} + \dfrac{\boxed{}}{5} = \dfrac{3}{\boxed{}}$

$\dfrac{1}{\boxed{}} + \dfrac{6}{12} = \dfrac{7}{\boxed{}}$

BRAIN BOX

You can add fractions with the same **denominators** by adding the **numerators**. Their sum becomes the new numerator. The denominator remains the same.

Example:

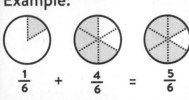

$\dfrac{1}{6} + \dfrac{4}{6} = \dfrac{5}{6}$

Fraction Frenzy

Subtract the fractions.

$$\frac{2}{3} - \frac{1}{3} = \frac{\boxed{}}{\boxed{}}$$

$$\frac{4}{5} - \frac{2}{5} = \frac{\boxed{}}{\boxed{}}$$

$$\frac{5}{7} - \frac{1}{7} = \frac{\boxed{}}{\boxed{}}$$

$$\frac{9}{12} - \frac{7}{12} = \frac{\boxed{}}{\boxed{}}$$

$$\frac{7}{8} - \frac{5}{8} = \frac{\boxed{}}{\boxed{}}$$

$$\frac{4}{6} - \frac{3}{6} = \frac{\boxed{}}{\boxed{}}$$

$$\frac{13}{15} - \frac{7}{15} = \frac{\boxed{}}{\boxed{}}$$

$$\frac{8}{9} - \frac{5}{9} = \frac{\boxed{}}{\boxed{}}$$

$$\frac{3}{4} - \frac{2}{4} = \frac{\boxed{}}{\boxed{}}$$

$$\frac{7}{10} - \frac{1}{10} = \frac{\boxed{}}{\boxed{}}$$

Candice cut a rectangular birthday cake into 16 pieces. Her brother and sister ate a total of 5 pieces. Write a fraction to show what part of Candice's cake was left.

BRAIN BOX

You can **subtract** fractions with the same denominator by subtracting the numerators. The denominator will remain the same.

Example:
$$\frac{5}{7} - \frac{2}{7} = \frac{3}{7}$$

In the Shade

Look at the shape and fraction on each card. Circle the shape that shows an **equivalent fraction**. Write that equivalent in the colored boxes.

Identifying equivalent fractions

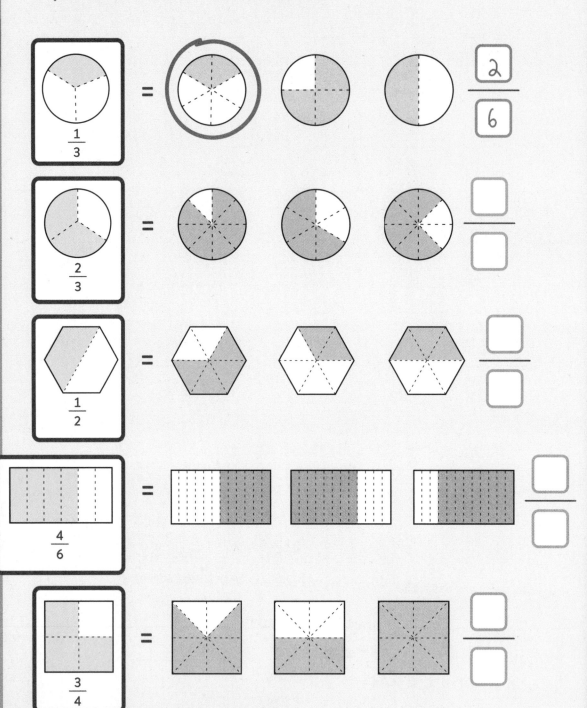

$\dfrac{2}{6}$

BRAIN BOX

Fractions that stand for the same amount are called **equivalent fractions**. Look at the shaded parts.

$\frac{1}{2}$ is equivalent to $\frac{2}{4}$

Whole Parts

Write the number 1 as a fraction using each figure.

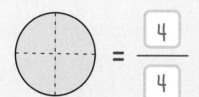 = $\dfrac{4}{4}$

○ = $\dfrac{\ \ }{\ \ }$

▭ = $\dfrac{\ \ }{\ \ }$

△ = $\dfrac{\ \ }{\ \ }$

▢ = $\dfrac{\ \ }{\ \ }$

▭ = $\dfrac{\ \ }{\ \ }$

FRACTIONS AND DECIMALS

Equivalent fractions

> **HINT:** Remember that any number multiplied by 1 always stays the same. 1 written as a fraction can be $\frac{1}{1}$ or $\frac{2}{2}$ or $\frac{3}{3}$ and so on.

Fill in the missing parts.

$\dfrac{2}{5} \times \dfrac{2}{2} = \dfrac{4}{10}$

$\dfrac{1}{7} \times \dfrac{2}{2} = \dfrac{\ \ }{\ \ }$

$\dfrac{1}{2} \times \dfrac{4}{4} = \dfrac{\ \ }{\ \ }$

$\dfrac{4}{5} \times \dfrac{3}{3} = \dfrac{\ \ }{\ \ }$

$\dfrac{3}{6} \times \dfrac{\ \ }{\ \ } = \dfrac{6}{12}$

$\dfrac{3}{8} \times \dfrac{\ \ }{\ \ } = \dfrac{6}{16}$

$\dfrac{1}{3} \times \dfrac{\ \ }{\ \ } = \dfrac{3}{9}$

$\dfrac{2}{4} \times \dfrac{2}{2} = \dfrac{\ \ }{\ \ }$

BRAIN BOX

When 1 is written as a fraction, the numerator and denominator are equal.

Example:

$\dfrac{2}{2}$ and $\dfrac{3}{3}$

Equivalent fractions are two different fractions that show the same number.

Example: $\dfrac{4}{8}$

and

$\dfrac{1}{2}$

You can find an equivalent fraction by multiplying the numerator and the denominator by the same number.

Example: $\dfrac{1}{2} \times \dfrac{2}{2} = \dfrac{4}{8}$

Up, Up, Up!

Fill in the boxes to find an **equivalent fraction** with the denominator of 12.

FRACTIONS AND DECIMALS

Putting fractions in ascending order

$$\frac{2}{3} \times \frac{\boxed{4}}{\boxed{4}} = \frac{\boxed{8}}{12}$$

$$\frac{2}{4} \times \frac{\boxed{}}{\boxed{}} = \frac{\boxed{}}{12}$$

$$\frac{4}{4} \times \frac{\boxed{}}{\boxed{}} = \frac{\boxed{}}{12}$$

$$\frac{5}{6} \times \frac{\boxed{}}{\boxed{}} = \frac{\boxed{}}{12}$$

$$\frac{1}{6} \times \frac{\boxed{}}{\boxed{}} = \frac{\boxed{}}{12}$$

$$\frac{1}{3} \times \frac{\boxed{}}{\boxed{}} = \frac{\boxed{}}{12}$$

On the left, write the equivalent fractions in order from smallest to largest. Then write the original fractions in order from smallest to largest.

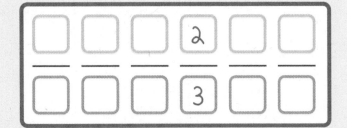

Musical Numbers

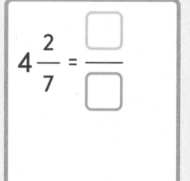

Change each **mixed number** to an **improper fraction**. Show your work.

$1\frac{2}{4} = \frac{\square}{\square}$

$1 \times 4 = 4$
$4 + 2 = 6 \rightarrow \frac{6}{4}$

$5\frac{1}{3} = \frac{\square}{\square}$

$4\frac{5}{6} = \frac{\square}{\square}$

Changing mixed numbers to fractions

$3\frac{3}{4} = \frac{\square}{\square}$

$2\frac{1}{2} = \frac{\square}{\square}$

$4\frac{2}{7} = \frac{\square}{\square}$

$3\frac{5}{8} = \frac{\square}{\square}$

$6\frac{3}{5} = \frac{\square}{\square}$

$1\frac{5}{6} = \frac{\square}{\square}$

BRAIN BOX

A **mixed number** is a whole number plus a fraction.

Example: $4\frac{2}{3}$

To change a mixed number to a fraction:

Step 1: Multiply the whole number by the denominator.
$4 \times 3 = 12$

Step 2: Add that number to the numerator.
$12 + 2 = 14$

Step 3: Write your answer above the denominator.
$\frac{14}{3}$

The resulting fraction is called an **improper fraction**, because the numerator is bigger than the denominator.

Change It Back

Change each improper fraction to a mixed number.
Show your work.

**Changing
fractions to
mixed numbers**

$\frac{7}{5}$ = $\boxed{1}$ $\dfrac{\boxed{2}}{\boxed{5}}$

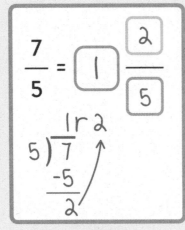

$$\begin{array}{r} 1\,r\,2 \\ 5\overline{)\,7} \\ -5 \\ \hline 2 \end{array}$$

$\frac{7}{2}$ = $\boxed{}$ $\dfrac{\boxed{}}{\boxed{}}$

$\frac{7}{3}$ = $\boxed{}$ $\dfrac{\boxed{}}{\boxed{}}$

$\frac{8}{7}$ = $\boxed{}$ $\dfrac{\boxed{}}{\boxed{}}$

$\frac{18}{4}$ = $\boxed{}$ $\dfrac{\boxed{}}{\boxed{}}$

$\frac{14}{6}$ = $\boxed{}$ $\dfrac{\boxed{}}{\boxed{}}$

$\frac{10}{4}$ = $\boxed{}$ $\dfrac{\boxed{}}{\boxed{}}$

$\frac{15}{2}$ = $\boxed{}$ $\dfrac{\boxed{}}{\boxed{}}$

$\frac{11}{8}$ = $\boxed{}$ $\dfrac{\boxed{}}{\boxed{}}$

BRAIN BOX

An **improper fraction** can be changed to a mixed number. | **Example:** $\frac{15}{2}$ |

Step 1: Divide the numerator
by the denominator.

$$\begin{array}{r} 7\,r\,1 \\ 2\overline{)\,15} \\ -14 \\ \hline 1 \end{array}$$

Step 2: The quotient is the whole number.
The remainder is the numerator. The
denominator stays the same.

$$\frac{15}{2} = 7\frac{1}{2}$$

More or Less

Add or subtract these mixed numbers.

$8\frac{1}{3} + 5\frac{1}{3} = \boxed{}\ \frac{\boxed{}}{\boxed{}}$

$10\frac{1}{3} + 3\frac{1}{3} = \boxed{}\ \frac{\boxed{}}{\boxed{}}$

$6\frac{7}{8} - 4\frac{1}{8} = \boxed{}\ \frac{\boxed{}}{\boxed{}}$

$8\frac{1}{4} + 2\frac{2}{4} = \boxed{}\ \frac{\boxed{}}{\boxed{}}$

Adding and subtracting mixed numbers

$9\frac{5}{7} - 4\frac{4}{7} = \boxed{}\ \frac{\boxed{}}{\boxed{}}$

$7\frac{6}{8} - 5\frac{5}{8} = \boxed{}\ \frac{\boxed{}}{\boxed{}}$

$7\frac{1}{5} + 2\frac{2}{5} = \boxed{}\ \frac{\boxed{}}{\boxed{}}$

$5\frac{9}{10} - 4\frac{1}{10} = \boxed{}\ \frac{\boxed{}}{\boxed{}}$

$6\frac{2}{4} + 8\frac{1}{4} = \boxed{}\ \frac{\boxed{}}{\boxed{}}$

$1\frac{1}{5} + 7\frac{2}{5} = \boxed{}\ \frac{\boxed{}}{\boxed{}}$

$3\frac{2}{8} + 1\frac{5}{8} = \boxed{}\ \frac{\boxed{}}{\boxed{}}$

$7\frac{8}{10} + 5\frac{3}{10} = \boxed{}\ \frac{\boxed{}}{\boxed{}}$

BRAIN BOX

To add mixed numbers with like denominators: | Example: $5\frac{3}{7} + 2\frac{1}{7} = 7\frac{4}{7}$

Step 1: Add the fractions.
$\frac{3}{7} + \frac{1}{7} = \frac{4}{7}$

Step 2: Add the whole numbers.
$5 + 2 = 7$

Step 3: Combine to write the mixed number.
$7\frac{4}{7}$

To subtract mixed numbers with like denominators: | Example: $6\frac{6}{9} - 4\frac{2}{9} = 2\frac{4}{9}$

Step 1: Subtract the fractions.
$\frac{6}{9} - \frac{2}{9} = \frac{4}{9}$

Step 2: Subtract the whole numbers.
$6 - 4 = 2$

Step 3: Combine to write the mixed number.
$2\frac{4}{9}$

Tenths Another Way

Write the fraction for each figure. Then write the equivalent decimal.

Tenths in decimals

$= \dfrac{3}{10} = .3$

$= \dfrac{}{} = \square$

$= \dfrac{}{} = \square$

$= \dfrac{}{} = \square$

$= \dfrac{}{} = \square$

$= \dfrac{}{} = \square$

BRAIN BOX

A **decimal** is another way to write any fraction that has a denominator of 10, 100, 1,000, etc.

Example: $\dfrac{2}{10} = .2$

decimal point   tenths

In decimals, the first digit to the right of the decimal point stands for **tenths**. Since this number is .2, we would say it is two-tenths.

$.2 =$ two-tenths $= \dfrac{2}{10}$

Hundredths

Write the fraction for each figure. Then write the equivalent decimal.

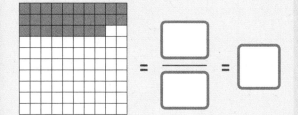

$$= \frac{12}{100} = .12$$

$$= \frac{\boxed{}}{\boxed{}} = \boxed{}$$

$$= \frac{\boxed{}}{\boxed{}} = \boxed{}$$

$$= \frac{\boxed{}}{\boxed{}} = \boxed{}$$

Hundredths in decimals

Write the decimal for each fraction.

$$\frac{15}{100} = \boxed{} \qquad \frac{43}{100} = \boxed{} \qquad \frac{60}{100} = \boxed{}$$

HINT: The numerator is less than 10!

$$\frac{30}{100} = \boxed{} \qquad \frac{22}{100} = \boxed{} \qquad \frac{7}{100} = \boxed{}$$

$$\frac{75}{100} = \boxed{} \qquad \frac{19}{100} = \boxed{} \qquad \frac{99}{100} = \boxed{}$$

BRAIN BOX

The second digit to the right of the decimal point stands for **hundredths**.

Example: $.25 = \frac{25}{100}$
tenths hundredths

If there are fewer than 10 hundredths in a decimal, you write a 0 in the tenths column.

Example: $.01 = \frac{1}{100}$
tenths hundredths

Down, Down, Down

Write the smallest decimal at the bottom of the page.
Write the other decimals down along the side of the
mountain in order from largest to smallest.

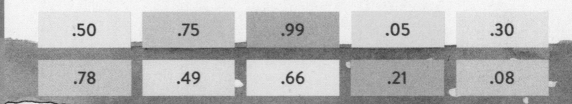

| .50 | .75 | .99 | .05 | .30 |
| .78 | .49 | .66 | .21 | .08 |

Decimals in
descending
order

.99

BRAIN BOX

You can **compare decimals** by looking at the
numbers in the tenths place. The higher the number,
the larger the decimal. If two or more decimals
have the same number in the tenths place, look at
the number in the hundredths place. The higher the
number, the larger the decimal.

Different and Equal

Write the **fraction** for each figure. Then write the equivalent **decimal**. Hint: Each grids contain 100 squares.

Matching fractions and decimals

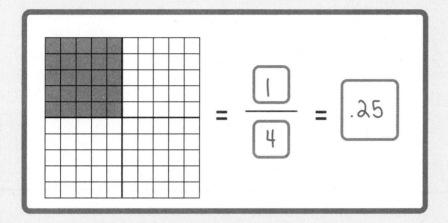

$$= \frac{1}{4} = \boxed{.25}$$

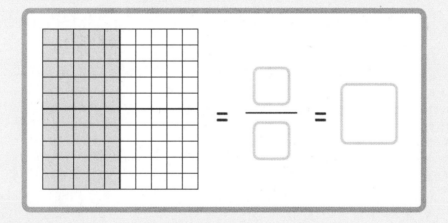

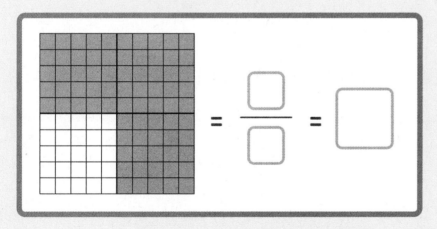

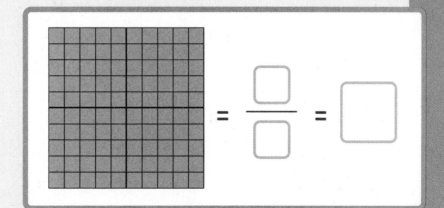

Big Time

Color each row of figures to show the decimal or fraction. Then circle the bigger number in each row.

FRACTIONS AND DECIMALS

Comparing fractions and decimals

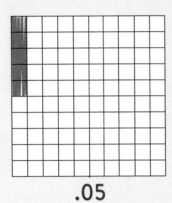 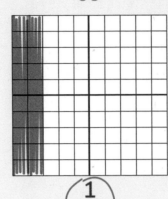

$$\frac{1}{5} \times \frac{20}{20} = \frac{20}{100} = .2$$

.05

$\left(\dfrac{1}{5}\right)$

HINT: Since these grids are divided into one hundred squares, convert the fractions into hundredths to help you figure out how many squares to color.

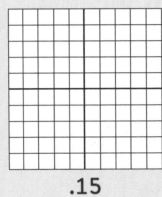 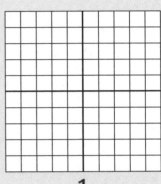

.15

$\dfrac{1}{10}$

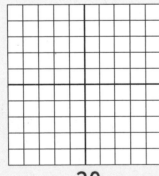 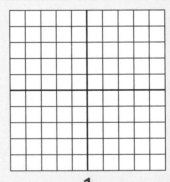

.30

$\dfrac{1}{2}$

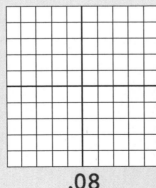 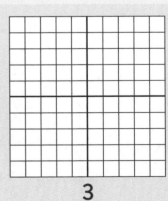

.08

$\dfrac{3}{4}$

More Money

Multiply the money. Be sure to write the dollar sign in your answers.

$5.32 × 5 —— $26.60	$1.50 × 8	$3.85 × 5	$4.00 × 7	$7.24 × 6

Multiplying money

$3.89 × 2	$2.75 × 9	$9.95 × 4	$5.41 × 6	$7.00 × 5

$2.44 × 12	$6.05 × 10	$1.74 × 22	$8.25 × 50	$6.39 × 34

In 1891, a Seated Liberty half-dollar was worth $0.50. Today, it's worth 300 times that. How much is it worth now? _____

BRAIN BOX

When you see a multiplication problem with a decimal, multiply as usual, ignoring the decimal point.

Example:
$3.57
× 3
——
1,071

When you're done, count how many digits are to the right of the original decimal.

$3.57

Put the decimal point into your answer the same number of digits in from the right.

$10.71

Less Money

Divide to find the quotient. Show your work.

Dividing money

```
        $1.43
     3)$4.29
      -3 ↓|
        12↓
       -12
         09
         -9
          0
```

5)$5.00

6)$0.78

2)$15.00

7)$1.47

4)$7.60

2)$1.68

8)$0.88

5)$9.05

6)$4.26

Check the answer to the first problem by writing out a multiplication problem. Multiply the quotient by the divisor. Your answer should be the dividend.

```
   $1.43
 ×    3
  $4.29
```

HINT: When you divide into a decimal, first put the decimal point in your answer. Keep the whole numbers to the left of the decimal point.

Suzanne, Raquel, and Orlando made $17.49 selling popcorn. They divided the money evenly. How much did each person get?

GEOMETRY AND MEASUREMENT

What's your angle? No, really: Geometry has a lot of angles, and you can learn more about them in this section. Get your knowledge in shape and circle back to the lessons in this chapter anytime you need to!

PARENTS Working with lines, shapes, angles, and polygons helps your child build their comprehension of geometric shapes. They will also calculate measurements of volume, weight, temperature, and time. The applications of geometry and measurement are relevant in our everyday lives. Activities such as cooking, building models, and mapping a room are fun ways to practice these skills as a family.

PLACE A
STICKER
HERE

For additional resources, visit www.BrainQuest.com/grade4

Label the Lines

Label each **line segment** by its endpoints. Mark the shortest segment AB and the longest segment FG. Mark the other segment CD.

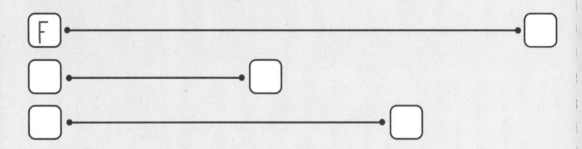

Line segments

Draw two line segments. Name each segment by labeling both endpoints.

Draw two lines. Name each line by labeling two points on the line.

BRAIN BOX

A **line** goes in both directions and is named by any two points on the line. Points are usually labeled with letters, such as A, B, C, or D.

For example:

⟵•——•⟶ = line AB or BA
  A B

A **line segment** is named by its two endpoints. For example:

•————• = line segment CD or DC
C   D

Along the Same Lines

Draw a circle around each set of **parallel** lines.

Parallel and perpendicular lines

Draw a circle around each set of **perpendicular** lines.

BRAIN BOX

Parallel lines are lines that are the same distance apart at every point and can never meet or cross.

Perpendicular lines are lines that intersect at a 90° angle, which is called a right angle.

Many Sides

Write the number of sides below each **polygon**.

Understanding polygons and angles

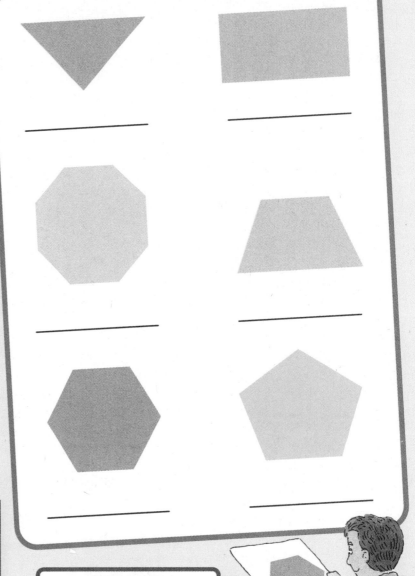

_____   _____

_____   _____

_____   _____

BRAIN BOX

A **polygon** is a closed shape with three or more straight sides and the same number of angles.

An **angle** is formed wherever two line segments meet.

Right Angle   **Acute Angle** (less than 90°)

Obtuse Angle (more than 90°)

BRAIN FACT
Poly is a prefix that means "many." **Gon** comes from a Latin word meaning "angle."

Write the name of each angle.

_____   _____

_____

Triangles

Circle each **isosceles** triangle.

Circle each **scalene** triangle.

Circle each **equilateral** triangle.

BRAIN BOX

A **triangle** is a closed figure with three straight sides.

Every triangle has three angles. **Tri** is a prefix that means "three."

In an **equilateral triangle,** all three sides are the same length.

In an **isosceles triangle,** two of the three sides are the same length.

In a **scalene triangle,** no three sides are the same length.

So Many Sides

Read about **polygons**. Then label each polygon.

A **polygon** is a closed figure with three or more straight sides and the same number of angles. Polygons include:

- **Quad**rangle = 4 sides
- **Penta**gon = 5 sides
- **Hexa**gon = 6 sides
- **Hepta**gon = 7 sides
- **Octa**gon = 8 sides

_____   _____   _____

_____   _____   _____

_____   _____   _____

BRAIN FACT
A nine-sided polygon
is called a **nonagon**.

Shape Up!

Read about **four-sided figures.** Then label each figure.

A **rectangle** is a four-sided figure that has four right angles.

A **square** is a rectangle with four equal sides.

A **quadrangle** (or **quadrilateral**) is a four-sided polygon that is not a rectangle.

Meet the Circle

Read about **circles**.

> A **circle** is a closed curved line on which every point is the same distance from the center.
>
> The **radius** is a line segment from the center of the circle to any point on the edge.
>
> The **diameter** is a line segment that passes through the center of the circle and whose ends touch the circle's edge.

Draw a **radius** on the circle from point A. Label the endpoint B.

Then draw a diameter through the circle. Label it DE.

A •

Through the Middle

Use the figure to answer the questions.

Radius and
diameter

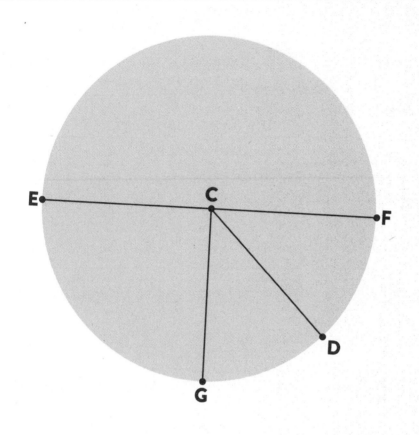

Name all the radii of this circle.

<u>CD</u>   ____   ____   ____

____ is the diameter of this circle.

Which radius forms an acute angle with
the diameter? ____

A diameter divides a circle in ____ .

> **FUN FACT:**
> The plural of *radius*
> is *radii* (ray-dee-ai).
> It's from Latin!

The Ruler

Cut out the ruler at the bottom of the page. Use it to measure the length in **inches** of each object below. Be sure to include either abbreviation for the word *inches* in your answer.

Measuring by inches

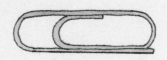

_____   _____

_____

_____

Using the ruler, draw a dot exactly two inches to the right of the red dot.

•——————————————————

Draw a dot exactly 4" to the right of the green dot.

•——————————————————

BRAIN BOX

An **inch** mark is written like this: "

The word **inch** is abbreviated like this: **in**

You can use either one to indicate inches.

> Example:
> **3"** or **3 in**

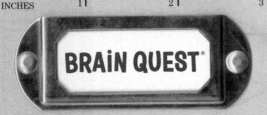

Going Metric

One edge of the ruler you cut out is a **centimeter** ruler. Use it to measure the length of each item below to the nearest centimeter. Be sure to include the abbreviation for the word *centimeters* in your answer.

Measuring by centimeters

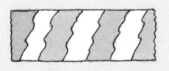
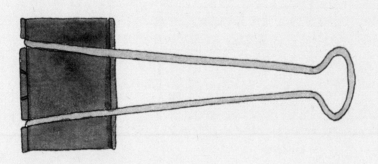

_____

_____   _____   _____

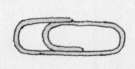
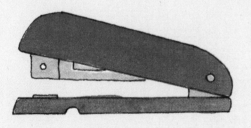

_____

BRAIN FACT
The USA, Liberia, and Myanmar are the only three countries in the world that don't use the metric system!

Measure the length of the flashlight. Write the length in inches and in centimeters.

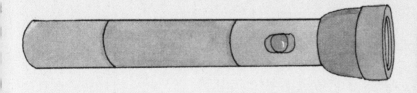

_____

BRAIN BOX

Centimeters, meters, and **kilometers** are the units of length in the metric system. The abbreviation for centimeters is **cm**. The abbreviation for meters is **m**. The abbreviation for kilometers is **km**.

Add the Sides

Write the **perimeter** below each polygon.

Understanding perimeter

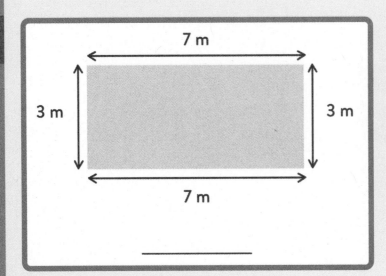

7 m

3 m   3 m

7 m

_____

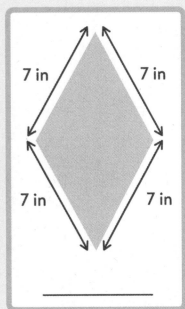

7 in   7 in

7 in   7 in

_____

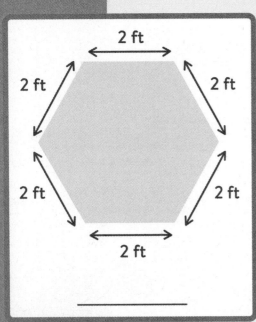

2 ft

2 ft   2 ft

2 ft   2 ft

2 ft

_____

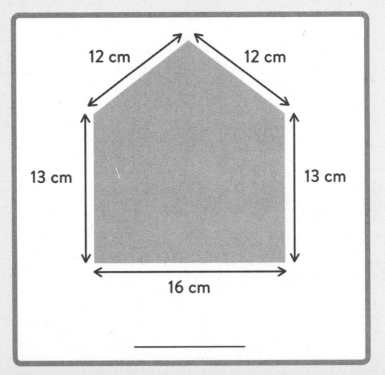

12 cm   12 cm

13 cm   13 cm

16 cm

_____

BRAIN BOX

The **perimeter** is the distance around a figure. You can find the perimeter by adding the lengths of the sides.

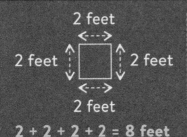

2 feet

2 feet   2 feet

2 feet

2 + 2 + 2 + 2 = **8 feet**

The perimeter of the square is **8 ft.**

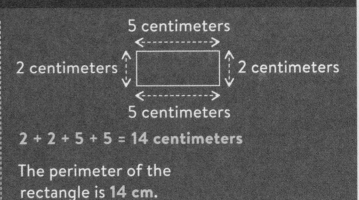

5 centimeters

2 centimeters   2 centimeters

5 centimeters

2 + 2 + 5 + 5 = **14 centimeters**

The perimeter of the rectangle is **14 cm.**

Length Times Width

Read about **area**. Then solve the problems.

The **area** of a figure is the number of square units inside a figure. You can find the area of a rectangular figure by using this simple formula:

length × width = area

For example, this polygon is 4 inches long and 5 inches wide.

4 inches × 5 inches = 20 square inches

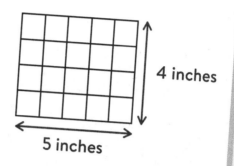

4 inches

5 inches

Finding area

Find the **area** of each shape below. Be sure to write the correct abbreviation as part of your answer.

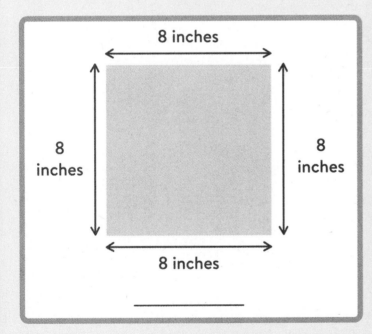

8 inches

8 inches

8 inches

8 inches

_____

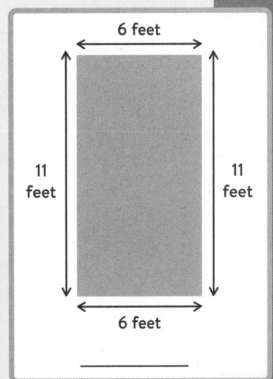

6 feet

11 feet

11 feet

6 feet

_____

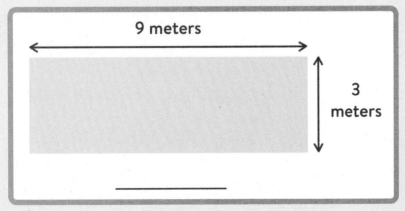

9 meters

3 meters

_____

BRAIN BOX

The abbreviation for square inches is **sq in.**

The abbreviation for square feet is **sq ft.**

Different Shape, Same Size

Find the **area** of each figure. Be sure to write the correct abbreviation as part of your answer.

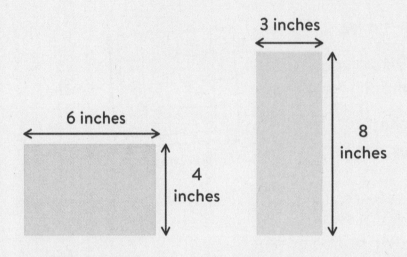
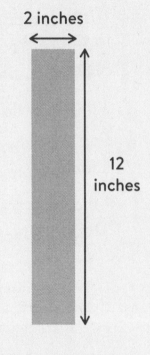

6 inches

4 inches

3 inches

8 inches

2 inches

12 inches

_____   _____   _____

Answer the questions.

Do the three polygons above have different shapes? _____

Do 6 × 4 and 12 × 2 have the same product? _____

Do 8 × 3 and 12 × 2 have the same product? _____

Do the three polygons have the same area? _____

List the factors of 24: _____ _____ _____ _____ _____ _____

If you drew a rectangle that was 24 inches long by 1 inch wide, what would its area be? _____

Can polygons of different shapes have the same area? _____

Three Dimensions

Read about **three-dimensional solids.**

Polygons are figures that have **two dimensions: length** and **width. Solids** are figures that have **three dimensions: length, width,** and **height.**

This figure has two dimensions: length and width

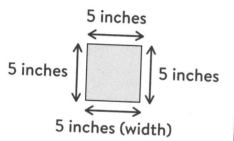

5 inches

5 inches   5 inches

5 inches (width)

This figure has three dimensions: length, width, and height

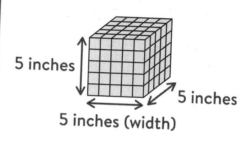

5 inches

5 inches

5 inches (width)

Write the length, width, and height of each figure.

length _____
width _____
height _____

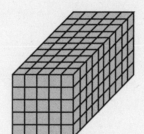

length _____
width _____
height _____

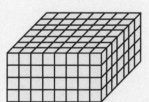

length _____
width _____
height _____

length _____
width _____
height _____

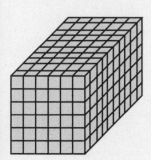

length _____
width _____
height _____

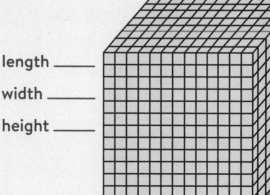

length _____
width _____
height _____

What's Inside?

Read about **volume** and **cubic units**.

> **Volume** tells you how many units will fit inside a solid. These units are called **cubic units**.
>
> Find the volume of a solid rectangular figure with this formula:
>
> **length × width × height = cubic units**

Finding volume

Find the number of **cubic inches** in each figure.

Be sure to write the correct abbreviation as part of the answer.

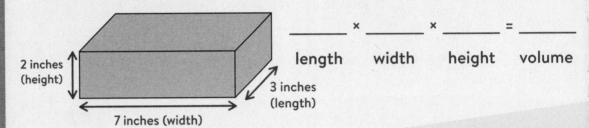

_____ × _____ × _____ = _____
length   width   height   volume

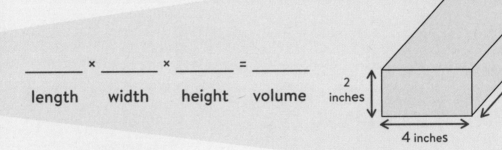

_____ × _____ × _____ = _____
length   width   height   volume

_____ × _____ × _____ = _____
length   width   height   volume

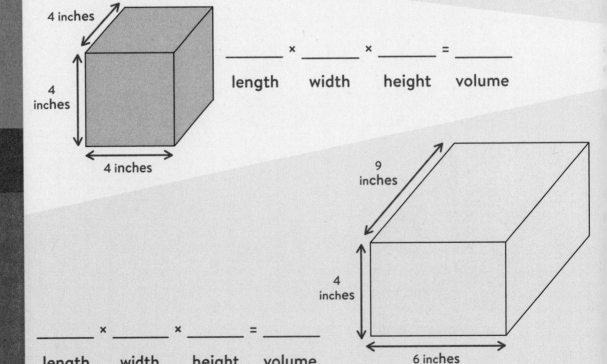

_____ × _____ × _____ = _____
length   width   height   volume

BRAIN BOX

Cubic units can be written as **cubic inches (cu in)** or **cubic feet (cu ft)**.

From Cups to Gallons

Answer the questions about **liquid volume**. Show your work.

  **1 cup (c)** = 8 ounces (oz)

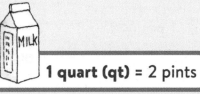 **1 quart (qt)** = 2 pints

 **1 pint (pt)** = 2 cups

1 gallon (gal) = 4 quarts

Liquid volume

Jackson drank one pint of milk for breakfast.
How many cups of milk did he drink? _____

Mr. Zonda starts his daylong hike with one gallon
of water divided into four equal containers.
How much does each container hold? _____

Elena's mother asked her to add a half cup
of water to the beans. How many ounces of
water did Elena add? _____

Mrs. Beverly brought two quarts of juice
to class. How many cups of juice could
she pour for the students? _____

These containers are arranged from smallest
to largest. Label each container using the
measurements at the top of the page.

_____   _____   _____   _____

BRAIN BOX

Liquid volume is
measured in:

ounces (oz)

cups (c)

pints (pt)

quarts (qt)

gallons (gal)

Ounces to Tons

Answer the questions about **weight**. Show your work.

| 1 pound (lb) = 16 ounces (oz) | 1 ton = 2,000 pounds (lbs) |

Weight
measurements

How many ounces are in 5 pounds?

_____

How many pounds are in 48 ounces?

_____

Emily's backpack weighed 7 pounds and 3 ounces.
Joseph's backpack weighed 12 pounds and 15 ounces.
How much did the two backpacks weigh together?

_____

BRAIN BOX

Weight can be measured in **ounces (oz)** and **pounds (lbs)**.

You can add, subtract, multiply, or divide pounds and ounces just as you would any other numbers. When you have pounds and ounces, you might have to change pounds into ounces before you can do the math.

Mouse the elephant weighs $2\frac{1}{2}$ tons.
How many pounds does he weigh?

_____

Samuel's pumpkin weighed 17 pounds.
Butler's pumpkin weighed 13 pounds and 7 ounces.
How much more did Samuel's pumpkin weigh?

_____

Hot and Cold

Read about **temperature**.

Temperature is measured in units called degrees. The symbol for degrees is °.

In the US, we measure temperature on a **Fahrenheit** thermometer.

Other countries measure temperature on a **Celsius** thermometer.

On the Fahrenheit scale:
- water freezes at 32°
- water boils at 212°
- normal body temperature is 98.6°

On the Celsius scale:
- water freezes at 0°
- water boils at 100°
- normal body temperature is 37°

Draw a blue line across both thermometers at their freezing point.

Draw a red line across both thermometers at their boiling point.

Draw a purple line across both thermometers at the normal body temperature point.

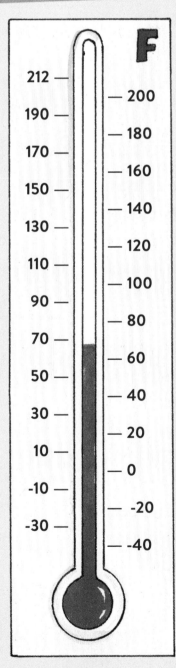

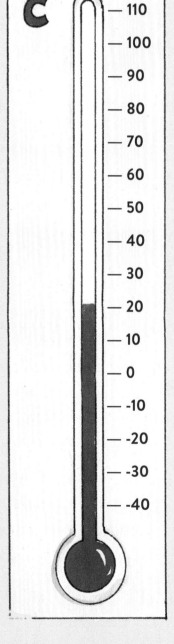

224

From Now to Then

Write the **time** on each line. All clocks show the time as a.m.

_____   _____   _____

Answer each question. Show your work.

How much time has elapsed
between the yellow clock
and the green clock?   _____

How much time has elapsed
between the purple clock
and the green clock?   _____

How much time has elapsed
between the yellow clock
and the purple clock?   _____

PROBABILITY AND DATA

It's in the cards: There is a high probability you will do an amazing job in this section! Probability refers to the chance of something happening. So let's roll the dice and dive into charts, graphs, tables, and more.

PARENTS In this section, your child will practice calculating the chances, or probability, of something happening. They will interpret different visualizations of data, including graph and chart types. Point out examples of graphs you see in a weather report. Share real-world examples of where and how probability is used, like the coin toss at a football game or a spinner on a board game. This real-world practice will help provide meaning and context for their learning.

For additional resources, visit www.BrainQuest.com/grade4

What Are the Chances?

Use the picture to answer the questions about **probability**.

Probability

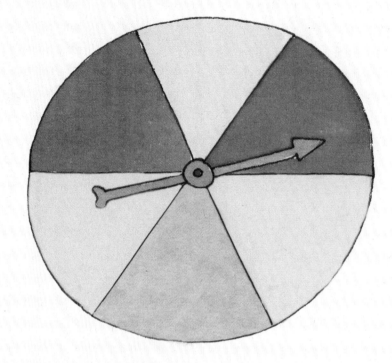

What are the chances of the hand landing on green? ___1:6___

What are the chances of the hand landing on red? _____

What are the chances of the hand landing on yellow? _____

BRAIN BOX

Probability is the likelihood or chance that something will happen.

For example, a coin has two sides: heads and tails. If you toss a coin into the air and let it fall, the chances that it will come up heads are one in two. This probability is written as a ratio: **1:2**.

Use the picture to answer the questions.

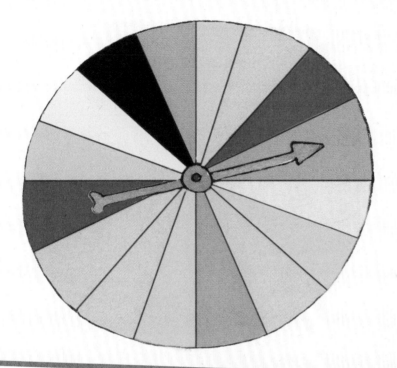

Probability

What are the chances of the hand landing on red? _____

What are the chances of the hand landing on orange? _____

What are the chances of the hand landing on black? _____

What are the chances of the hand landing on blue? _____

What are the chances of the hand landing on green? _____

What are the chances of the hand landing on yellow? _____

In the Cards

Answer the questions based on the cards shown in the picture.

Probability

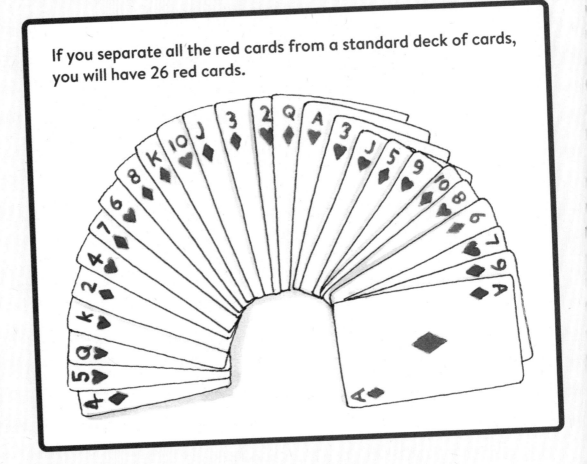

If you separate all the red cards from a standard deck of cards, you will have 26 red cards.

What are your chances of drawing a diamond? _____

What are your chances of drawing a heart? _____

What are your chances of drawing a black card? _____

What are your chances of drawing a king? _____

What are your chances of drawing an ace of hearts? _____

Lift the Flap

Answer the following questions.

P R O B A B I L I T Y

P R O B L E M S

Probability

Suppose a prize worth $1,000 is hidden under the letters in PROBABILITY.

What are the chances that it's hidden under the O? _____

What are the chances that it's hidden under a B? _____

What are the chances that it's hidden under an I? _____

Suppose the prize is hidden under the letters in PROBLEMS. What are the chances that it's hidden under the M? _____

What is the probability that it's hidden under the S? _____

Now suppose that the prize is hidden under one of the letters of either word. How many letters are there altogether? _____

What are the chances that the prize is hidden under a P? _____

What is the probability that it's hidden under a B? _____

What are the chances that it's hidden under a T? _____

Which letter has the highest probability of having the prize hidden under it? _____

Bar graphs

Puppies and Parakeets

Answer the questions using the **bar graph**.

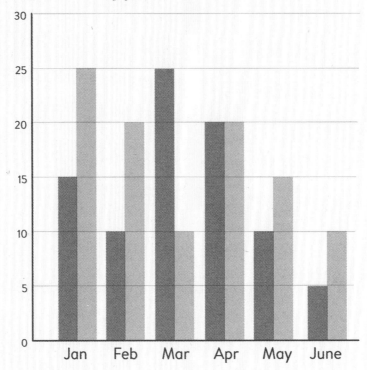

Puppies and Parakeets

KEY
puppies
parakeets

BRAIN BOX

A **bar graph** is a picture, diagram, or drawing that shows how two or more things are related. Some graphs have a **key**. The **key** gives you information you need to understand the graph.

This bar graph shows how many _____ and _____ visited Main Street Vets in half a year.

The half year was from _____ to _____ .

What color bar is used to show puppy visits? _____

What was the largest number of visits in any one month? _____

What month had the most puppies visit? _____

What was the largest number of parakeet visits in any one month? _____

What month had the most parakeet visits? _____

Which pet had the lowest one-month total? _____

Which month was that? _____

In the half year, a total of _____ puppies and a total of _____ parakeets visited Main Street Vets.

Energy Savers!

This year, the De La Hoya family worked to reduce their household energy use. The bar graph shows how much their electric bill was in certain months last year versus how much it was during the same months this year.

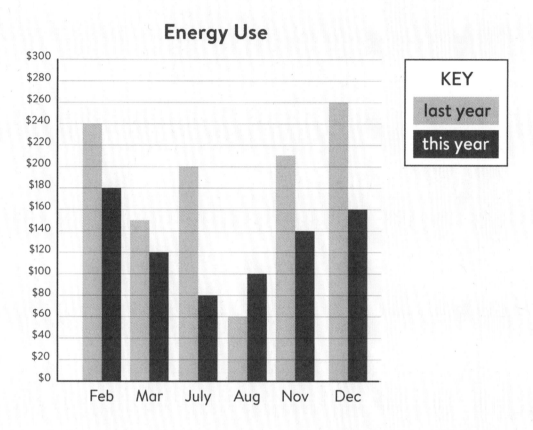

Energy Use

KEY
last year
this year

Answer each question using the **bar graph** they created.

In which month shown on the bar graph did the De La Hoya family lower their electric bill the most? By how much? _____

In which month did they lower their electric bill the least? By how much?

_____

Which was the only month in the bar graph in which they used more electricity this year than last year? How much did their bill increase from that month last year to that month this year? _____

In March, the family lowered their electric bill by $30. In which month did they lower it by exactly twice that much? _____

How much money did they save in total for all the months shown?

_____

Line graphs

Lost Gloves

The **line graph** shows the number of gloves turned in to the Lost and Found. Answer the following questions using the graph.

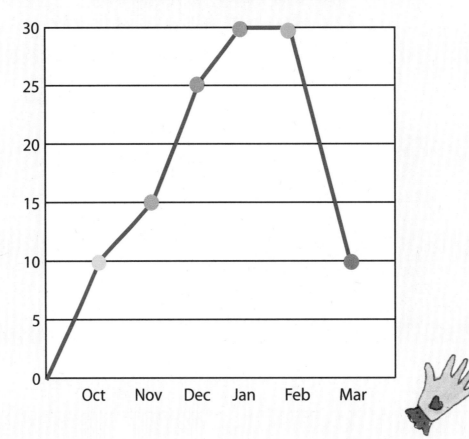

Number of Lost Gloves

This line graph shows the relationship between two things: the number of lost gloves and _____ .

How many gloves were turned in to the Lost and Found in October?

_____

How many gloves were turned in in November? _____

As the weather got colder in December, were more or fewer lost gloves turned in to the Lost and Found than in November? _____

What happened in March, as the weather got warmer? _____

Getting There

Answer the questions below by referring to the information shown in the **pie chart**.

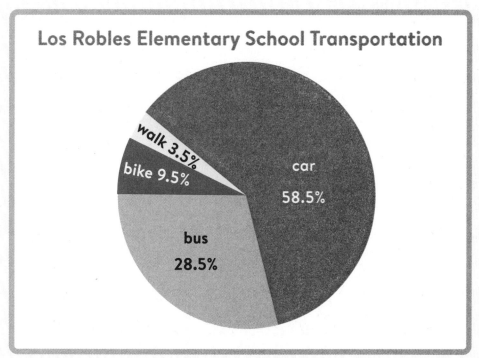

Los Robles Elementary School Transportation

- walk 3.5%
- bike 9.5%
- car 58.5%
- bus 28.5%

Understanding
pie charts

This pie chart gives data about how kids at the _____
_____ get to school every day.

The _____ section of the pie chart is the largest.
It represents transportation by _____ .

The second-largest section of the pie chart is _____ .
It represents transportation by _____ .

Almost 10% of kids _____ to school.

What percentage of students walk to school? _____

If the kids who take the bus to school biked instead, what percentage of the population would bike? _____

If half of the students who rode in cars to school started walking instead, what percentage of students would walk, bike, or take the bus to school? _____

BRAIN BOX

A **pie chart** is a circle graph divided into sections, like a pie. Pie charts are an excellent way to show **parts** or **percentages** of the whole.

Homework vs. Screen Time

Make your own **bar graph** comparing how much time you spend doing homework to how much time you spend on a screen in one week.

Bar graphs

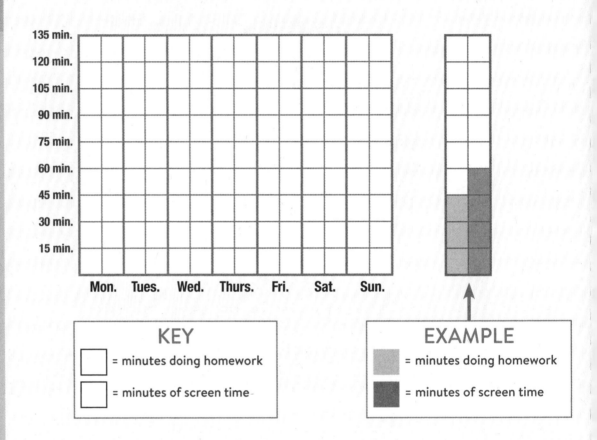

KEY	
☐	= minutes doing homework
☐	= minutes of screen time

EXAMPLE	
▨	= minutes doing homework
▨	= minutes of screen time

After you've finished the graph, answer the questions.

What is the total number of minutes you spent on homework? _____

What is the total number of minutes you spent using screens? _____

On what day did you spend the most time on screens? _____

On what day did you do the most homework? _____

WORD PROBLEMS

Word problems are no problem at all! They're really just short stories about math. The key to solving them is to identify the important numbers and which operation(s) to use. You've got this.

PARENTS Your child will apply math skills from earlier sections to a variety of word problems in this section. An important math practice is to make sense of problems and persevere in solving them. If your child gets stuck or frustrated, suggest using physical objects or drawings to make the math more concrete.

PLACE A STICKER HERE

For additional resources, visit www.BrainQuest.com/grade4

Collecting Numbers

Solve the word problems. Use the extra space on the cards to show your work.

Math skills

Ted and Truman held a contest to see who could collect more baseball caps. Ted collected three caps in April, four in May, none in June, eight in July, three in August, and four in September. Truman collected one in April, seven in May, three in June, none in July, four in August, and three in September. How many caps did each boy collect?

Ted = _____ caps

Truman = _____ caps

What is the place value of the 2 in 124,683?

What is the difference between 75,238 and 118,500?

Write the digits 1 through 6 in reverse order to create a large number. Place a comma where it belongs. The number is:

How many zeros are in five million?

Chloe makes extra money by baking brownies and selling them. In one week, she earned $43.61. What was the average amount of money she earned every day that week?

Number Games

Solve the word problems.

Math skills

Logan plays number games with his pen pal in China. One day, Logan wrote this sequence to his pen pal:

4   9   15   22

His pen pal wrote back the next three numbers. What were they?

Rhonda is a bank teller who handled $254,794 in a 10-hour shift. Aiden, another teller, handled $214,689. How much more money did Rhonda handle than Aiden?

On Friday, Ethan sold 17 chocolate cookies for $1.25 each. How much money did he make that day?

What is the sum of 234 and 87 rounded to the nearest ten?

Subtract 55 from 188. Then multiply by 3. What number do you get?

Round 594,768 to the nearest ten thousand.

Fractured Fractions

Solve the word problems.

Erika baked 7 pies and cut each pie into 7 pieces. She sold each piece for $1.65. At the end of the day, she had sold $\frac{3}{7}$ of a pie. How much did Erika earn that day?

Philip pitched $1\frac{1}{3}$ innings on Monday and $3\frac{1}{3}$ innings on Wednesday. How many innings did he pitch in all?

Roberto and his sister Elena go shopping at a farmers market. Elena asks Roberto to buy $\frac{1}{4}$ pound of chives and $\frac{1}{2}$ pound of cilantro. How many ounces of chives should Roberto buy?

Write these numbers in order from the smallest to the largest.

3.03   .30   0.03   3.30

Four friends worked together as dog walkers, sharing the profits. At the end of the month, they had earned a total of $1,179.36. How much did each friend make?

Morning Rush

Solve the word problems.

Every morning, Mr. Jackson takes the 7:03 train to work. It arrives at the downtown station at 7:57. How many minutes is Mr. Jackson on the train?

Mrs. Cohen takes the 6:42 train to work. It arrives at the downtown station at 7:57. How many minutes is Mrs. Cohen on the train? Write the answer as hours and minutes.

Write 7.3 as a mixed number.

Convert $\frac{2}{10}$ to a decimal.

Makayla mixes $\frac{5}{8}$ cup of syrup with $\frac{5}{8}$ cup of water and $\frac{6}{8}$ cup of juice. How many cups is the finished drink?

Streets and Angles

Solve the word problems.

Math skills

Hester ran $\frac{7}{8}$ of a mile on Monday, $\frac{9}{8}$ on Wednesday, and $\frac{7}{8}$ on Friday. How far did she run that week?

What's the difference between 8.7 and 5.9?

Which line segment is $3\frac{1}{2}$ inches long? Use your BQ ruler.

A •————————————• B

C •——————————————• D

E •————————————————• F

Write the numbers 3, 4, and 5 as six different three-digit numbers.

When Jaime got to the corner, he realized that the street he was about to cross was perpendicular to the street next to him. This meant that the corner he was standing on was:

an acute angle

an obtuse angle

a right angle

Perimeters

Solve the word problems.

Math skills

François draws a rectangle that is 34 centimeters long and 21 centimeters wide. What is the perimeter of the rectangle?

Every morning, Mia walks her Saint Bernard puppy around the outside of a park. She walks 750 feet in one direction and 1,325 feet in another direction. Then she walks another 750 feet and another 1,325 feet. What is the perimeter of the park that Mia walks?

Write the number of sides for each figure:

octagon

quadrangle

hexagon

triangle

pentagon

heptagon

If one side of a square is 9 meters, what is its perimeter?

In one week, Drexel Dumpsters collects 8,000 pounds of garbage. How many tons of garbage is that?

Jasmine lives in an apartment building that has 8 equal sides. Each side is 8 yards. What is the perimeter of the building?

Carpeted Area

Solve the word problems.

Stefani wants to get new carpeting in her bedroom. Her bedroom is 9 feet by 10 feet. How many square feet is that?

Maxie's room is 72 square feet. The carpeting she wants is sold by the square yard. Since 9 square feet equals 1 square yard, how many square yards of carpeting does Maxie need?

The cost of the carpeting is $8.99 a square yard. Julio needs 10 square yards. How much change will he get back if he pays with a $100 bill?

Kenji knows that the perimeter of a rectangle is 780 feet. He also knows that the length of the rectangle is 200 feet. What width does he give for the rectangle?

Tamar knows that the perimeter of a square is 384 centimeters. What is the length of one side of the square?

Preston is building a small box that is 55 centimeters by 35 centimeters. What is the area of the box?

Hiroko must pour cups of spring water into quart containers. She fills 17 quart containers. How many cups did she pour?

SOCIAL STUDIES

Ready to flex your social studies skills? Let's read all kinds of maps, travel back in time to learn some interesting history, and find out more about the world around us.

PLACES I WANT TO VISIT

PARENTS Your child will use their reading, writing, and researching skills to expand their understanding of government, economics, geography, and history. Encourage your child to take inspiration from this chapter and create a list of places they'd like to visit one day. Ask them which parts in this section they would like to know more about.

PLACE A STICKER HERE

Seven Continents

Look at a **world map** in a book or online to label the seven continents and the five major oceans of the world.

World map

Ask a trusted
adult before
you go online.

Earth Covers

Use the **map key** to answer the questions about Earth's landscape.

The northern part of Africa is mainly _____ .

Which two continents have the most desert? _____

Antarctica is mostly _____ .

Does Asia have more grasslands or mountains? _____

Using a
map key

The three continents that have the largest mountain ranges
are _____ , _____ , and
_____ .

Is there more land north of the equator or south
of the equator? _____

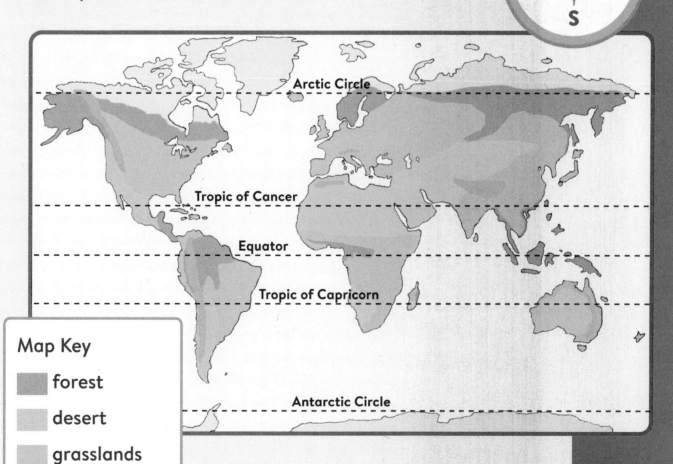

Map Key

forest

desert

grasslands

tundra or ice

mountains

Arctic Circle

Tropic of Cancer

Equator

Tropic of Capricorn

Antarctic Circle

N
W   E
S

The Thirteen Colonies

Read about the original **thirteen colonies.** Use the map to answer the questions.

What was the southernmost colony? _____

The colonies were situated along the eastern seacoast. What ocean did they border? _____

Which very large colony was north of Pennsylvania? _____

Which small colony is west of Rhode Island and east of New York? _____

Which colony is north of North Carolina? _____

The Original Thirteen Colonies

The thirteen colonies were formed on land where hundreds of Indigenous societies had existed for thousands of years. In 1607, the first wave of settlers left England for North America. They settled in an encampment in Virginia they called Jamestown and began to displace the Indigenous people who lived there.

The Pilgrims followed soon after. They arrived on a ship called the *Mayflower* and called their settlement New England.

Over the next hundred years, waves of European settlers arrived and built settlements on Indigenous land, establishing what became known as the original thirteen colonies.

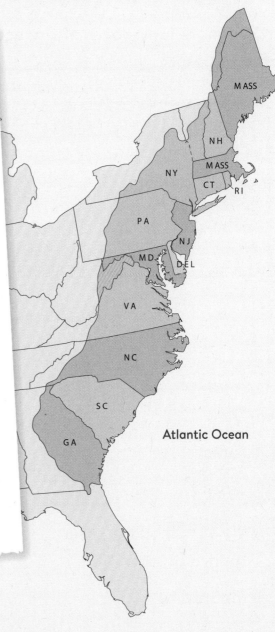

Atlantic Ocean

Gulf of Mexico

July 4, 1776

Read about the **Declaration of Independence.**

SOCIAL STUDIES

Reading an original document

Many people in the thirteen colonies believed they were being treated unjustly by the king of England. On July 4, 1776, representatives from each colony met to sign a document. In it, they listed their reasons for separating from Great Britain to create a brand-new nation: the United States of America. This document is the Declaration of Independence.

Draw a line connecting each quote from the Declaration of Independence to the correct explanation of it.

King George of England "has kept among us, in times of peace, Standing Armies without the Consent of our legislatures."	Colonists were not allowed to sell goods, like grains, furs, and fish to other countries.
King George is "quartering large bodies of armed troops among us."	Colonial families were forced to let British soldiers live with them and eat their food.
King George is "cutting off our Trade with all parts of the world."	The colonists were forced to pay taxes but were not allowed to vote on whether or not they wanted the taxes.
King George is "imposing Taxes on us without our Consent."	The British Army was stationed throughout the colonies without permission from the colonists.

The Oregon Trail

Read about the **Oregon Trail**. Then, answer the questions.

The Oregon Trail

The Oregon Trail was a two-thousand-mile path between Independence, Missouri, and Oregon City, near what is today Portland, Oregon. Much of the trail followed three rivers—the Platte, the Snake, and the Columbia—with a string of natural landmarks serving as guideposts along the way.

From the early 1840s to the late 1860s about 400,000 settlers used the Oregon Trail on their way west to Oregon Territory, or California. In 1848, gold was found at Sutter's Mill in California, and people flocked west to search for more. Other settlers were moving west to build homesteads and establish farms. In 1862, the US government started giving away farmland for free to encourage more US citizens to settle there.

The terrain along the Oregon Trail was uneven and rough. Many settlers traveled west in covered wagons that could not easily cross rivers or mountains and didn't protect them against extreme weather. If the journey took too long, the settlers faced the danger of getting stuck on the trail during winter.

The western territories and the land surrounding the Oregon Trail were home to many different Indigenous nations, including the Nimiipuu (Nez Perce) and Walla Walla peoples. When westward expansion began, the US government forced Indigenous nations off their homelands and onto reservations and rancherias (smaller reservations). They took millions of acres of land from the original inhabitants and gave it to the settlers. By mining, farming, and hunting, the settlers used up natural resources and polluted the rivers.

In 1884, the newly built Union Pacific railway replaced the Oregon Trail as the best route west. For most settlers it was a safer and faster alternative.

How long was the Oregon Trail? Where did it start and end?

_____

_____

Which three rivers did the trail follow?

_____

_____

What are two reasons settlers wanted to head west?

_____

_____

Why was covered wagon a strenuous way to travel along
the Oregon Trail?

_____

_____

What happened to Indigenous nations, like the Nimiipuu
and Walla Walla, when settlers moved west? What happened
to the land?

_____

_____

What technological advancement replaced the Oregon Trail
in 1884?

_____

_____

Making Sense of the Census

Read about the **US census**.

The US Census

The US census counts the number of people in all fifty states, the District of Columbia, and the US territories. It asks specific questions about each person in a household, including name, age, date of birth, and race. The US Constitution requires that the population be counted by a census every ten years.

The first national count of the US population was undertaken in 1790. It counted the populations of the following states (here called "districts"): Vermont, New Hampshire, Maine, Massachusetts, Rhode Island, Connecticut, New York, New Jersey, Pennsylvania, Delaware, Maryland, Virginia, Kentucky, North Carolina, South Carolina, and Georgia.

The 1790 Census put the state populations into five categories*: free white men sixteen and older, free white men sixteen and younger, free white women, other free people, and enslaved people.

DISTICTS	Free white Males of 16 years and upwards, including heads of families.	Free white Males under sixteen years.	Free white Females, including heads of families.	All other free persons.	Slaves.	Total.
Vermont	22435	22328	40505	255	16	85539
N. Hampshire	36086	34851	70160	630	158	141885
Maine	24384	24748	46870	538	NONE	96540
Massachusetts	95453	87289	190582	5463	NONE	378787
Rhode Island	16019	15799	32652	3407	948	68825
Connecticut	60523	54403	117448	2808	2764	237946
New York	83700	78122	152320	4654	21324	340120
New Jersey	45251	41416	83287	2762	11423	184139
Pennsylvania	110788	106948	206363	6537	3737	434373
Delaware	11783	12143	22384	3899	8887	59094
Maryland	55915	51339	101395	8043	103036	319728
Virginia	110936	116135	215046	12866	292627	747610
Kentucky	15154	17057	28922	114	12430	73677
N. Carolina	69988	77506	140710	4975	100572	393751
S. Carolina	35576	37722	66880	1801	107094	249073
Georgia	13103	14044	25739	398	29264	82548
	807094	791850	1541263	59150	694280	3893635

*The categories listed from left to right in the top row of the table read: "free white males of 16 years and upwards, including heads of families", "free white males under 16 years", "free white females, including heads of families", "all other free persons", and "slaves". The total population of each category is listed in the bottom row. The total population of each district is in the column farthest to the right.

Use the image of the 1790 census population on the opposite page to answer these questions.

In 1790, how many total people were counted in the United States?

_____

Which "district" had the largest total population?

_____

Which "district" had the smallest total population?

_____

Which two "districts" were the only ones without an enslaved population?

_____

Which category had the greatest total number of people?

_____

Which category had the smallest total number of people?

_____

In which four "districts" was the enslaved population larger than any other category of people counted?

_____

_____

_____

Who could the category "all other free persons" have been referring to?

_____

_____

_____

Looking at primary sources

BRAIN BOX

A census is an official count or survey of a population. The results of the US census are used to make decisions about the number of seats each state can have in the US House of Representatives. The results are also used to decide how money from the federal government will be distributed to communities for important public services such as schools, hospitals, roads, fire departments, and more.

50 States

Study the map of the United States. Then answer the questions.

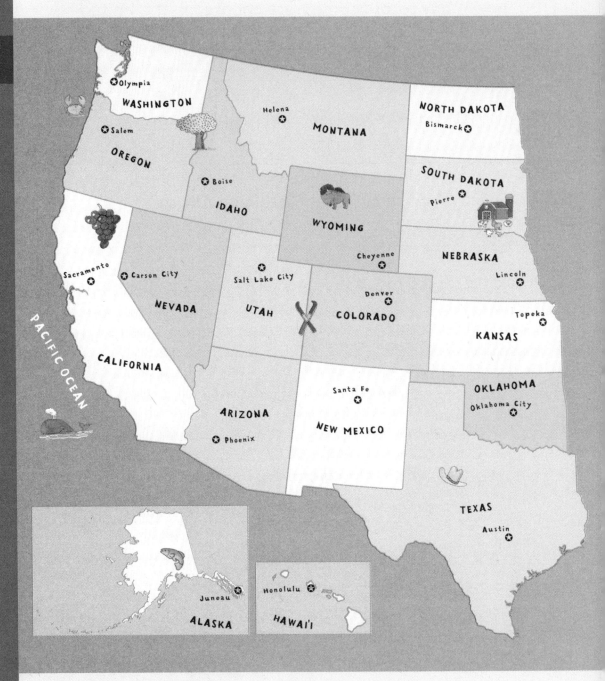

What is the name of your state?

_____

Write the names of the states that border your state.

_____

_____

_____

Geography skills

There is one place in the United States where four states meet.
They are called the Four Corners. Can you name them?

_____

What state is a chain of islands?

_____

What state is farthest east on the US mainland?

_____

Your State

Research your state in an atlas, an encyclopedia, or on the internet. Fill in as much information as you can on the lines below.

Events in Kansas History

State facts

State name:	
Joined the Union on:	
State nickname:	
Capital city:	
State flower:	
State tree:	
State bird:	
State mammal:	
State insect:	
State rock:	
If your state has had a centennial celebration (100th anniversary of statehood), when was it?	
If it hasn't yet, when will it be?	
If your state has had a bicentennial celebration (200th anniversary of statehood), when was it?	
If it hasn't, when will it be?	

Ask a trusted adult before you go online.

Know Your History

Use one library source and one online source to research an important event in the history of your state.

Use the **idea web** below to organize your research. Write the state event in the center. Fill each of the smaller circles with a detail about the event. Look for dates, key people involved, the location, and so on.

State facts

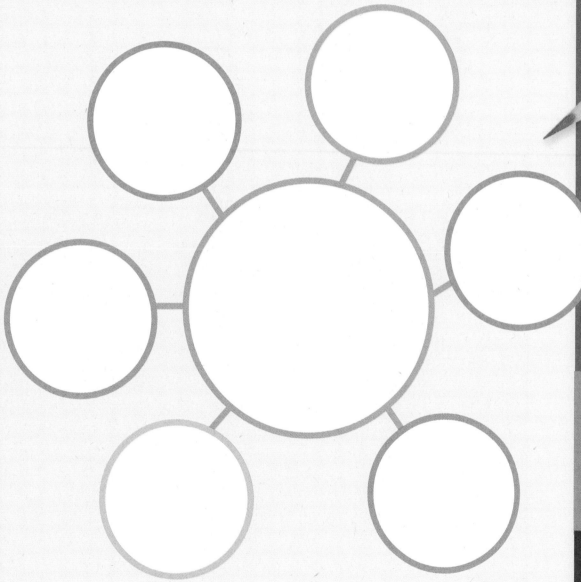

Ask a trusted adult before you go online.

BRAIN BOX

You can organize your research by making an **idea web.**

Dear Friend,

Write a letter to a friend about your state's important historic event. Use the idea web on page 255 to organize your writing and remember important details.

State facts

Dear _____ ,

Sincerely,

SCIENCE

From the biggest planets in our solar system to the smallest particles in the universe, science is all around us. Let's learn about space, our home planet, energy, animal adaptations, and more!

PARENTS This section explores life, physical, earth, and space sciences. Your child will apply their language arts skills to learn about science concepts and practices, building a foundation for deeper science learning in middle and high school biology, chemistry, and physics classes. Have your child record questions that arise as they complete these pages and encourage them to seek answers independently.

PLACE A STICKER HERE

For additional resources, visit www.BrainQuest.com/grade4

The Universe

Read about the **universe** and **galaxies**.

The Big Picture

Everything that exists—our world, our sun, our galaxy, all of outer space, and even time—lives within the universe. Scientists believe that the universe began with a huge explosion, the Big Bang, more than 13 billion years ago. Out of that explosion, the stars and galaxies and planets came into being.

There are hundreds of billions of galaxies in the universe. There are hundreds of billions of stars in every galaxy. There are also other celestial bodies, like planets, asteroids, comets, satellites, black holes, clouds of cosmic dust and gas called nebulae, and what scientists call "dark matter," which is all the stuff we cannot see.

There are three types of galaxies: spiral, elliptical, and irregular. Our solar system is part of the Milky Way galaxy, which is a spiral galaxy.

BRAIN FACT
Another word for *universe* is **cosmos**, which means "order." The universe is bound by gravity, which brings order to the way the universe functions.

Answer the questions.

Name at least five types of celestial bodies in the universe.

_____

_____

Name the three types of galaxies.

_____

_____

Scientists believe that the universe began with an explosion billions of years ago. This is called the _____ theory.

What are nebulae?

_____

_____

What do scientists call the stuff in the universe we can't see?

_____

What is the name of our galaxy?

_____

What is another word for *universe*?

_____

The Solar System

Read about the **solar system**. Then read about the planets on the following page.

A Tour of Our Solar System

Our solar system is made up of the sun, which is at the very center of our system, and the eight planets—plus dwarf planets, asteroids, and meteors—that orbit the sun.

The eight planets that orbit the sun are Mercury, Venus, Earth, Mars, Jupiter, Saturn, Uranus, and Neptune. A good way to remember the order of the planets is to remember this sentence:

My Very Educated Mother Just Showed Us Neverland.

Answer the questions about the planets.

Which planet looks blue because of its methane gas?

_____

Which planet orbits the sun in eighty-eight days?

_____

Which is the largest planet in the solar system? _____

What dwarf planet is no longer considered to be a major planet in our solar system? _____

Which planet is known as the red planet?_____

Which major planet is covered in an icy layer of clouds?

_____

Which planet is third from the sun?_____

Which planet is known for its beautiful rings? _____

Which planet is the hottest? _____

The solar system

Earth, our home planet, is the third planet from the sun. It takes 365 days to orbit the sun.

Earth has one moon.

Pluto used to be considered a planet but is now called a dwarf planet. It takes Pluto 247.7 Earth years to orbit the sun. That means a Plutonian year is 90,410 days long!

Pluto has five moons.

The last major planet in the solar system is Neptune. The blue color of Neptune is due to methane gas in its atmosphere, which absorbs all the red light. A constant storm rages over Neptune, with winds blowing ten times faster than the worst hurricanes on Earth. It takes almost 165 Earth years for Neptune to orbit the sun.

Neptune has fourteen moons.

Saturn is known for its beautiful rings, which are chunks of ice and rocks as small as the head of a pin or as large as an elephant. It takes Saturn 29.5 Earth years to orbit the sun.

Saturn has eighty-two known moons.

Uranus is a frozen planet completely covered in an icy layer of clouds. It takes Uranus eighty-four Earth years to orbit the sun.

Uranus has twenty-seven moons.

Jupiter is the fifth planet from the sun and the largest planet in the solar system. It is 318 times the size of Earth and is made up of gases that give it a red and orange glow. A great red spot in the center of Jupiter is a giant cloud swirling in the opposite direction of all the other clouds. It takes Jupiter 11.87 Earth years to orbit the sun.

Jupiter has seventy-nine known moons.

Venus, the second planet from the sun, is covered in a thick layer of clouds. These clouds are made of sulfuric acid, which trap the heat of the sun on the surface of Venus and make it our solar system's hottest planet.

Venus has no moons.

Mars, the fourth planet from the sun, is known as the red planet because of its desertlike landscape. Its land has long grooves made by rivers that flowed there four billion years ago. There might have once been life on Mars, though the atmosphere is too thin to support life now. It takes Mars nearly 687 Earth days to orbit the sun.

Mars has two moons.

Mercury, the planet closest to the sun, looks a lot like our moon. It is covered in craters, and it has no atmosphere. It takes Mercury eighty-eight Earth days to orbit the sun.

Mercury has no moons.

The Moon

Read about the **moon**.

It takes the moon twenty-seven days and seven hours
to go around Earth once. As it orbits Earth, the moon is
illuminated by the sun in different ways, depending how
the sun, Earth, and moon line up. Each of the different
"looks" of the moon is called a lunar phase.

SUNLIGHT

Last
Quarter
(Half Moon)

Waning
Crescent

Waning
Gibbous

New Moon

Full Moon

Waxing
Crescent

Waxing
Gibbous

First
Quarter

(Half Moon)

Use the diagram on page 262 to answer the questions.

When the moon is between the sun and Earth, it is completely shadowed. This lunar phase is called a _____ .

A _____ appears as a complete circle in the night sky.

There are two times in a lunar cycle when we see only a sliver of the moon. These are called the _____ and _____ phases.

Another term for a last quarter moon and a first quarter moon is a _____ .

How long does it take the moon to orbit Earth?

_____

Where do you think the word *month* comes from?

_____

A gibbous moon is when more than half the moon is visible.

A _____ comes before the full moon phase.

A _____ comes after a full moon phase.

BRAIN FACT
Waxing means growing.
Waning means shrinking.

A View from Above

Read about planet **Earth**.

Blue Marble

On December 7, 1972, the crew of the Apollo 17 spacecraft took this picture on their way to the moon, 28,000 miles from Earth. Called Blue Marble, this image helped change the way people saw and understood our home planet.

The Blue Marble image was the first full photo of Earth ever taken. Before this image was shared across the world, no one had ever seen Earth from above—a sphere of land, water, and swirling clouds suspended in a sea of black space.

Look at the image for a moment. Can you point to the coastline of Africa? How about the Arabian Peninsula? Or the polar ice cap at the southernmost part of the globe? Can you identify areas of desert?

There's no mistaking the feature that makes Earth unique in our solar system: liquid water. Earth is the only planet in our solar system on which life exists. About 71% of the surface of Earth is covered in water, something all organisms (living things) need to survive. There are trillions of organisms on the "water planet" (as Earth is known), including plants, animals, bacteria, and fungi. Earth's abundant water is actually the reason this famous photo is called Blue Marble!

Look at these images of landforms and bodies of water. Label each image with the correct word below.

glacier   desert   lake   plateau

mountain range   ocean   island

Earth

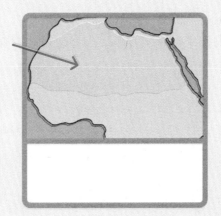

BRAIN BOX

Landforms are physical features on the surface of the Earth that make up its terrain.

Shapers of the Earth

Read about natural forces that shape the earth in the cards below. Then label each card with a word from the colored boxes.

Natural forces

| glacier | flood | volcano | hurricane | earthquake | wind |

[_____]

This powerful ocean storm causes great damage when it hits land. Katrina, for example, washed away Louisiana beaches and submerged some islands.

[_____]

This is an overflowing of water outside its normal boundaries. It can uproot trees, wash away topsoil, and wipe out towns.

[_____]

This force causes the earth to move suddenly and violently along fault lines. In 1812, the Mississippi River's course was changed by one of these.

[_____]

Unlike some natural forces that cause immediate changes in Earth's surface, this force works over time. It can carve rocks into strange shapes.

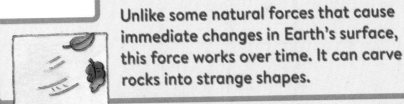

[_____]

This huge sheet of ice scrapes basins into the earth and creates lakes. The Great Lakes were formed by this force.

[_____]

When this erupts, lava is sent into the air and down its sides. In the ocean, one of these can form an island or island chain, such as Hawai'i.

BRAIN BOX

Landforms can be shaped by natural forces, such as volcanic activity, earthquakes, and wind.

Rocks and Minerals

Read about **rocks** and **minerals**. Then answer each question with a word from the colored boxes below.

> A **mineral** is a substance whose physical properties are the same throughout.

> A **rock** is an aggregate (combination) of minerals. A rock might not have the same physical properties throughout.

Knowing rocks and minerals

lava	granite	copper	shale	talc	graphite

Ten thousand years ago this mineral was used to make tools because it can be hammered into shape. It conducts electricity well, and you probably have some of it in your piggy bank in the form of pennies. It is called _____ .

When a volcano erupts it spews this very hot and liquid igneous rock. It is called _____ .

This is one of the softest of all minerals. It can be ground up and made into a body powder or talcum powder. It is called _____ .

_____ is the most common sedimentary rock, formed from mud or clay. You can see the layers in this rock, and sometimes they break off easily. This rock is used to make bricks and cement.

This soft metamorphic rock is used to make pencils. It is slippery and can be used to lubricate machinery. This rock is called _____ .

This igneous rock is very common on Earth. It is made of quartz, feldspar, and mica, and you can see the crystals in the rock. This rock, called _____, is often used for kitchen countertops.

Everything's Related

Read about **solids**, **liquids**, and **gases**.

Why Matter Matters

Everything in the universe is made up of either matter or energy. Matter is everything that takes up space. It is made up of tiny particles called atoms and molecules that are so small they can only be seen with powerful microscopes. No matter how big or small, matter has mass—it can be weighed even if it's as light as a feather.

Matter has three common states:

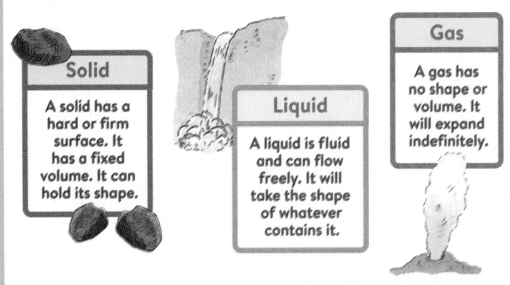

Solid

A solid has a hard or firm surface. It has a fixed volume. It can hold its shape.

Liquid

A liquid is fluid and can flow freely. It will take the shape of whatever contains it.

Gas

A gas has no shape or volume. It will expand indefinitely.

Sometimes the state of matter is determined by temperature. For instance, water is a liquid. When water is frozen it becomes ice, which is a solid. When water is boiled it becomes steam, which is a gas.

Identify each state of matter by writing **solid**, **liquid**, or **gas** next to it.

a desk _____

an icicle _____

mist _____

milk _____

maple syrup _____

helium in a balloon _____

Read about **energy.** Then answer the questions.

It's All Relative

Energy is everything in the universe that is not matter. It's not a solid, a liquid, or a gas—and it's everywhere around us. It's what gets everything in the universe going. Heat, light, sound, and motion are all different forms of energy. Energy can change forms, but it can never be made and it can never be ended. In fact, the most important scientific principle is called the law of the conservation of energy, which states that energy can be neither created nor destroyed, but it can be transformed from one form to another.

Energy can be converted into matter, and matter can be converted into energy. For instance, although we can't see it, we know there is a core of matter at the very center of the sun. The fiery glow that surrounds the sun is caused by that core of matter being converted into energy. This is what causes all stars to shine.

It was Albert Einstein who, in 1905, first theorized that all matter contained the possibility of being converted into energy. He came up with an equation to figure out how much energy any amount of matter might actually contain. He found that even the tiniest amounts of mass could be converted into huge amounts of energy.

$$e = mc^2$$

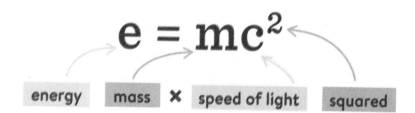

energy   mass **×** speed of light   squared

His theory on the relationship between matter and energy revolutionized the way scientists viewed the universe. Much of what we know about how the universe works today is due to the work of Albert Einstein.

What does the law of the conservation of energy state?

_____

What causes the sun to glow?

_____

When did Einstein write his theory about matter and energy?

_____

Kinetic and Potential

Read about the two types of **energy**. Then answer the questions.

Kinetic energy is the energy of motion. Everything that is moving or that causes other things to move has kinetic energy.

Examples of **kinetic energy**:
- electricity, because electrical charges cause things to move
- magnets, because magnetic forces cause things to move
- light, heat, and wind, because these energies cause things to move
- sound, since sound is caused by vibrations that are carried on sound waves

Potential energy is energy that can be put into motion. It is energy that is stored and waiting to happen.

Examples of **potential energy**:
- gasoline, propane, and petroleum (chemical energy)
- coils and springs that have been compressed and rubber bands that have been stretched (mechanical energy)
- the energy stored inside an atom (nuclear energy)
- a boulder at the top of a hill, since it could be pushed off the hill and roll downward (gravitational energy)

Write **K** next to the things that have **kinetic energy**.
Write **P** next to the things that have **potential energy**.

an apple hanging from a tree _____

an apple falling from a tree _____

a bolt of lightning _____

a windmill _____

gasoline _____

Answer the questions.

Kinetic energy is the energy of _____ .

A rubber band that is stretched—but has not been released—is an example of _____ energy.

Once the rubber band has been released and goes flying through the air, its energy turns into _____ energy.

Why does this happen?
_____

Why is sound considered a type of kinetic energy?
_____

Name three other examples of kinetic energy.
_____
_____
_____

Name three examples of potential energy.
_____
_____
_____

What kind of potential energy is stored inside an atom?
_____

Root to Flower

Read about the different **parts of a plant**. Label each card with a word from the colored boxes below.

| stem | seeds | fruit | bud |

| flower | root | leaf |

Plant parts

This part of the plant is a young flower, leaf, or stem that hasn't yet unfurled. It grows at the end of a stem or along a stem.

This part of the plant absorbs light, water, and air so the plant can produce food.

This part of the plant carries the water and nutrients from the roots to the leaves and the rest of the plant. It is aboveground and acts as a support system for the rest of the plant. It holds the leaves of the plant high so that the plant can get light from the sun.

This part of the plant is found underground. It absorbs nutrients and water from the soil to feed the rest of the plant. It can also store food that the plant needs.

Label each card with a word from the colored boxes.

This part of the plant is where reproduction of the plant takes place. Its scent or colorful petals help attract animals like bees, which pollinate the plant so it can produce seeds.

New plants grow from these, which are actually tiny embryos of the plant. They often grow in the fruit of the plant and are protected by a coating. They are dispersed by wind, water, animals, or people.

This part of the plant is where the seeds develop once a flower has been pollinated. It is a ripened ovary of the plant.

Answer these questions about plants.

What part of a plant is underground?

_____

What part of a plant is used to help disperse seeds so that new plants can grow?

_____

Name three things the stem of a plant does.

_____
_____
_____

Circle of Life

Look at the pictures that show the **life cycle of a plant.** Label each stage with a word or phrase from the colored boxes.

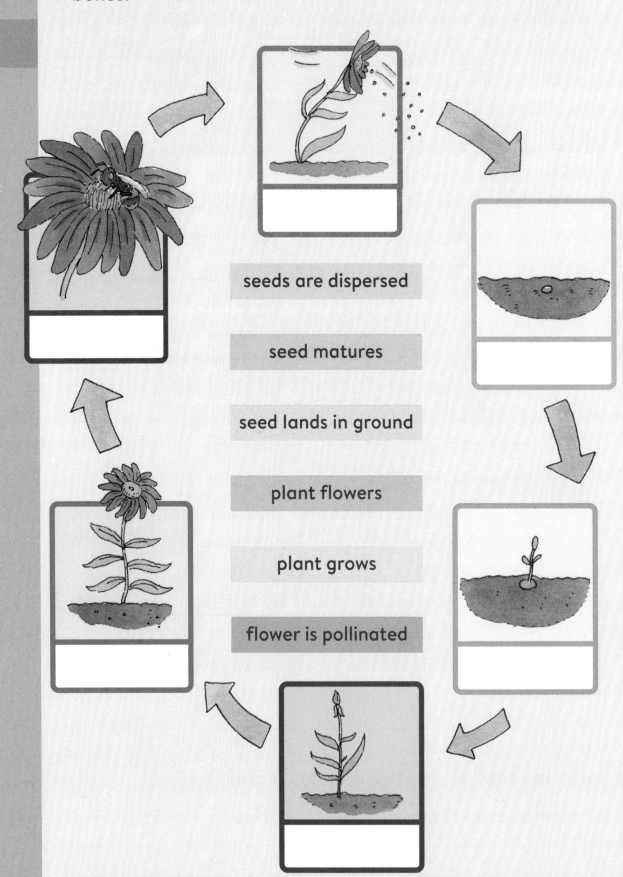

seeds are dispersed

seed matures

seed lands in ground

plant flowers

plant grows

flower is pollinated

Fitting In

Help explain **food webs** by completing each sentence with a word from the colored boxes below.

herbivores	soil	bacteria	carnivores

bottom	food	omnivores

Food Web

All living things are linked together by food webs. Living things that make their own _____ are called producers. Plants are producers. They are at the _____ of food webs. Animals that eat plants are called _____ . Animals that eat other animals are called _____ . Animals that eat both plants and animals are called _____ . Decomposers such as _____ are living things. They break down dead things into very small particles that become part of the _____ . Plants need the soil to grow.

BRAIN BOX

These prefixes are from Latin words.

herb(a)- means green plants

carni- means meat or flesh

omni- means all

Plant Survival

Draw a line from the plant to its description.

This plant is a fruit. It grows very low to the ground. In order to spread, it has special horizontal stems called runners.

This plant has developed spines in order to protect itself from animals that would like to eat it.

This plant lives in northern forests where there is heavy snowfall. Its branches point downward so that the snow falls off and doesn't break them.

This plant lives in temperate zones. As cold weather approaches, it drops its leaves. Because the tree doesn't have to provide water and nutrients to its leaves, it can conserve energy over the winter.

This plant's leaves are supported by water. Its roots are anchored to pond bottoms.

Specialized features of plants

BRAIN BOX

In order to survive in a particular environment, plants develop special features.

Animal Survival

Write the letter of the correct animal on each line.

B

A

C

Specialized features of animals

D

E

F

_____ This animal lives in the desert. It stores large supplies of fat in its hump so that it can survive when there is no food for it to eat.

_____ This animal has a thick layer of fat so that it can survive in very cold weather.

_____ This animal's long beak allows it to drink the nectar of deep flowers.

_____ This animal's very long legs allow it to wade into water to find food.

_____ This animal uses its scent to protect itself from predators.

_____ The pattern of this predator's fur coat allows it to hide as it hunts.

BRAIN BOX

In order to survive in a particular environment, animals develop special features.

Eye See . . .

Read the text below. Then label the diagram of the eye on the opposite page.

Can you see with your eyes closed? Of course not! The reason? There is no light entering your eye.

Light is reflected by the objects around you. When your eyes are open, that reflected light enters them. The eye has many important parts that work together to help you see and decode the world around you:

The **cornea** is the clear covering on the surface of the eye.

The cornea allows light rays to pass through to the **pupil**, the black hole in the middle of the **iris** (the colored part of your eye).

Tiny muscles in the iris control the size of your pupils, opening and closing them depending on the amount of light present. Pupils grow larger in low light and smaller in bright light.

After passing through the iris, light goes through the **lens**.

The lens focuses light on the **retina**, the back surface of the eyeball, which changes the light rays into electrical signals.

These electrical signals are carried along the **optic nerve** to the brain.

Try This

Find a handheld mirror. Head somewhere sunny or bright, and look in the mirror. Are your pupils large (dilated) or small (constricted)? Now go somewhere with very dim light, such as a bathroom with a small nightlight. Again, look in the mirror. Have your pupils changed their size? Record your observations here.

_____

_____

_____

Label the diagram using the words below.

| cornea | pupil | lens |
| iris | retina | optic nerve |

The eye

BRAIN FACT
The pygmy slow loris has huge eyes that let in a lot of light. This tree-dwelling primate needs as much light as it can get because it is a **nocturnal** animal. Nocturnal animals are mostly active after dark, so they need special adaptations. Many nocturnal animals also have a layer of tissue at the back of their eye called a **tapetum lucidum.** This tissue reflects visible light back to the retina and helps these animals see in low light.

Ask and Observe

Circle the highlighted word that correctly completes each final sentence on the cards below.

Louis Pasteur was a French scientist who lived from 1822 to 1895. He wondered what caused broth and milk to spoil. At the time, people said that "spontaneous generation" caused both broth and milk to spoil. They also believed that something inside spoiled hay created mice and that something inside dew created aphids. The explanation of "spontaneous generation" was a/an scientific unscientific approach to the problem because it assumed the answer and did not experiment.

When Pasteur asked himself why milk and broth spoil, he wondered if something entered the milk or broth and spoiled it. His beginning explanation—that something entered the broth and spoiled it—is an example of a hypothesis conclusion .

Pasteur boiled broth to purify it. Then he sealed the boiled broth in airtight containers. This meant that no air could get into the broth. Pasteur was concluding testing to see whether something inside the broth spoiled the broth.

The result was that the broth did not spoil. Pasteur proved that whatever spoiled broth, it did not come from inside outside the broth.

This experiment proved disproved the theory of "spontaneous generation."

BRAIN BOX

A person using the **scientific method**:

1. asks a question

2. constructs a **hypothesis**, an explanation that works as a starting point

3. tests the hypothesis by doing experiments

4. analyzes the results

5. draws a conclusion

Pasteur's next step was to expose the broth to air. After he did this, the broth spoiled. Pasteur proved that what caused the broth to spoil was in the air heat .

Pasteur also concluded that what spoiled the broth was visible invisible to the naked eye.

At this time in Europe, some scientists believed that invisible things called germs caused spoilage and some diseases. Pasteur's experiment helped prove disprove that there were germs in the air and that they could cause spoilage or disease.

Understanding the scientific method

Pasteur's experiment is a good example of the scientific unscientific method.

Louis Pasteur wondered if something could be done to the invisible organisms in milk so that it would not spoil so quickly. He and another scientist, Claude Bernard, conducted a series of tests in which they heated milk to different temperatures. They discovered that heating milk to a certain temperature for a certain time destroyed some of the yeasts, molds, and other bacteria in the milk. The milk would then last longer and people would not get sick from the bacteria. The process that Pasteur and Bernard started is still used today. It is called pasteurization photosynthesis .

Science Crossword

Read each clue below. Write the answer in the crossword puzzle.

Science crossword

Across

1. Our galaxy is called the _____ .

3. Matter has three common states: solid, _____ , and gas.

5. A vast cover of ice called a _____ can cut valleys, rivers, and lakes into the land.

7. _____ theorized that all matter contained the possibility of being converted into energy.

9. The colored part of your eye is the _____ .

10. The _____ is everything that exists— all space, galaxies, and time.

Down

2. A _____ gibbous moon is when more than half the moon is visible after a full moon.

4. A violent tropical storm is called a _____ .

6. There are two types of energy: _____ and potential.

8. The _____ is the part of the plant that carries water and nutrients from the roots to the rest of the plant.

TECHNOLOGY

Every day you solve problems: How will you reach the book on the highest shelf? If you have homework, a birthday party, and sports practice in one afternoon, how will you get it all done? Computer science is a form of problem-solving too!

PARENTS In this section, your child will practice problem-solving and computational thinking. Share a story about a time when you had to try multiple times to achieve a solution. The next time a task doesn't go according to plan, ask your child: What else could you try? Can you break this problem into smaller parts? Questions like these help foster a creative and flexible problem-solving mindset.

PLACE A STICKER HERE

Daily Shortcuts

Many things you do every day, like brushing your teeth, take multiple steps. In computer programming, these steps are called **commands**. All of the commands together accomplish one **function**: They make your teeth clean!

Put the commands in the Brush Teeth function in order.

BRUSH TEETH

rinse brush	_____
wet toothbrush	_____
take out toothbrush and toothpaste	1
put toothpaste on toothbrush	_____
put toothbrush and toothpaste away	_____
brush teeth for two minutes	_____

BRAIN BOX

Computers follow a sequence of steps called **commands**. A group of commands that accomplishes a specific goal is a **function**. Functions can be used over and over again in a computer program.

Functions can also be used as commands. There are several commands that make up the Get Ready for Bed function. Put the commands below in order.

fall asleep	pull up the covers	crawl into bed

turn off the light	brush teeth

GET READY FOR BED

_____

_____

_____

_____

fall asleep

Functions

Write the commands for a function called Socks and Shoes. Check your "code" by following the commands to put on socks and shoes.

SOCKS AND SHOES

_____

_____

_____

_____

Emoji Grid

You can find each emoji's location by its **coordinates**. Coordinates are a pair of numbers showing the distance from the center of the grid, called the **origin**.

To find a coordinate, start at the origin, then count the number of squares left or right. Coordinates to the left of the origin are negative numbers.

 is 4 squares to the right of the origin, so the first number in the coordinate is 4.

To find the second number in the coordinate, start at the origin, then count the number of squares up or down. Coordinates below the origin are negative numbers.

 is 2 squares above the origin, so the second number in the coordinate is 2.

ORIGIN

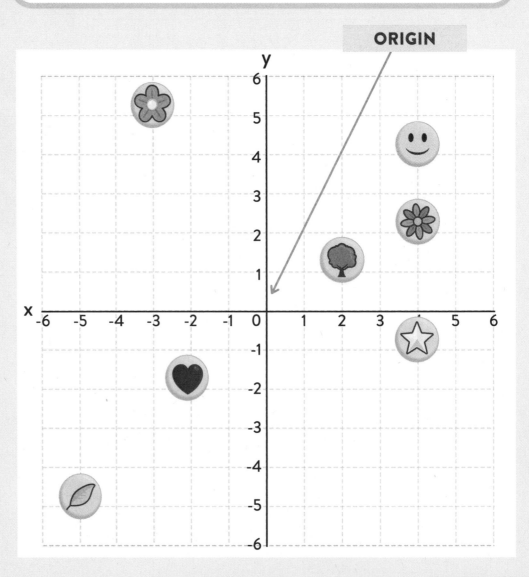

To identify where the emoji is located on the grid, write the coordinates using this format:

_____4_____ , _____2_____

the number of the first coordinate   the number of the second coordinate

Write the coordinates for the 🙂 emoji on the lines:

_____ , _____

Find the coordinates for the other emojis and write them on the lines.

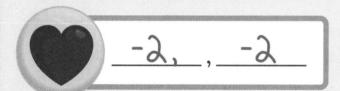
-2, , -2

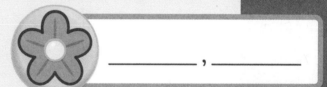
_____ , _____

_____ , _____

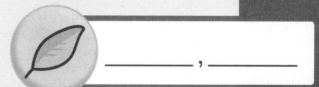
_____ , _____

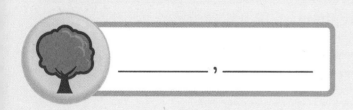
_____ , _____

BRAIN BOX

Every computer screen is broken into a grid. Programmers use **coordinates** on this grid to place text or graphics, such as emojis, on the screen in the correct location.

Running on Empty

A driver mapped the shortest route to the gas station. The green line on this map shows the route, with each section of road labeled in kilometers (km). Use your finger to trace the route. Circle the incorrect step in the directions below.

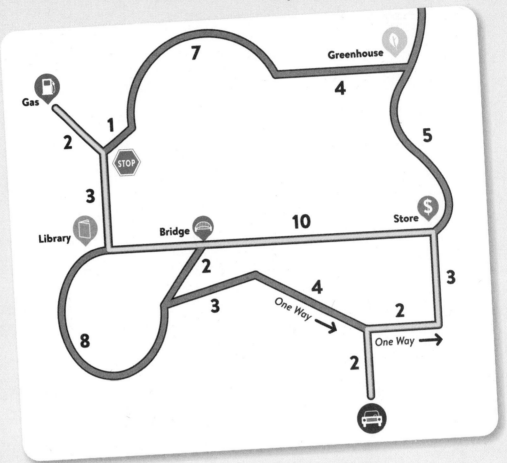

Go straight 2 km.

Turn right on the one-way street, then go 2 km.

Turn left and go 3 km.

Turn right at the store, then go 10 km, passing over the bridge.

Turn right at the library, then go 3 km.

Make a left at the stop sign, then go 2 km.

Arrive at the gas station.

Total distance: 22 km

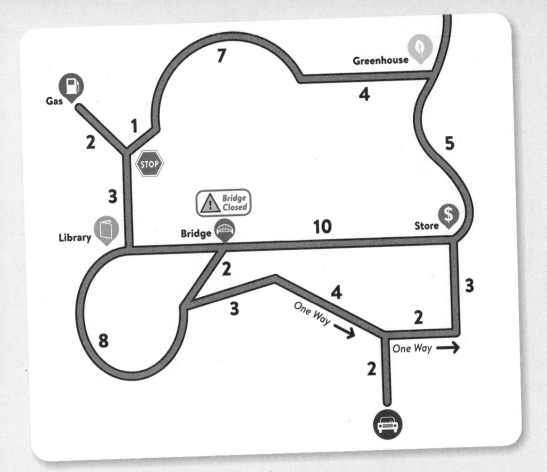

Uh oh! Now the bridge is closed. Find a different path to the gas station. Write the new directions below and record the total number of kilometers for this trip.

Total distance: _____

Jacko's Polygons

This sprite is named Jacko. Two students wrote algorithms for Jacko so that it would draw a polygon. Follow the students' algorithms exactly as they are written on the graph to draw each polygon.

To make diagonal lines that go up and to the right, use the command **Move 1U 45 degrees**

⬚ = one unit (1U)

◹ = 45 degrees

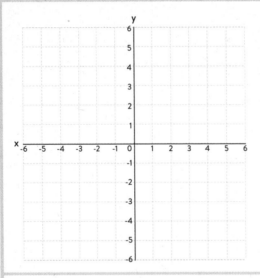

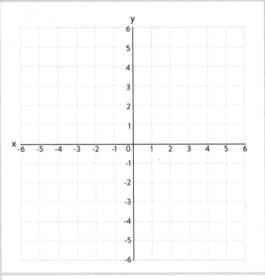

Algorithm A	Algorithm B

To draw a square:

• Go to point 0, 0

• Place pencil on paper

• [Move 1U left] 4 times

• [Move 1U up] 4 times

• [Move 1U right] 4 times

• [Move 1U down] 4 times

• Lift pencil off paper

To draw a triangle:

• Go to point 0, 0

• Place pencil on paper

• [Move 1U left] 4 times

• [Move 1U 45 degrees right] 4 times

• [Move 1U down] 4 times

• Lift pencil off paper

BRAIN BOX

A **sprite** is a computer graphic element, like a character. It can be static (not moving) or animated (moving).

Modify **Algorithm A** on the previous page so that Jacko makes a square that's 50 units long on each side.

_____

_____

_____

_____

_____

_____

Write an algorithm using commands from the previous page to program Jacko to draw the rhombus.

_____

_____

_____

_____

_____

_____

_____

_____

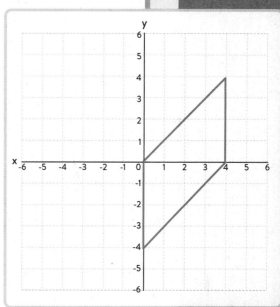

BRAIN BOX

Computer programmers can take a shortcut by **modifying** existing code that they already know works. They look for patterns in the code and make changes so the computer does a new task.

Don't Overshare

Jordyn made an invitation to post online. Circle three pieces of information that Jordyn should not include if they are going to post it on the internet.

Online, it's usually okay to share some personal information but not private information. **Personal information**, like the title of your favorite book, might be the same for other people. But **private information**, like your street address, is unique to you.

Label each piece of information below as **personal** or **private**.

Privacy and cybersecurity

| Your favorite movie | _____ |

| How many cousins you have | _____ |

| Your email address | _____ |

| Your pet's name | _____ |

| Your computer password | _____ |

| Your gender | _____ |

| Your complete birthday (day, month, and year) | _____ |

BRAIN BOX

It is important that you keep some information **private**, which means not sharing it with anyone else. Your password, as well as anything that can be used to identify you, should be shared only with trusted adults.

Code Breaker

In this code, each letter in the alphabet is represented by another letter.

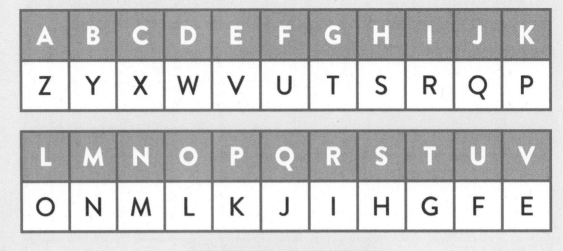

A	B	C	D	E	F	G	H	I	J	K
Z	Y	X	W	V	U	T	S	R	Q	P

L	M	N	O	P	Q	R	S	T	U	V
O	N	M	L	K	J	I	H	G	F	E

W	X	Y	Z
D	C	B	A

Learn some fun facts about computer history by decoding these messages.

GSV URIHG XLNKFGVI NLFHV DZH NZWV LU DLLW.

_____

_____

_____

VZIOB XLNKFGVIH DVIV YRT VMLFTS GL UROO HVEVIZO ILLNH.

_____

_____

_____

ANSWER KEY

Some problems have only one answer. Some problems have many answers. Turn the page to check your work.

SPELLING AND VOCABULARY

pg. 8

A Night to Remember
By Malia

It had been a tuff few weeks! Our band had been practicing a lot to get redy for our winter concert. Every day, we eether met before school or stayed after to practice. It was hard work, but we beleeved in ourselves. The nite of the concert, each roe of the auditorium was filled with our frends and families. (We were afrade the heavy rane would keep them away.) I gess we're ready, I thawt. We were nervis, but we plade our best. The music was joyus. I was so pleesed with our performance. And we went out for pizza afterward! Mostly, I was happy because I tried my best. I will tresure the memory of that evening forever!

tough	rain
ready	guess
either	thought
believed	nervous
night	played
row	joyous
friends	pleased
afraid	treasure

pg. 9

double	short u
although	long o
neighbor	long a
weather	short e
treasure	short e
does	short u
symbols	short i
height	long i
young	short u
people	long e
thread	short e
chief	long e

pg. 10

knob; knock; kneel; wrists; wrinkled; gnome; wrench; wreath

pg. 11

keys; school; check; collar; blanket; basket; couch; kite; truck; cage

pg. 12

pg. 13

col/or/ful 3	af/ter/ward 3
prob/lem 2	slip/pe/ry 3
swal/low 2	near/est 2
par/a/chute 3	fre/quent 2
au/to/mo/bile 4	curl/y 2
spot/less 2	dis/re/spect 3
ex/cel/lent 3	awk/ward 2
pres/i/dent 3	jour/ney 2
mil/lion 2	in/stant 2
u/su/al/ly 4	mes/sen/ger 3
bunk 1	en/cy/clo/pe/di/a 6

pg. 14

plain plane; ate eight; hare has hair; earn an urn; rained reins; beech by the beach; herd heard; rain reigned; muscled my mussels; bored by the board

pg. 15

I Want to Visit the Galápagos
By Akira

If I could go anywhere, I wood go two the Galápagos Islands. These islands are in the eastern Pacific Ocean, along the equator. I have wanted to visit them for sew long. Their are so many animals that are knot found anywhere else. Did you no that Galápagos tortoises can live up to 150 years and sleep up to 16 ours a day? And marine iguanas found in the Galápagos are the only see swimming lizards in the hole world! If I was able to visit, I would definitely knead to look four Galápagos sea lions, witch usually stay close to shore. But of awl the animal species, I think the waved albatross is the won I find most interesting. These birds don't waive at you, but they have the largest wingspan of any bird in the Galápagos. Pears of them mate for life, and when they are courting, they make a noise that sounds like a cow's moo!

would	whole
to	need
so	for
there	which
not	all
know	one
hours	wave
sea	pairs

pg. 16

view
leap
ordinary
quickly
within
stop
throw
snack
help
tale

pg. 17

pg. 18

always (never); more (less); love (hate); more (fewer); fewer (more); never (always); easy (difficult); far (near); glad (sad)

pg. 19

(answers may vary)
rough; talkative; answers; different; brave; reward; appear; public

pg. 20

(answers may vary)

uncommon	miscalculate
recapture	overexpose
misfortune	misrepresent
uneventful	undisturbed
overachieve	unexcited
revisit	relocate

pg. 21

(answers may vary)
disappear: to become invisible
disloyal: unfaithful
dishonest: untruthful
disorderly: chaotic, cluttered
disinfect: to make clean, sanitize

pg. 22

government; clueless; fearless; westward; playful; equipment; hopeful; worthless; successful; upward

pg. 23

laugh a b l e — something that can be easily broken
break a b l e
fiend i s h — very bad or cruel
power l e s s — somewhat green
name l e s s — anonymous
harm l e s s — pleasant or delightful
green i s h — easy to read, or legible
read a b l e — funny or amusing
enjoy a b l e — endearing
lov a b l e — not dangerous
— helpless

pg. 24

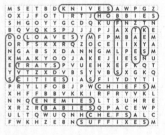

hygienn — personal cleanliness
multiply — increase in number
boundaries — something indicating a limit
javelin — long slender shaft thrown in field events
anxious — uneasy or worried
penthouse — upper or top floor of a building
individual — single or separate
pollution — harmful substance in the air, water, or soil
modify — change
approximate — estimate or make a guess

pg. 25

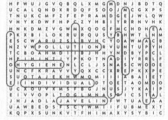

encyclopedia; merchandise

pg. 26

infuriate; renew; rhombus; insert; elevation; guarantee; establish; gristle; engrave; relevant

pg. 27

(answers may vary)
generous: giving and sharing often
concentrate: to focus
awkward: lacking skill; clumsy
accelerate: to speed up
gradual: taking place slowly
ignore: to refrain from noticing
refund: to give back or repay
locate: to find the place or location
harvest (verb): to gather a crop
despise: to regard with contempt

pg. 28

(This is only a partial list.)
incomprehensibility: mop, hens, yes, cop, pine, come, income
uncopyrightable: bat, table, tip, top, bit, pie, copyright
otolaryngologist: tag, long, sit, tool, yarn, logo, glaring

LANGUAGE ARTS

pg. 30

fingerprint	cupcake	
motorbike	football	raincoat
toothpaste	flashlight	
	grasshopper	hairbrush

pg. 31

suffixes	hobbies	knives
chefs	monkeys	donkeys
chiefs	babies	trays
enemies	families	taxes
cities	loaves	keys

(word search grid)

pg. 32

boats	umbrellas
churches	visitors
brushes	artists
newspapers	torches
bicycles	princes
threads	gearboxes
wrenches	princesses
foxes	benches
millions	compasses
quilts	hours

pg. 33

can't	isn't
I'm	couldn't
shouldn't	he's
you're	weren't
I'll	didn't
aren't	you'll

pg. 34

the car's fender
the dragon's breath
the woman's scarf
Xander's books
the gremlin's ideas
Orma's calendar
the man's plans
the tundra's smell
the explorer's hardships
the keyboard's stickiness
the oak's leaves

pg. 35

(answers may vary)
The computers' screens were flashing.
The whales' song was sad.
The mechanics' wrench was greasy.
A bear ate the campers' gear.
The flowers' petals were blown away.
The catcher caught the pitchers' throws.
The reporters' stories won first prize.
I read the poets' poems.
The clowns' noses were bright blue.
The dragons' breath was really stinky.

pg. 36

My Favorite Animal
By Carlos
What animal looks like it borrowed a ducks bill, an otters furry body, and a beavers flat tail? Its the puzzling platypus! Found either at the waters edge or in lakes, rivers, and streams in eastern Australia and Tasmania, the platypus is one of natures most curious creatures. Besides its interesting appearance, the platypus is one of only two mammals that lays eggs. (The echidna is the other.) Male platypuses have a sharp, venomous spur on each back leg. Scientists think they use these spurs to compete with other male platypuses during breeding season. A platypuss webbed front feet allow it to paddle, and its beaver-like tail helps it steer as it moves through the water hunting for worms, crustaceans, and insects. Its bill has cells that help it sense movements and electrical fields given off by its prey.

duck's
otter's
beaver's
It's
water's
nature's
platypus's

pg. 37

Dear Gretchen,
Hi! How are you? I hope you're having fun at camp! Everything's the same as usual around here. My sister's room is even more of a mess now that we're on vacation. Her shoe^{x}s are all over the floor, and so are her sweaters. Lily's^x trench coat is on top of the bed's canopy—how it got there, I don't know. Maybe she doesn't even know it's there! On top of that, all the poster^{x}s on her wall are torn.
My twin brothers' room is neat. Everything is in its place. Yesterday I wanted to borrow a sweatshirt from Lily, but hers was under the bed. So I borrowed either Jack's or John's sweatshirt instead. Unfortunately, they noticed. "It's gone!" they shouted. "Who took it?" After I confessed, they ordered me to stay out of their bedroom. "Nothing that's ours is your^{x}s!" they said. Well, I'll show them. I'm knitting myself a sweater. It's beautiful! The sweater will be all mine. So there!
Anyway, I miss you and hope your bunkmate isn't as much of a slob as Lily.
Love, Emily
P.S. Here's a photo of Lily's messy bed!

pg. 38

1-don't; 2-do; 3-don't; 4-do;
5-don't; 6-do; 7-do; 8-do;
9-don't; 10-do; 11-do

pg. 39

The Sahara desert covers the northern third of the continent.
Victoria Falls is located along the Zambezi River, on the border between Zambia and Zimbabwe.
Mount Kilimanjaro, in northeastern Tanzania, is the highest free-standing mountain in the world.
The Ituri Forest is a tropical rain forest. It is home to hyenas, antelopes, elephants, monkeys, chimpanzees, and many bird species.
The two longest rivers in Africa are the Nile, in northern Africa, and the Congo River, in central Africa.

pg. 40

Three books written by Kwame Alexander are The Crossover, Booked, and Rebound.
Kids interested in marine mammals might like the TV series called Secrets of the Whales.
A Sporting Chance is a book by Lori Alexander about how a scientist named Ludwig Guttmann created the Paralympic Games, a sporting event for athletes with physical disabilities.
Some movies about spelling bees include the fictional film Akeelah and the Bee and a documentary called Spellbound.
E. B. White wrote Charlotte's Web, a book about the friendship between a pig and a spider.
Lin-Manuel Miranda said he was inspired to write the musical Hamilton after reading a biography called Alexander Hamilton by Ron Chernow.
The Invention of Hugo Cabret is a book by Brian Selznick that was later turned into a movie called Hugo.

pg. 41

"Have you ever been on a roller coaster?" asked Shane. "No," admitted Caitlin, "but my cousin has been on the American Eagle, the Demon, and the Iron Wolf."
"Those are fun," said Shane, "but not nearly as awesome as the Raging Bull!"
"Is it scary?" asked Caitlin.
"Not too scary," answered Shane. "The first drop is 208 feet, but the speed is only 73 miles an hour." Shane shrugged. "I've been on coasters that go over 100 miles an hour—zoom!" Shane stopped talking. He looked at Caitlin. "Hey," he said, "you look kind of green. Don't worry about it. You'll be okay."
"Are you sure?" asked Caitlin.
"Sure," said Shane. "If you get too scared, just close your eyes!"
"Gulp," said Caitlin.

pg. 42

Anthea suddenly screamed, "Cyril! Come quick! It's alive! It'll get away! Quick!"
They all hurried back.
"It's a rat, I think," said Robert. "Father says they infest old places—and this must be pretty old if the sea was here thousands of years ago."
"Perhaps it is a snake," said Jane.
"Let's look," said Cyril, jumping into the hole. "I'm not afraid of snakes. If it is a snake I'll tame it, and it will follow me everywhere, and I'll let it sleep round my neck at night."
"No, you won't," said Robert firmly. He shared Cyril's bedroom. "But you may if it's a rat."
"Oh, don't be silly," said Anthea "it's not a rat, it's MUCH bigger. And it's not a snake. It's got feet; I saw them; and fur."

pg. 43

Earth's ocean is divided into five separate bodies of water: the Atlantic, the Pacific, the Indian, the Arctic, and the Southern oceans.
The ocean has zones where different plants and animals live. The three zones closest to the water's surface are the sunlight zone, the twilight zone, and the midnight zone.
The ocean is home to a diverse array of plants, mammals, invertebrates, fish, and more.

Some creatures, such as the sea star, the sea squirt, and the sea cucumber, can regrow body parts after losing them!
Many types of coral—including elkhorn, staghorn, and lettuce—can be found in the ocean.
There are about fifty thousand species of mollusks, including octopuses, cuttlefish, and squid.
Hawksbill, green, and Kemp's ridley are three endangered species of sea turtle.
Many people, such as scientists, conservationists, and citizens like you, are working to protect ocean ecosystems.

pg. 44

"Did you hear the concert?" asked my brother Rob.
"What concert?" I asked as I glanced at pages eleven, twelve, thirteen, and fourteen of the book I was reading.
"My drum concert," answered Rob.
"No," I answered. "I'm reading Harry Potter and the Goblet of Fire."
"Cool!" said my brother. "It's even better than Harry Potter and the Prisoner of Azkaban."
"My plan is to read all seven books by the end of August," I said.
"I have a plan too," said Rob.
And then he told me that his plan was to start a rock band, become a rock star, and make millions of dollars by the end of August.
"Good luck with that," I replied.
"Now can I finish reading my book?"

pg. 45

Concrete nouns: bread, table, napkin, chef, tomato, spices, chair, pizza, water
Abstract nouns: friendship, emotion, appetite, happiness, conversation, excitement, generosity

pg. 46

"Bugs bug me!" James shouts as he swats the insects.
I love when my friends laugh at the jokes I tell.
Jackson loads the boat while Jason raises the sails.
I buff the trophy until it gleams.
"I knead bread all day long, but I don't need to," Dad jokes.
Ginny matches all the socks, folds them, and stuffs them into her backpack.
Until Chris returns my football, I will hide his helmet.

pg. 47

dug; drew; went; rode; held; grew; kept; gave
got; drank; rang; slept; hurt; heard; thought; laid

pg. 48

Yes
No
No
Yes
Yes
No
No
Yes
Yes
Yes
No
Yes

pg. 49

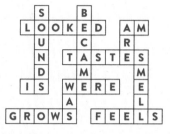

pg. 50

Many large cities have underground spaces. The speedy subway trains in Washington, DC, travel deep underground, and you can tour Seattle's old underground streets. But you can't visit Chicago's famous underground—it is sealed off. Chicago's underground is a fascinating series of tunnels. Digging began in 1899. Workers laid telephone cables and railroad tracks. The narrow tracks and wide tunnels allowed easy delivery of freight to many hotels and businesses.
Few people in Chicago knew or thought about the complex network of tunnels—until 1992, when the Chicago River burst through a small crack and flooded the huge tunnels. Hundreds of frightened employees evacuated tall office buildings as river water gurgled into ancient basements and sloshed up winding staircases.
If Chicago had repaired the leak when it was first reported, the cost would have been ten thousand dollars. But the city didn't repair it and the river broke through. The cost of repairing all damages came to one billion dollars.

pg. 51

hot, hotter, hottest
kind, kinder, kindest
smelly, smellier, smelliest
quick, quicker, quickest
nasty, nastier, nastiest
breezy, breezier, breeziest
funny, funnier, funniest
easy, easier, easiest

pg. 52

That basset hound has the saddest face I've ever seen.
The mechanic said that my car's problem was more troublesome than yours.
Layla is the most starstruck fan I know.
Today's sky is darker than yesterday's.
Who will prove more loyal, you or me?
There goes the most honest person on the block.
David's bike is more valuable than mine.
If you ask me, Tangia is too outspoken. She's the most outspoken person in the whole school.

pg. 53

Turtles <u>move</u> slowly.

When did you <u>arrive</u> at school this morning?

No, an alien has <u>never</u> <u>visited</u> me.

Serena always <u>looks</u> both ways before she crosses a street.

I feel that I <u>have</u> <u>been</u> here before.

Ari felt sick yesterday, but today he is feeling better.

He <u>picked up</u> the glass vase carefully so it wouldn't break.

Damien came home, but then he <u>left</u>.

She <u>whistled</u> happily while she worked.

My dog <u>looked</u> hungrily at the can of food.

pg. 54

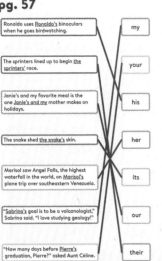

pg. 55

The batter held the bat firmly.

The astronaut looked at me strangely.

The collie dug a hole swiftly.

Don't answer people meanly.

Tegan divided the cookies fairly.

The flimsy tree swayed weakly.

My mother kissed me on the head tenderly.

Tell the truth boldly.

pg. 56

(answers may vary)

them

his/their

It

his/theirs

us

it

they

She/They, her/their

her/their

It, their

pg. 57

Ronaldo uses <u>Ronaldo's</u> binoculars when he goes birdwatching.	my
The sprinters lined up to begin <u>the sprinters'</u> race.	your
Janie's and my favorite meal is the one <u>Janie's and my</u> mother makes on holidays.	his
The snake shed <u>the snake's</u> skin.	her
Marisol saw Angel Falls, the highest waterfall in the world, on <u>Marisol's</u> plane trip over southeastern Venezuela.	its
"<u>Sabrina's</u> goal is to be a volcanologist," Sabrina said. "I love studying geology!"	our
"How many days before <u>Pierre's</u> graduation, Pierre?" asked Aunt Céline.	their

pg. 58

Sea otters hold hands while (they're) sleeping on water so they don't drift away from each other.

A coyote commonly uses (its) howl to communicate with other coyotes.

As they grow, hermit crabs exchange (their) shells for bigger ones.

No matter how swift your stroke, (you're) no match for a dolphin: They can go more than 30 miles an hour!

A giraffe has seven bones in (its) neck.

Glasswing butterflies have transparent wings to avoid detection by (their) predators.

A ruby-throated hummingbird can beat (its) wings up to two hundred times per second!

All tigers have unique stripe patterns on (their) coats. No two are the same!

An axolotl can regrow (its) limbs.

If (you're) wondering what kind of plant a coral is . . . (it's) not a plant at all! A coral is actually an animal.

pg. 59

Mary laid the book **on** the table.

The socks were **under** Jaylen's bed.

He drove **by** the park on his way to work.

Vicki walks to class **with** Olivia.

The shy poodle hid **behind** the sofa.

She likes to sit in **between** her mother and her father.

"Hey! Who took the costume **from** my locker?"

The pioneers set out **for** the western territories.

We walked **over** the bridge to get to the other side of the river.

Do you ever wonder what lies **below** the ocean surface?

pg. 60

"The flowerpot fell (on) my head," said the defendant.

Kris hid (behind) the bushes.

Sebastian stepped (outside) the line.

Hannah left (without) her lunch.

I parked my bike (near) the gym doors.

Emily was (among) the top five swimmers.

David raced (down) the ramp and (up) the stairs.

"You have (until) tomorrow," said the teacher.

We always eat breakfast (at) 7:30.

Grace received a letter (from) China.

My sister drew a line (along) the edge.

Angela climbed (up) the hill.

Put the ball (in) the basket.

Prepositions:
on; behind; outside; without; near; among; down; up; until; at; from; along; up; in

Objects:
head; bushes; line; lunch; doors; swimmers; ramp; stairs; tomorrow; 7:30; China; edge; hill; basket

pg. 61

Hurricanes are strong storms that can have winds of up to 150 miles an hour or more.

At one time hurricanes could not be predicted, but the development of technology such as radar and satellites has changed that.

At the National Hurricane Center, scientists use weather satellites to watch storms that are forming and track their movement.

Satellite data can tell scientists where the eye of a storm is going, so they won't be surprised if it changes direction.

Scientists can predict where hurricanes are going, so people have a chance to evacuate before the storm arrives.

Before these predictions, people had to depend on their own observations of wind direction and ocean currents.

pg. 62

(answers may vary)

Because I lost my notebook, I couldn't turn in the lesson.

Mr. Pilsen says he hates chocolate, yet he ate a whole pound of it.

Nobody has talked to Dylan since he moved to Alaska.

While I counted zucchini, the gardener read a magazine.

Max threw the ball to second base instead of third, so the runner scored.

"Unless you agree to wash the dishes, you won't eat," said the cook.

If he makes this free throw, Clive will win the prize.

Either I lost my new gloves, or I left them at Dana's.

Daniel agreed to help me, but Caleb didn't.

pg. 63

(answers may vary)

We wanted to have a picnic, but the rain spoiled our plans.

I like to swim, but my brother doesn't.

The dog chased the truck, and the cat followed.

Learn to swim, because if you don't, you will sink.

Victor asked me for a dollar, so I gave him one.

pg. 64

<u>We rode our bikes with Elijah, and then we played baseball with Jeremiah.</u>
compound

<u>Our team won, so we celebrated.</u>
compound

<u>My puppy bit the mail carrier.</u>
simple

<u>Maria and Hannah hid the cookies.</u>
simple

<u>The dragon's breath smelled like mint, but his feet smelled like wet cardboard.</u>
compound

<u>The bear destroyed the picnic tables and the garbage bins.</u>
simple

<u>Juan and Ryder spelled better than Clancy and Marco did.</u>
simple

<u>I changed my name to Javier, so that's what you should call me.</u>
compound

pg. 65

The tugboat pushed and pushed <u>until it could push no more</u>.

Omar called me <u>after I had gone to bed</u>.

<u>When Rolf growls</u>, everybody stands still.

I learned Arabic <u>after I visited my grandfather</u>.

<u>Unless we run very fast</u>, we will miss the bus.

<u>Although I like football</u>, I love soccer.

<u>Before Vanessa said hello</u>, Candace said goodbye.

You will win a hundred dollars <u>if you answer correctly</u>.

<u>Now that I'm in fourth grade</u>, I make my own lunch.

<u>When you take a photo</u>, first frame your shot in the viewer.

Jonathan sets the table <u>while his father makes dinner</u>.

pg. 66

READING

pg. 68

Jays; Thursday; Giants;

Monday, Wednesday, and Thursday;

Sandusky and Taylor;

Yes. They play on different nights.

pg. 69

- potato chips, apple butter, bread
- tear a hole in the potato chip bag to release the air inside
- no
- one slice of bread
- after spreading the apple butter

pg. 70

7 batteries; 2 legs; 1 torso

6 fangs; 5 cape; 3 arms; 4 head

pg. 71

6; 5; 1; 96; 110; 1

pg. 73

mixture: something made by stirring two or more things together

absolutely: most certainly; without a doubt

form: a shape

category: a group of things within a larger group

separate: to pull apart; to divide into parts

challenge: something very difficult

competition: a contest; a struggle to win something

engineers: people who design things such as bridges

pg. 74

(answers may vary)
- Kristen Bartos
- She was honored for her service to animals.
- Tuesday
- City Hall
- because she is a devoted vet
- with a statue
- veterinarian
- Chauncey Smith
- Bassport

pg. 75

- The bridge curves in places.
- The bridge crosses over water.
- The bridge connects Shanghai and Nanjing.

pg. 76

This sentence doesn't confuse me.

<u>My sister misses the bus.</u>

<u>Our team lost the game.</u>

<u>Nadya took the key and locked the door.</u>

<u>My camera fell and shattered.</u>

I threw away the box.

<u>Stephen felt better.</u>

<u>The horse bucked.</u>

<u>Jesse calls his cat.</u>

pg. 77

Elk are the second-largest type of deer.
All told, there are hundreds of several kinds of marsupials.
Dogs are descended from wolves.
The onager is an interesting animal.

pg. 79

(answers may vary)
- A cow's color and patterns will help you tell one breed from another.
  - The Holstein is a white cow with large black blobs of color all over its body.
  - The Ayrshire is a white cow covered with red spots.
- Another way to tell the different breeds apart is by unusual features.
  - The Brahman has a large hump and ears that hang downward.
  - The Chianina is all white and the largest cow breed in the world.
- If you look more closely, you will notice other differences.
  - The Guernsey has yellow ears.
  - The Pinzgauer is orange around the eyes.

pg. 80

(answers may vary)
- Angus will dig for treasure.
- John will crash into the board.

pg. 81

persuade; inform; entertain
inform: *How to Fix Almost Anything; Butterflies of North America; Prehistoric Life on Earth*
entertain: *Ancient Folktales and Myths; Silly Jokes for the Whole Family; King Arthur and the Knights of the Round Table*
persuade: *Why YOU Should Be an Eco-Warrior!; Golden Retrievers: Why They Are the Best Dogs Ever!; Top Ten Reasons to Visit Spain Now*

pg. 82

- buy a Glow-Glow T-shirt
- exaggeration
- appealing to emotions

pg. 83

opinion
fact
fact
opinion
opinion
fact
fact
opinion
opinion
fact
fact
fact

pg. 84

yes; first; second

pg. 85

Atlantic and Pacific

The Atlantic Ocean is the second-largest ocean on Earth. It covers about 20% of the Earth's surface. In addition, the Atlantic is the saltiest of the oceans. It got its name from Atlas, a Greek god.

The Pacific Ocean is the largest ocean on Earth, covering 32% of the Earth's surface. In fact, the Pacific covers more area than all the land on Earth. It is warmer than the Atlantic. It was named by the explorer Ferdinand Magellan. The name Pacific means *peaceful*.

pg. 86

Cause: Because Declan left his repair kit behind.
Cause: Because Declan could not repair his flat tire
Effect: He was not able to play in the game.
Cause: Because Declan did not play

pg. 87

because; Since; caused; Because of; so; Due to; As a result of

pg. 88

nonfiction
fiction
nonfiction
nonfiction
nonfiction
fiction
nonfiction
nonfiction
nonfiction
fiction
fiction
nonfiction

pg. 89

- home; Metropolitan Museum of Art; New York City
- February; Jackson Hole, Wyoming
- 1930; Mexico; southern California; farm camp
- summer; 1963; Flint, Michigan; Birmingham, Alabama

pg. 90

a; c
a; b
b; c

pg. 91

- speech; enthusiastic; silence; Merrie
- actions; carefully
- thoughts; has little confidence in himself

pg. 93

kind
an old toy
happy
concerned
worried

pg. 94

(answers may vary)
Kyle sees a message on his computer screen.
Kyle types, "Your name isn't Hal."
The computer makes a loud sound.
Kyle jumps back and folds his arms over his head.
At last the sound stops.
Kyle sits down and begins typing.

pg. 96

snake
file
file; angry
bites; file
It is useless to attack a nonliving thing.

pg. 97

boy
villagers
villagers; lies
A liar will not be believed, even when speaking the truth.

pg. 98

- Grungo the Giant couldn't be counted on to do anything because he always had his head in the clouds.
- Yoshi won the prize because he kept his nose to the grindstone.
- Shane is a dog in the manger about kids using his swimming pool.

pg. 99

cool as a cucumber
Greek to me
the way the cookie crumbles
on his high horse
on pins and needles
hit the books
wolf in sheep's clothing
out of the woods

pg. 101

(answers may vary)
- because he put out every fire in the village
- in the underworld
- because everything she touched burst into flame
- because he kept dropping her fingernails into a stream
- Māui turned into a hawk
- by rubbing twigs from a kaikomako tree together

pg. 103

Robert Burns wrote that his love was like a red, red rose.
Celia was as graceful as Godzilla.
Our teacher's understanding of history is as deep as the Pacific.
After Aiden tried to shave, his face looked like a jigsaw puzzle.
The two-year-old raced around the room like a hamster on its wheel.
"I wandered lonely as a cloud" was written by Wordsworth.
The football fluttered through the air like a sick duck.
The tired dog huffed and puffed like a steam engine.
My sister dances like a puppet.
The distant pueblos were as tiny as anthills.

pg. 104

fluff, stuff, cuff
enough
above, shove, glove

pg. 105

5
7
5
Earth
They slide on slime and have eyes on stalks.
sliding, slime, stalks; eyes, eat; green, garden

pg. 106

wolf
nose, knows
smell, hearing, sight
size, stand
eyes, size
the photographer

pg. 107

two
no
when they address each other as sister or brother
eat a seal or a walrus
eat grass and berries
3; 5

pg. 108

WRITING

pgs. 110–126

(answers may vary)

pg. 127

authoritative
not authoritative
authoritative
not authoritative
authoritative
authoritative

pg. 135

(answers may vary)
My dog is scratching himself because he has fleas.
Kayla and Cyrah are friends, but Kayla and Iniko are not friends.
I earn money by doing chores and washing the car.
Omar went to the farmers market for fresh vegetables, which he needed to make a salad.
My state has a state flower, a state bird, and a state insect.
Indigenous people gave the Mississippi River its name, which means "Great River," because it is a powerful river.

pg. 136

(answers may vary)
The directions of US interstate highways are easy to understand. All the even-numbered highways travel east to west. I-80 starts in New York City and ends up in San Francisco. All the odd-numbered highways run north and south. I-35 begins in Texas and ends in Minnesota.

pg. 137

(answers may vary)
- The knight charged the castle because the drawbridge was going up.
- Jeans are very popular because they are stylish and comfortable.
- I don't like heights, but we live on the 25th floor.
- Gophers are cute, and they are awesome diggers.
- The planets travel around the sun in an ellipse, which is an oval shape.
- Lance drops candy wrappers everywhere because he is a litterbug.
- The remote control stopped working because its battery was dead.

pg. 138

To make a chocolate milkshake, you need milk, chocolate ice cream, and a blender. First, put two scoops of ice cream in the blender, then add one-half cup of milk. Second, close the lid of the blender. (If you don't, you'll get milk everywhere!) Third, press the MIX button for six or seven seconds. Next, press the LIQUEFY button for another six or seven seconds. Finally, take the lid off the blender. Pour the milkshake into a glass. Yum!

300

pg. 140

Deserts cover one-fifth of Earth's land surface. Most people think of them as being hot and dry, but an area doesn't have to be hot or dry to be called a desert. A desert is the name for a place that gets very little rainfall—less than 10 inches per year. ¶ The two largest deserts in the world are in Earth's polar regions: the Arctic and the Antarctic. At the southern end of the globe lies the Antarctic Desert—the world's largest desert. It is about 5.5 million square miles and covers the continent of Antarctica. Scientists there have recorded temperatures as low as –144°F! ¶ The second-largest desert in the world is the Arctic Desert. It has a surface area of about 5.4 million square miles. Extending across the northern end of the globe, it covers parts of Norway, Finland, Sweden, Canada, Alaska, Iceland, Greenland, and Russia. The lowest recorded temperature during Arctic winter is –93.3°F!

pg. 141

Rita Dove was the first Black American to be Named poet laureate (LAW-ree-at) of the united states. A poet laureate is selected by the librarian of the US Congress to encourage people to appreciate reading and writing Poetry. They usually do this by giving talks and readings. Dove was poet laureate from 1993 to 1995.

Rita Dove loved reading when she was a Child. She was a high school Presidential Scholar, an honor given to the country's most distinguished students. Rita Dove attended college at Miami University in ohio, graduating summa cum laude—meaning With highest honors. She also studied in germany and at the University of iowa.

Rita Dove has won many Awards and written many Books, including *On the Bus with Rosa Parks* and *Thomas and Beulah*, which won the Pulitzer Prize for poetry. Rita Dove is also a teacher. She is a professor at the University of virginia.

MATH SKILLS

pg. 144

4⑥	ones
⑥14	hundreds
16⑧	tens
4,⑥02	hundreds
⑥,190	thousands
⑥	ones
①,542	thousands
①45	hundreds
4,32①	ones
9,8①0	tens
5,③02	hundreds
9,14③	ones
7③5	tens
③,447	thousands

pg. 145

5,147: 5,000 + 100 + 40 + 7
7,975: 7,000 + 900 + 70 + 5
8,331: 8,000 + 300 + 30 + 1
2,704: 2,000 + 700 + 0 + 4
1,228: 1,000 + 200 + 20 + 8
6,977: 6,000 + 900 + 70 + 7
3,812: 3,000 + 800 + 10 + 2
5,548: 5,000 + 500 + 40 + 8
45,239
23,476
57,557
81,623
46,908
15,192
32,839
79,712
94,344

pg. 146

89,251
97,347
25,176

pg. 147

35 rounds up to 40
58 rounds up to 60
64 rounds down to 60
17 rounds up to 20
88 rounds up to 90
12 rounds down to 10
55 rounds up to 60
42 rounds down to 40
76 rounds up to 80
39 rounds up to 40
8 rounds up to 10
94 rounds down to 90

pg. 148

689 rounds up to 700
231 rounds down to 200
449 rounds down to 400
758 rounds up to 800
391 rounds up to 400
862 rounds up to 900
2,854 rounds up to 3,000
7,125 rounds down to 7,000
5,550 round up to 6,000
1,820 rounds up to 2,000
3,437 rounds down to 3,000
6,501 rounds up to 7,000

pg. 149

780,000
815,000
100,000
564,200
1,600,000
3,850,000
7,600,000
238,000
600,000
1,500,000

pg. 150

6 12 18 24 30 36 (+6)
4 8 7 11 10 14 13 (+4, −1)
8 20 32 44 56 68 80 (+12)
20 19 17 14 10 5 (−1, −2, −3, −4, −5,...)
12 13 15 18 22 27 33 (+1, +2, +3, +4, +5, ...)
27 37 32 42 37 47 42 (+10, −5)
7 8 11 16 23 32 43 (+1, +3, +5, +7, +9, ...)
50 45 48 43 46 41 44 (−5, +3)

pg. 151

Helena 30
Graham 20
Victoria 30
Enzo 20
Kathleen 20
Pham 10
Morgan 40
Pham
Morgan
Pham
Enzo
Morgan

pg. 152

40 + 30 = 70   30 − 10 = 20
10 + 10 = 20   50 − 30 = 20
0 + 60 = 60   50 − 20 = 30
10 + 20 = 30   30 − 20 = 10
40 + 50 = 90   70 − 30 = 40
10 + 70 = 80   90 − 40 = 50
10 + 90 = 100   80 − 30 = 50

pg. 153

10 + 11 = 5 + 16   28 − 4 < 18 + 10
4 − 1 = 7 − 4   45 − 9 = 6 × 6
7 + 8 > 8 + 5   4 + 4 < 4 × 4
2 + 13 < 7 + 9
17 + 9 > 28 − 5
10 + 2 = 6 + 6
12 − 2 < 9 + 9

pg. 154

III   LIII
V   XXIV
X   CLVII
VIII   DXXI
XX   MDLV

pg. 155

2; 3; 5; 7; 11; 13; 17; 19; 23

pg. 156

−200
−17
−3,189
−1,500
−20
−$18.50
−$8,000,000

pg. 157

4
−4
yes
5
5
−4
10
−6
12

← -12 -11 -10 -9 -8 -7 -6 -5 -4 -3 -2 -1 0 1 2 3 4 5 6 7 8 9 10 11 12 →

pg. 158

10:17
12:15
7:30
1:40
8:19
10:33
5:50
12:45
12:00
3:30

ADDITION AND SUBTRACTION

pg. 160

483	999	686
365	887	825
567	575	859
789	255	762

pg. 161

2,664	788	857	765
878	6,281	4,516	6,681
9,022	6,281		
8,372	6,281		

pg. 162

| 8,997 | 3,013 | 4,870 |
| 7,701 | 5,839 | 5,664 | (14,161) |

△ 1,275   9,948
3,535   9,390
12,799

pg. 163

11,857	21,961	40,393
92,054	10,587	84,491
84,728	72,459	63,624
90,214	88,005	72,133

pg. 164

141	122	111
935	150	512
202	112	33
115	34	110
935
33
902
yes

pg. 165

136	427	284
	478	3,821
7,523	6,567	5,450

pg. 166

6,375 − 3,174 = 3,201
2,347 − 205 = 2,142
9,042 − 16 = 9,026
8,755 − 7,418 = 1,337
5,555 − 4,446 = 1,109
5,120 − 386 = 4,734
9,722 − 8,876 = 846
5,413 − 1,019 = 4,394
4,144 − 876 = 3,268
2,781 − 2,764 = 17

pg. 167

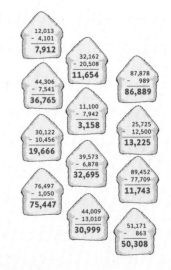

12,013 − 4,101 = 7,912
32,162 − 20,508 = 11,654
87,878 − 989 = 86,889
44,306 − 7,541 = 36,765
11,100 − 7,942 = 3,158
25,725 − 12,500 = 13,225
30,122 − 10,456 = 19,666
39,573 − 6,878 = 32,695
89,452 − 77,709 = 11,743
76,497 − 1,050 = 75,447
44,009 − 13,010 = 30,999
51,171 − 863 = 50,308

pg. 168

21,142	22,053		
67,331	15,054	77,294	63,330
20,948	31,210	19,946	
6,630	7,425	52,659	

MULTIPLICATION AND DIVISION

pg. 170
2 × 2 = 4
3 × 4 = 12   2 × 4 = 8
10 × 3 = 30
2 × 6 = 12

pg. 171
4   15   30   12   54
9   32   8   27   63
56   25   12   20
36   42   3
0   49

pg. 172
4 × 8 = 32   6 × 6 = 36   3 × 5 = 15
7 × 7 = 49   4 × 5 = 20   5 × 5 = 25

12
1 × 12 = 12
2 × 6 = 12
3 × 4 = 12
1   12   2   6   3   4

9
1 × 9 = 9
3 × 3 = 9
1   9   3

16
1 × 16 = 16
2 × 8 = 16
4 × 4 = 16
1   16   2   8   4

15
1 × 15 = 15
3 × 5 = 15
1   15   3   5

18
1 × 18 = 18
2 × 9 = 18
3 × 6 = 18
1   18   2   9   3   6

8
1 × 8 = 8
2 × 4 = 8
1   8   2   4
40
28
18
50
22

pg. 173
60   60   160   400   490
1,500   1,800   900   800   3,600
1,800   3,600   3,500   3,200   1,000
3,000   20,000   12,000   64,000   12,000
8,000   35,000   81,000   30,000
42,000

pg. 174
245   144   99   288   372
133   222   720   371   110
252   356   464   204   639
132   308   25   108   201

pg. 175
1,398   760   2,808   1,771   1,152
2,058   1,520   4,608   3,265   3,464
7,568   1,848   2,282   3,078   4,672

pg. 176
726   165   2,257   400   492
736   294   580   143   1,365
27 × 17 = 459 tropical fish

pg. 177
1,960   2,490   3,549   540
3,886   1,170   2,448   2,183
2,646   2,332   5,100   4,071
19 × 12 = 228 fish food pellets

pg. 178
4,914   11,376   41,657   22,365
13,640   28,435   10,982   43,674
103 × 12 = 1,236 eggs

pg. 179
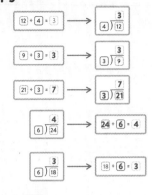

pg. 180
11   6   10   5   11
23   10   8   34   7
7   5
7   9
7   9

pg. 181
12r1   6r1   8r4   2r1   2r5
24r2   13r3   9r3   5r4   5r6
10r4   12r3   3r6   18r3   11r2

pg. 182
18r1   35r1   15r4
7r7   8r3   10r5
9r4   12r1   12r3

pg. 183
166   168   61r5
18r3   68   171r2
24r3   52r8   36r3
789 ÷ 3 = 263 T-shirts

pg. 184
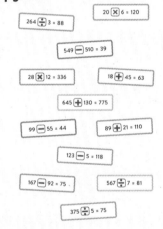

264 ÷ 3 = 88
20 × 6 = 120
549 − 510 = 39
28 × 12 = 336
18 + 45 = 63
645 + 130 = 775
99 − 55 = 44
89 + 21 = 110
123 − 5 = 118
167 − 92 = 75
567 ÷ 7 = 81
375 ÷ 5 = 75

pg. 185
4 + 20 = 24
8 + 14 = 22
12 + 6 = 18
15 − 11 = 4
3 + 4 − 7 = 0
47 − 36 = 11

pg. 186
Sum	Average
36	12
92	46
44	11
530	265
280	70
78	26
378	189
272	68
330	110
52	13

FRACTIONS AND DECIMALS

pg. 188
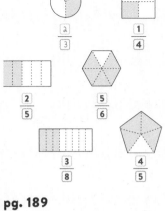

$\frac{2}{3}$ $\frac{1}{4}$
$\frac{2}{5}$ $\frac{5}{6}$
$\frac{3}{8}$ $\frac{4}{5}$

pg. 189
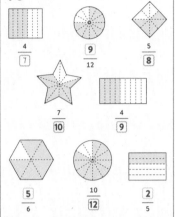

$\frac{4}{7}$ $\frac{9}{12}$ $\frac{5}{8}$
$\frac{7}{10}$ $\frac{4}{9}$
$\frac{5}{6}$ $\frac{10}{12}$ $\frac{2}{5}$

Thomas cut a round birthday cake into eight pieces. He ate three of the pieces. Write a fraction to show what part of the cake Thomas ate. $\frac{3}{8}$

pg. 190
$\frac{2}{3}$ $\frac{6}{7}$
$\frac{3}{4}$ $\frac{7}{8}$
$\frac{2}{5}$ $\frac{7}{10}$
$\frac{3}{6}$ $\frac{9}{12}$

$\frac{1}{10} + \frac{6}{10} = \frac{7}{10}$ $\frac{3}{8} + \frac{2}{8} = \frac{5}{8}$
$\frac{1}{4} + \frac{1}{4} = \frac{2}{4}$ $\frac{1}{3} + \frac{1}{3} = \frac{2}{3}$
$\frac{3}{7} + \frac{1}{7} = \frac{4}{7}$ $\frac{1}{6} + \frac{2}{6} = \frac{3}{6}$
$\frac{2}{5} + \frac{1}{5} = \frac{3}{5}$ $\frac{1}{12} + \frac{6}{12} = \frac{7}{12}$

pg. 191
$\frac{1}{3}$ $\frac{2}{5}$
$\frac{4}{7}$ $\frac{2}{12}$
$\frac{2}{8}$ $\frac{6}{8}$
$\frac{6}{15}$ $\frac{3}{9}$
$\frac{1}{4}$ $\frac{6}{10}$

Candice cut a rectangular birthday cake into 16 pieces. Her brother and sister ate a total of 5 pieces. Write a fraction to show what part of Candice's cake was left. $\frac{11}{16}$

pg. 192
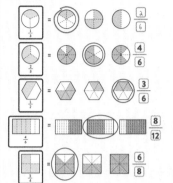

$= \frac{2}{6}$
$= \frac{4}{6}$
$= \frac{3}{6}$
$= \frac{8}{12}$
$= \frac{6}{8}$

pg. 193
$\frac{4}{4}$ $\frac{8}{8}$
$\frac{5}{5}$ $\frac{3}{3}$
$\frac{2}{2}$ $\frac{10}{10}$
$\frac{2}{2}$ $\frac{2}{14}$
$\frac{4}{8}$ $\frac{12}{15}$
$\frac{2}{2}$ $\frac{2}{2}$
$\frac{3}{3}$ $\frac{4}{8}$

pg. 194
$\frac{2}{3} \times \frac{4}{4} = \frac{8}{12}$
$\frac{2}{4} \times \frac{3}{3} = \frac{6}{12}$
$\frac{4}{4} \times \frac{3}{3} = \frac{12}{12}$
$\frac{5}{6} \times \frac{2}{2} = \frac{10}{12}$
$\frac{1}{6} \times \frac{2}{2} = \frac{2}{12}$
$\frac{1}{3} \times \frac{4}{4} = \frac{4}{12}$

$\frac{2}{12}$ $\frac{4}{12}$ $\frac{6}{12}$ $\frac{8}{12}$ $\frac{10}{12}$ $\frac{12}{12}$
$\frac{1}{6}$ $\frac{1}{3}$ $\frac{2}{4}$ $\frac{2}{3}$ $\frac{5}{6}$ $\frac{4}{4}$

pg. 195
$\frac{6}{4}$ $\frac{16}{6}$ $\frac{29}{6}$
$\frac{15}{4}$ $\frac{5}{2}$ $\frac{30}{7}$
$\frac{29}{8}$ $\frac{33}{5}$ $\frac{11}{6}$

pg. 196
$1\frac{2}{5}$ $3\frac{1}{2}$ $2\frac{1}{3}$
$1\frac{1}{7}$ $4\frac{2}{4}$ $2\frac{2}{6}$
$2\frac{2}{4}$ $7\frac{1}{2}$ $1\frac{3}{8}$

pg. 197
$13\frac{2}{3}$ $13\frac{2}{3}$
$2\frac{6}{8}$ $10\frac{3}{4}$
$5\frac{1}{7}$ $2\frac{1}{8}$
$9\frac{3}{5}$ $1\frac{8}{10}$
$14\frac{3}{4}$ $8\frac{3}{5}$
$4\frac{7}{8}$ $12\frac{11}{10}$

pg. 198

$\frac{3}{10} = .3$

$\frac{7}{10} = .7$

$\frac{8}{10} = .8$

$\frac{9}{10} = .9$

$\frac{5}{10} = .5$

$\frac{6}{10} = .6$

pg. 199

$\frac{12}{100} = .12$ $\qquad$ $\frac{36}{100} = .36$

$\frac{28}{100} = .28$ $\qquad$ $\frac{50}{100} = .50$

.15 .43 .60

.30 .22 .07

.75 .19 .99

pg. 200

.99
.78
.75
.66
.50
.49
.30
.21
.08
.05

pg. 201

$\frac{1}{4} = .25$

$\frac{2}{4} = .5$

$\frac{3}{4} = .75$

$\frac{4}{4} = 1.0$

pg. 202

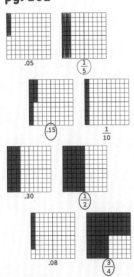

pg. 203

$26.60 $12.00 $19.25 $28.00 $43.44
$7.78 $24.75 $39.80 $32.46 $35.00
$29.28 $60.50 $38.28 $412.50 $217.26
The Seated Liberty half-dollar is worth $150 today.

pg. 204

$1.43 $1.00 $.13 $7.50 $.21
$1.90 $.84 $.11 $1.81 $.71
$1.43 × 3 = $4.29
$17.49 ÷ 3 = $5.83

GEOMETRY AND MEASUREMENT

pg. 206

Examples of line segments:

Examples of lines:

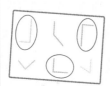

pg. 207

pg. 208

3 $\qquad$ 4
8 $\qquad$ 4
6 $\qquad$ 5
acute $\quad$ right $\quad$ obtuse

pg. 209

pg. 210

quadrangle $\quad$ hexagon $\quad$ octagon
quadrangle $\quad$ pentagon $\quad$ heptagon
heptagon $\quad$ hexagon $\quad$ quadrangle

pg. 211

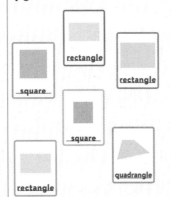

square $\quad$ rectangle $\quad$ rectangle $\quad$ square $\quad$ rectangle $\quad$ quadrangle

pg. 212

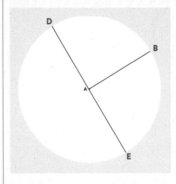

pg. 213

CE $\quad$ CF $\quad$ CG $\quad$ CD
EF
CD
half

pg. 214

$1\frac{1}{2}$ in $\qquad$ 1 in
5 in
7 in

pg. 215

10 cm
5 cm $\qquad$ 4 cm $\qquad$ 3 cm
7 cm $\qquad$ 4 cm
4 in $\qquad$ 10 cm

pg. 216

20 m $\qquad$ 28 in
12 ft $\qquad$ 66 cm

pg. 217

64 sq in $\qquad$ 66 sq ft
27 sq m

pg. 218

24 sq in $\quad$ 24 sq in $\quad$ 24 sq in
yes
yes
yes
yes
6 $\quad$ 4 $\quad$ 3 $\quad$ 8 $\quad$ 2 $\quad$ 12
24 sq in
yes

pg. 219

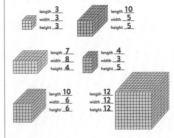

pg. 220

3 × 7 × 2 = 42 cubic in
8 × 4 × 2 = 64 cubic in
4 × 4 × 4 = 64 cubic in
9 × 6 × 4 = 216 cubic in

pg. 221

2 cups
1 quart
4 oz
8 cups
1 cup $\quad$ 1 pint $\quad$ 1 quart $\quad$ 1 gallon

pg. 222

80 oz
3 lbs
20 lbs, 2 oz
5,000 lbs
3 lbs, 9 oz

pg. 223

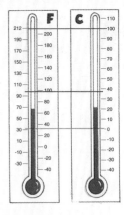

pg. 224

9:13 $\quad$ 10:45 $\quad$ 12:53
1 hour, 32 minutes
2 hours, 8 minutes
3 hours, 40 minutes

PROBABILITY AND DATA

pg. 226

1:6
2:6
3:6

pg. 227

2:16
3:16
1:16
4:16
4:16
2:16

pg. 228

13:26
13:26
0:26
2:26
1:26

pg. 229

1:11
2:11
2:11
1:8
1:8
19
2:19
3:19
1:19
B

pg. 230

puppies; parakeets
Jan; June
green
25
Jan
25
Mar
parakeets
June
100; 85

pg. 231

July; $120
March; $30
August; $40
February
$340

pg. 232

months
10
15
more
There were fewer gloves lost.

pg. 233

Los Robles Elementary School
blue; car
green; bus
bike
3.5%
38%
70.75%

WORD PROBLEMS

pg. 236

22   18
ten thousands
        43,262
654,321
        6
$6.23

pg. 237

30   39   49
$40,105
$21.25   320
399
590,000

pg. 238

$4.95
$4\frac{2}{3}$
4
.03, .30, 3.03, 3.30
$294.84

pg. 239

54 minutes
1 hour, 15 minutes
$7\frac{3}{10}$
.2
2

pg. 240

$2\frac{7}{8}$ 2.8
EF
345 354 534 543 435 453
a right angle

pg. 241

François draws a rectangle that is 34 centimeters long and 21 centimeters wide. What is the perimeter of the rectangle? — 110 cm

Every morning, Mia walks her Saint Bernard puppy around the outside of a park. She walks 750 feet in one direction and 1,325 feet in another direction. Then she walks another 750 feet and another 1,325 feet. What is the perimeter of the park that Mia walks? — 4,150 ft

Write the number of sides for each figure:
octagon 8   quadrangle 4
hexagon 6   triangle 3
pentagon 5   heptagon 7

If one side of a square is 9 meters, what is its perimeter? — 36 m

In one week, Drexel Dumpsters collects 8,000 pounds of garbage. How many tons of garbage is that? — 4 tons

Jasmine lives in an apartment building that has 8 equal sides. Each side is 8 yards. What is the perimeter of the building? — 64 yards

pg. 242

90 sq ft   8 sq yards
$10.10
190 ft
96 cm   1,925 sq cm
68 cups

SOCIAL STUDIES

pg. 244

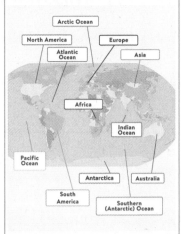

pg. 245

desert
Africa, Asia
tundra or ice
grasslands
South America; North America; Asia
north

pg. 246

Georgia (GA)
Atlantic Ocean
New York (NY)
Connecticut (CT)
Virginia (VA)

pg. 247

King George of England "has kept among us, in times of peace, Standing Armies without the Consent of our legislatures."

King George is "quartering large bodies of armed troops among us."

King George is "cutting off our Trade with all parts of the world."

King George is "imposing Taxes on us without our Consent."

Colonists were not allowed to sell goods, like grains, furs, and fish to other countries.

Colonial families were forced to let British soldiers live with them and eat their food.

The colonists were forced to pay taxes but were not allowed to vote on whether or not they wanted the taxes.

The British Army was stationed throughout the colonies without permission from the colonists.

pg. 249

(Answers may vary)
• 2,000 miles; Independence, Missouri, and Oregon City
• the Platte River, the Snake River, and the Columbia River
• The US government was giving away land to encourage people to colonize the western territories, and gold was discovered in California.
• The terrain was uneven and rough, and wagons could not easily cross rivers and mountains. Covered wagons also didn't protect against extreme weather.
• Indigenous nations were forced off their homeland onto reservations. Land was polluted and natural resources were used up.
• the Union Pacific Railway

pg. 251

3,893,635
Virginia
Delaware
Maine and Massachusetts
free white women
all other free persons
Maryland, Virginia, South Carolina, and Georgia
free people who were not white

pg. 253

Utah, Colorado, Arizona, New Mexico
Hawai'i
Maine

SCIENCE

pg. 259

• planets; asteroids; comets; satellites; black holes; nebulae; dark matter
• spiral; elliptical; irregular
• Big Bang
• clouds of cosmic dust and gas
• dark matter
• the Milky Way
• cosmos

pg. 260

Neptune
Mercury
Jupiter
Pluto
Mars
Uranus
Earth
Saturn
Venus

pg. 263

new moon
full moon
waxing crescent; waning crescent
half moon
27 days, 7 hours
the word moon
waxing gibbous; waning gibbous

pg. 265

lake
ocean
mountain range
desert
plateau
glacier
island

pg. 266

hurricane
flood
earthquake
wind
glacier
volcano

pg. 267

copper
lava
talc
shale
graphite
granite

pg. 268

solid
solid
gas
liquid
liquid
gas

pg. 269

• that energy can be neither created nor destroyed
• its core being is converted into energy
• 1905

pg. 270

P
K
K
K
P

pg. 271

(answers may vary)
• motion
• potential
• kinetic
• because once it starts moving, it has kinetic energy
• because sound travels on waves
• electricity; magnets; solar or wind energy
• gasoline; coils; springs; a boulder
• nuclear

pg. 272

bud
        leaf
stem
        root

pg. 273

flower
seeds
fruit

roots
fruits
It carries nutrients from the roots to the leaves. It supports the plants. It holds the leaves high so the plant can get sunlight.

pg. 274

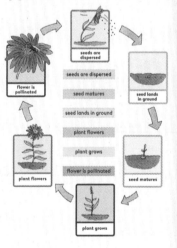

seeds are dispersed
seed lands in ground
seed matures
plant grows
plant flowers
flower is pollinated

pg. 275

Food Web
All living things are linked together by food webs. Living things that make their own food are called producers. Plants are producers. They are at the bottom of food webs. Animals that eat plants are called herbivores. Animals that eat other animals are called carnivores. Animals that eat both plants and animals are called omnivores. Decomposers such as bacteria are living things. They break down dead things into very small particles that become part of the soil. Plants need the soil to grow.

pg. 276

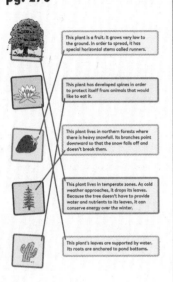

pg. 277

C
D
A
F
E
B

pg. 279

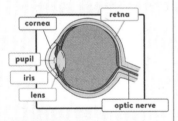

pg. 280

unscientific
hypothesis
testing
inside
disproved

pg. 281

air
invisible
prove
scientific
pasteurization

pg. 282

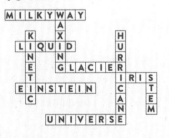

TECHNOLOGY

pg. 284

BRUSH TEETH	
rinse brush	5
wet toothbrush	2
take out toothbrush and toothpaste	1
put toothpaste on toothbrush	3
put toothbrush and toothpaste away	6
brush teeth for two minutes	4

pg. 285

brush teeth
crawl into bed
pull up the covers
turn off light
fall asleep

pg. 287

smiley face: 4, 4

heart: -2, -2
star: 4, -1
tree: 2, 1
blue flower: -3, 5
leaf: -5, -5

pg. 288

go left at the store

pg. 289

Go straight 2 km.
Turn right on the one-way street, then go 2 km.
Turn left and go 3 km.
Turn right at the store and go 5 km.
Turn left at the greenhouse, then go 12 km.
Turn right at the stop sign, then go 2 km.
Arrive at the gas station.
Total distance: 26 km

pg. 290

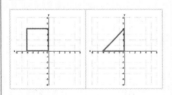

pg. 291

Go to point 0, 0
Place pencil on paper
[Move 1U left] 50 times
[Move 1U up] 50 times
[Move 1U right] 50 times
[Move 1U down] 50 times
Lift pencil off paper

Go to point 0, 0
Place pencil on paper
[Move 1U 45 degrees] 4 times
[Move 1U down] 4 times
Lift pencil off paper
Go to point 0, 0
Place pencil on paper
[Move 1U down] 4 times
[Move 1U 45 degrees] 4 times
Lift pencil off paper

pg. 292

pg. 293

personal
personal
private
personal
private
personal
private

pg. 294

THE FIRST COMPUTER MOUSE WAS MADE OF WOOD.

EARLY COMPUTERS WERE BIG ENOUGH TO FILL SEVERAL ROOMS.

BRAIN QUEST EXTRAS

You did it! Time to make a Brain Quest Mini-Deck so you can play and learn wherever you go. Fill out your certificate and hang your poster. Great work!

PARENTS Congratulations to you and your child! In this section you can help your child cut out the Brain Quest Mini-Deck and certificate and hang up their poster. Continue to make learning part of your everyday life beyond this book. Ask your child about what they are reading, continue to identify connections to science and technology during outings, and keep asking questions to encourage their curiosity and extend their learning.

CONGRATULATIONS!

You've finished the Brain Quest Workbook!

All your hard work paid off! Cut out these Brain Quest Smart Cards to make your own Mini-Deck.

You can play these anywhere—in the back of the car, at the park, or even at the grocery store. Remember: It's fun to be smart!®

QUESTIONS

 MATH
Divide 80 cents by 5. How much do you get?

 ENGLISH
"The cats paws were dirty." Which word needs an apostrophe?

 MATH
How do you abbreviate *centimeter*?

 ENGLISH
What does the contraction *won't* stand for?

BRAIN QUEST®

QUESTIONS

 MATH
Kyle is 5 feet 2 inches tall. What's his height in inches?

 ENGLISH
Find the proper nouns: "Mount Rushmore is in South Dakota."

 MATH
Examples of equivalent fractions are $\frac{2}{4}$, $\frac{4}{8}$, and $\frac{6}{12}$. True or false?

 ENGLISH
Say these words in alphabetical order: eggplant, yam, beet, tomato.

BRAIN QUEST®

QUESTIONS

 MATH
If 1 pound of pasta serves 4 kids, how many ounces of pasta does it take to serve 3 kids?

 ENGLISH
Which is the helping verb: b–e–e–n or b–e–a–n?

 MATH
How much is 56 × 4?

 ENGLISH
What is the plural of *calf*?

BRAIN QUEST®

QUESTIONS

 MATH
Do pints measure <u>size</u>, <u>weight</u>, or <u>volume</u>?

 ENGLISH
"My younger sister is in the pool." What is the complete subject of this sentence?

 MATH
Estimate the product by rounding the numbers in 29 × 52 to the nearest ten.

 ENGLISH
Which word means the opposite of *smooth*: <u>round</u>, <u>rough</u>, <u>rouge</u>?

BRAIN QUEST®

Brain Quest Mini-Deck

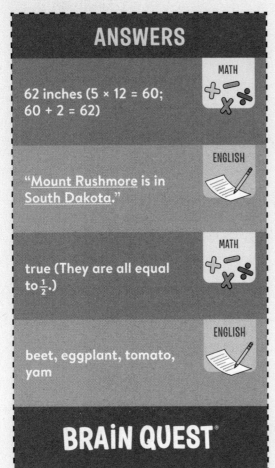

ANSWERS

MATH
62 inches (5 × 12 = 60; 60 + 2 = 62)

ENGLISH
"Mount Rushmore is in South Dakota."

MATH
true (They are all equal to ½.)

ENGLISH
beet, eggplant, tomato, yam

BRAIN QUEST

ANSWERS

MATH
16 cents

ENGLISH
"The cat's paws were dirty."
(the possessive noun)

MATH
cm

ENGLISH
will not

BRAIN QUEST

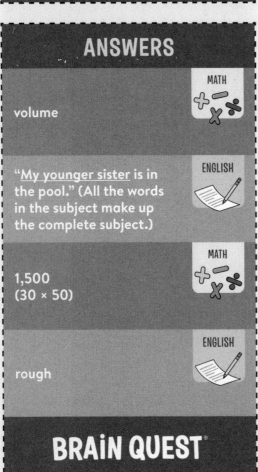

ANSWERS

MATH
volume

ENGLISH
"My younger sister is in the pool." (All the words in the subject make up the complete subject.)

MATH
1,500
(30 × 50)

ENGLISH
rough

BRAIN QUEST

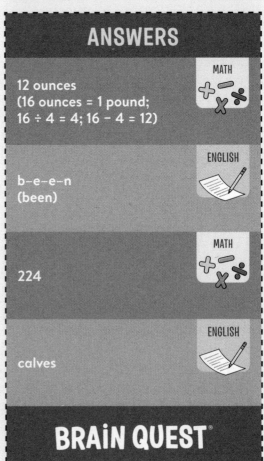

ANSWERS

MATH
12 ounces
(16 ounces = 1 pound; 16 ÷ 4 = 4; 16 − 4 = 12)

ENGLISH
b–e–e–n
(been)

MATH
224

ENGLISH
calves

BRAIN QUEST

Brain Quest Mini-Deck

QUESTIONS

 MATH Subtract 1,563 from 7,394.

 ENGLISH What word do you get when you spell *rats* backward?

 MATH Which is greater: 8 × 3 or 72 ÷ 6?

 ENGLISH Spell the month that follows January.

BRAIN QUEST®

QUESTIONS

 MATH Which number is the numerator in the fraction $\frac{6}{15}$?

 ENGLISH Which word stays the same in its plural form: cow, sheep, goat?

 MATH Subtract 62 from 232. Then divide by 5. What's the answer?

 ENGLISH How do you abbreviate 231 Waterfront Boulevard?

BRAIN QUEST®

QUESTIONS

 MATH Which number is the denominator in the fraction $\frac{12}{48}$?

 ENGLISH Which part of the word *reread* is the prefix?

 MATH Which number is a prime number: 4, 7, 9?

 ENGLISH Find the adjective in this sentence: "Ann's sweater is very soft."

BRAIN QUEST®

QUESTIONS

 MATH In the number 231,490, what is the place value of 1?

 ENGLISH Find a synonym of *confuse*: surprise, puzzle, alarm.

 MATH Which is a three-dimensional figure: a triangle or a sphere?

 ENGLISH What is the word for someone who studies stars?

BRAIN QUEST®

Brain Quest Mini-Deck

ANSWERS

MATH
6

ENGLISH
sheep

MATH
34
(232 − 62 = 170;
170 ÷ 5 = 34)

ENGLISH
231 Waterfront <u>Blvd</u>

BRAIN QUEST®

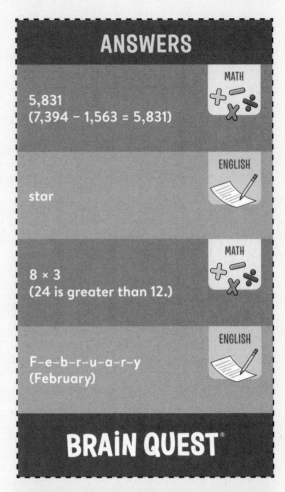

ANSWERS

MATH
5,831
(7,394 − 1,563 = 5,831)

ENGLISH
star

MATH
8 × 3
(24 is greater than 12.)

ENGLISH
F–e–b–r–u–a–r–y
(February)

BRAIN QUEST®

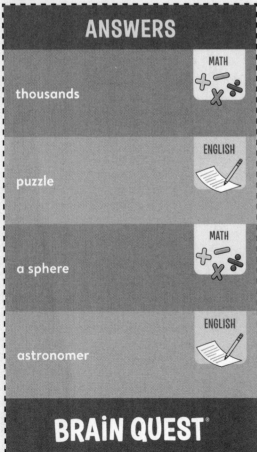

ANSWERS

MATH
thousands

ENGLISH
puzzle

MATH
a sphere

ENGLISH
astronomer

BRAIN QUEST®

ANSWERS

MATH
48

ENGLISH
re- (A prefix begins a word.)

MATH
7

ENGLISH
"Ann's sweater is very <u>soft</u>." (An adjective describes a noun.)

BRAIN QUEST®

Brain Quest Mini-Deck

QUESTIONS

 MATH
What is the average of 8, 9, 15, 20?

 ENGLISH
Which is correct? "I want that plums." or "I want these plums."

 MATH
What is the name of a shape with eight sides?

 ENGLISH
What does it mean to be *skating on thin ice*?

BRAIN QUEST®

QUESTIONS

 MATH
108 ÷ 12 = 9. Which number is the quotient?

 ENGLISH
Put the verb in the simple past tense: "Mr. Ramirez teaches us subtraction."

 MATH
Chitra went to college from 1998 to 2002. How many years was she there?

 ENGLISH
Correct this sentence: "I are not hungry."

BRAIN QUEST®

QUESTIONS

 MATH
Find the equivalent fractions in this group: $\frac{1}{3}$, $\frac{2}{3}$, $\frac{2}{6}$, $\frac{3}{6}$.

 ENGLISH
Find the antonym of *perfect*: <u>imperfect</u>, <u>unperfect</u>, <u>nonperfect</u>.

 MATH
How much money is 23¢ × 15?

 ENGLISH
Rearrange the letters in the word *earth* to form the word for an internal organ.

BRAIN QUEST®

QUESTIONS

 MATH
How much is 13 + 15 + 19?

 ENGLISH
Which is the first syllable of *marzipan*: m–a–r, m–a–r–z–i, p–a–n?

 MATH
How many years are in a half century?

 ENGLISH
In recipes, how is the word *teaspoon* abbreviated?

BRAIN QUEST®

Brain Quest Mini-Deck

ANSWERS

MATH

9

ENGLISH

"Mr. Ramirez <u>taught</u> us subtraction."

MATH

4 years
(2002 – 1998 = 4)

ENGLISH

"I <u>am</u> not hungry."

BRAIN QUEST

ANSWERS

MATH

13
(8 + 9 + 15 + 20 = 52;
52 ÷ 4 = 13)

ENGLISH

"I want these plums."
(*These* and *plums* are both plural.)

MATH

octagon

ENGLISH

to be doing something risky

BRAIN QUEST

ANSWERS

MATH

47

ENGLISH

m–a–r (mar • zi • pan)

MATH

50 years
(1 century = 100 years;
100 ÷ 2 = 50)

ENGLISH

tsp

BRAIN QUEST

ANSWERS

MATH

$\frac{1}{3}, \frac{2}{6}$

ENGLISH

imperfect

MATH

$3.45
(.23 × 15 = 3.45)

ENGLISH

heart

BRAIN QUEST

Brain Quest Mini-Deck

QUESTIONS

 MATH What is the average of 2, 4, 6, 8, 10?

 ENGLISH What silent letter do *plumber* and *thumb* have in common?

 MATH Find the numbers that are multiples of 3: 6, 13, 16, 24.

 ENGLISH If someone has written a biography, is it fiction or nonfiction?

BRAIN QUEST®

QUESTIONS

 MATH Joe has a quarter and 3 pennies. Eva has a dime, a nickel, and 6 pennies. Who has more?

 ENGLISH Which is listed first in the dictionary: anchor or anchovy?

 MATH What is the sum of 4.27 and .83?

 ENGLISH How many syllables are in the word *Mississippi*?

BRAIN QUEST®

QUESTIONS

 MATH Which is greater: $\frac{15}{2}$ or $\frac{40}{6}$?

 ENGLISH "Weekends are the funnest days." Find the mistake in this sentence.

 MATH The area of the room is 40 square feet. Its width is 8 feet. What is its length?

 ENGLISH Spell the plural of *goose*.

BRAIN QUEST®

QUESTIONS

 MATH Round the sum of 8.3 and 3.1 to the nearest whole number.

 ENGLISH Find the complete predicate: "Amir and Liam walked to the post office."

 MATH Is $\frac{21}{8}$ the same as $2\frac{5}{8}$, $2\frac{1}{2}$, or $2\frac{3}{8}$?

 ENGLISH Which should be written as one word: fire fighter, fire truck, fire hydrant?

BRAIN QUEST®

Brain Quest Mini-Deck

ANSWERS

 MATH

Joe (He has 28¢; Eva has only 21¢.)

 ENGLISH

anchor

 MATH

5.1
(4.27 + .83 = 5.1)

 ENGLISH

four syllables
(mis • sis • sip • pi)

BRAIN QUEST®

ANSWERS

 MATH

6
(2 + 4 + 6 + 8 + 10 = 30;
30 ÷ 5 = 6)

 ENGLISH

the letter *b*

 MATH

6, 24
(3 × 2 = 6; 3 × 8 = 24)

 ENGLISH

nonfiction

BRAIN QUEST®

ANSWERS

 MATH

11
(8.3 + 3.1 = 11.4;
Round down.)

 ENGLISH

"Amir and Liam <u>walked to the post office</u>." (The complete predicate is the verb and all the words that modify it.)

 MATH

$2\frac{5}{8}$
(8 goes into 21 two times, with 5 remaining.)

 ENGLISH

firefighter

BRAIN QUEST®

ANSWERS

 MATH

$\frac{15}{2}$
($\frac{15}{2} = \frac{45}{6}$)

 ENGLISH

"Weekends are the <u>funnest</u> days."
(The superlative form of fun is "most fun.")

 MATH

5 feet (40 ÷ 8 = 5)

 ENGLISH

g–e–e–s–e (geese)

BRAIN QUEST®

Brain Quest Mini-Deck

QUESTIONS

 MATH
Which is an improper fraction: $\frac{9}{8}$ or $\frac{7}{8}$?

 ENGLISH
If something is tricolored, how many colors does it have?

 MATH
The comic book series costs $24.99. You have $16.50. How much more do you need?

 ENGLISH
What is the last syllable in the word *whistle*?

BRAIN QUEST

QUESTIONS

 MATH
Which is greater: $\frac{2}{3} + \frac{1}{3}$ or $\frac{5}{6} + \frac{1}{6}$?

 ENGLISH
Which word is an example of onomatopoeia: <u>smile</u>, <u>growl</u>, <u>laugh</u>, <u>frown</u>?

 MATH
It's 34 minutes after 6:41 p.m. What time is it?

 ENGLISH
Which is the proper spelling: I–l–l–i–n–o–i–s or I–l–l–i–n–o–y?

BRAIN QUEST

QUESTIONS

 MATH
Subtract 26 from 233. Then divide by 9. What do you get?

 ENGLISH
Which part of the word *disgraceful* is the suffix?

 MATH
It snowed on 7 days in September. What fraction of the month was snowy?

 ENGLISH
Fix this sentence: "Jack go outside and plays with his dog."

BRAIN QUEST

QUESTIONS

 MATH
Bryony has one and a half dollars. Ali has 5 quarters and 10 pennies. Who has more?

 ENGLISH
Which silent letters do these words share: hedge, wedge, ledge?

 MATH
Is the sum of 22,425 + 6,423 + 150 <u>greater than</u> or <u>less than</u> 29,000?

 ENGLISH
Complete this analogy: *Portrait* is to *painting* as *novel* is to _____.

BRAIN QUEST

Brain Quest Mini-Deck

ANSWERS

MATH

They are equal. ($\frac{3}{3}$ and $\frac{6}{6}$ both equal 1.)

ENGLISH

growl

MATH

7:15 p.m.

ENGLISH

I–l–l–i–n–o–i–s

BRAIN QUEST

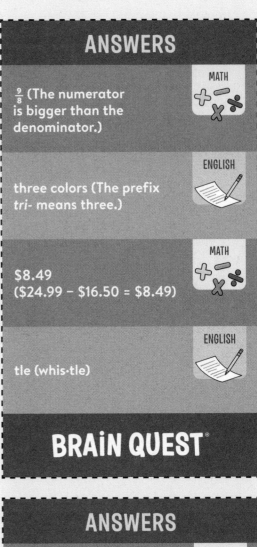

ANSWERS

MATH

$\frac{9}{8}$ (The numerator is bigger than the denominator.)

ENGLISH

three colors (The prefix *tri-* means three.)

MATH

$8.49
($24.99 – $16.50 = $8.49)

ENGLISH

tle (whis·tle)

BRAIN QUEST

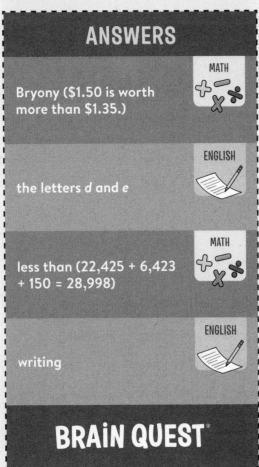

ANSWERS

MATH

Bryony ($1.50 is worth more than $1.35.)

ENGLISH

the letters *d* and *e*

MATH

less than (22,425 + 6,423 + 150 = 28,998)

ENGLISH

writing

BRAIN QUEST

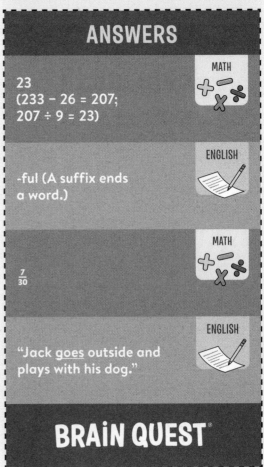

ANSWERS

MATH

23
(233 – 26 = 207;
207 ÷ 9 = 23)

ENGLISH

-ful (A suffix ends a word.)

MATH

$\frac{7}{30}$

ENGLISH

"Jack <u>goes</u> outside and plays with his dog."

BRAIN QUEST

Brain Quest Mini-Deck

QUESTIONS

MATH Find the two equivalent fractions in this group: $\frac{2}{2}$, $\frac{3}{9}$, $\frac{5}{12}$, $\frac{6}{18}$.

ENGLISH What two letters make the f sound in the word *enough*?

MATH If you have 62 nickels, how much do you have in dollars and cents?

ENGLISH Find the synonym of *forceful*: helpful, powerful, dreadful.

BRAIN QUEST®

QUESTIONS

MATH Add $\frac{5}{7}$ and $\frac{6}{7}$, then give your answer as a mixed number.

ENGLISH Which country comes first in the dictionary: United States or United Kingdom?

MATH Our group bought 6 movie tickets. Each cost $8.50. What was the total cost?

ENGLISH Spell the possessive form of *horse*.

BRAIN QUEST®

QUESTIONS

MATH If one train can carry 165 passengers, how many trains would you need to carry 1,320 passengers?

ENGLISH "Run quickly if you want to catch the bus." Which words are the action verbs?

MATH Does 85 ÷ 25 equal 3 with a remainder of 20 or 3 with a remainder of 10?

ENGLISH Which word has three syllables: anagram or enumerate?

BRAIN QUEST®

QUESTIONS

MATH 200° Fahrenheit is warmer than 100° Celsius. True or false?

ENGLISH What does it mean if you *get a kick out of* something?

MATH Find the product of 88 × 33.

ENGLISH Fix the verb in this sentence: "Liz see a snake yesterday."

BRAIN QUEST®

Brain Quest Mini-Deck

ANSWERS

MATH

$1\frac{4}{7}$
$(\frac{5}{7} + \frac{6}{7} = \frac{11}{7} = 1\frac{4}{7})$

ENGLISH

United Kingdom

MATH

$51.00
(6 × 8.50 = 51.00)

ENGLISH

h–o–r–s–e–'–s (horse's)

BRAIN QUEST

ANSWERS

MATH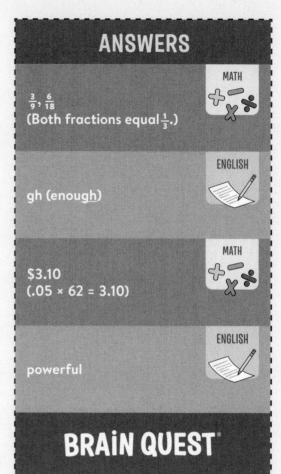

$\frac{3}{9}$, $\frac{6}{18}$
(Both fractions equal $\frac{1}{3}$.)

ENGLISH

gh (enough)

MATH

$3.10
(.05 × 62 = 3.10)

ENGLISH

powerful

BRAIN QUEST

ANSWERS

MATH

false (212° Fahrenheit is equal to 100° Celsius.)

ENGLISH

You enjoy it.

MATH

2,904

ENGLISH

"Liz saw a snake yesterday."

BRAIN QUEST

ANSWERS

MATH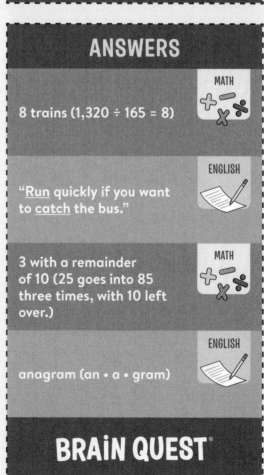

8 trains (1,320 ÷ 165 = 8)

ENGLISH

"Run quickly if you want to catch the bus."

MATH

3 with a remainder of 10 (25 goes into 85 three times, with 10 left over.)

ENGLISH

anagram (an • a • gram)

BRAIN QUEST

YOU DID IT!

CONGRATULATIONS! You completed every activity in the Brain Quest Grade 4 Workbook. Cut out the certificate and write your name on it. Show your friends! Hang it on the wall! You should be proud of your hard work.

CERTIFICATE OF ACHIEVEMENT

Earned by

_____

for completing all sections in the

BRAIN QUEST®
GRADE 4 WORKBOOK